Hockey and Philosophy

Edited by
Normand Baillargeon and Christian Boissinot

Hockey and Philosophy

Translated by Scott Irving

University of Ottawa Press
2015

uOttawa

The University of Ottawa Press gratefully acknowledges the support extended
to its publishing list by Heritage Canada through the Canada Book Fund, by
the Canada Council for the Arts, by the Ontario Arts Council, by the
Federation for the Humanities and Social Sciences through the Awards to
Scholarly Publications Programs and by the University of Ottawa.

Copy editing: Didier Pilon
Proofreading: Thierry Black
Typesetting: Édiscript enr.
Cover design: Lisa Marie Smith
Cover illustration: Aline Corrêa de Souza

Library and Archives Canada Cataloguing in Publication
Vraie dureté du mental. English
    Hockey and philosophy / edited by Normand Baillargeon
and Christian Boissinot; translated by Scott Irving.

(Philosophica)
Translation of: La vraie dureté du mental.
Includes bibliographical references.
Issued in print and electronic formats.
ISBN 978-0-7766-2289-7 (paperback).
ISBN 978-0-7766-2291-0 (pdf).
ISBN 978-0-7766-2290-3 (epub)

1. Hockey—Philosophy. 2. Hockey—Social aspects—Canada.
I. Boissinot, Christian, 1965-, editor II. Baillargeon, Normand, 1958-,
editor III. Irving, Scott, 1986-, translator IV. Title. V. Series: Collection
Philosophica

GV847.V7213 2015   796.96201   C2015-907128-3
                                                               C2015-907129-1

We acknowledge the financial support of the Government of Canada through
the National Translation Program of Book Publishing, an initiative of the
*Roadmap for Canada's Official Languages 2013-2018: Education, Immigration,
Communities*, for our translation activities.

Printed in Canada.

Table of Contents

3rd period
Ethical and aesthetic issues

Overtime

Shootout

Foreword
Thinker on the Rink

By Jean Dion

It was spring 2006. The Anaheim Ducks, still Mighty at the time, were trying for an improbable shot at the Stanley Cup. During the first round of the playoffs, the team's star goalie, Jean-Sébastien Giguère, suffering from an injury, fell into a slump. Giguère had brought his team to the cusp of victory three years earlier, but now there wasn't much choice: his replacement goalie had to be thrown into the lions' den. The replacement, Ilya Bryzgalov, was a Russian rookie who was almost completely unknown to anyone except the experts. But you never know with these things. It wasn't unheard of to see a goaltender come out of nowhere and end up winning the cup (just look at Ken Dryden and Cam Ward). Besides, it was play-off season; there wasn't any time to lose.

Bryzgalov answered with a 2-1 win the next game, followed by three back-to-back shutouts. The Ducks would perish in the semi-finals that year, but the young man made one heck of a name for himself in the process.

With all eyes on him, there was no disguising Bryzgalov's dom-inant personality trait: an extraordinary sense of calm, an unshake-able serenity. Goalies are typically thought of as the oddballs of hockey, the mavericks at the margins of the sport, isolated from their teammates and concerned with obscurities that never cross the average person's mind. But this was pretty extreme. A masked man who was even-keeled at all times, who never got worked up about anything? Come on. There was something almost suspicious about that unusual sense of calm. Some of his teammates even wondered whether deep down he cared about any of it. Five minutes before game time, the coach could arrive and tell Bryzgalov he was going between the posts, and he would reply with a simple "Okay."

After that 2-1 win against Calgary, Bryzgalov mentioned that even in the thick of it, he had never been stressed. "I wasn't nervous. Definitely not. It's hockey," he said. "Why am I supposed to be nervous? It's a game." The reporters asked him what the secret to his tranquility was. "If we lose," he replied, "it's not a reason to be grumpy because I know, for example, so many people in Africa who don't have any food and die from disease."

Then all was laid bare: "I like history," he continued. "I've been reading philosophy books for maybe five years. I like philosophy. It helps me in life. I find a couple of answers to my questions. I like ancient Greek philosophers like Socrates and Plato."[1] Sort of puts things into perspective.

Of course, certain journalists reported that Bryzgalov "read Socrates"—no easy task considering this pioneer of Western thought left little to nothing in the way of written works—but reports like these only served to highlight how unusual the behaviour was. Reactions ranged from astonishment to amusement: a pro athlete who dabbles in philosophy? Sharper tongues went further: an athlete who reads books? True, a few years prior there had been Phil Jackson, who coached the Los Angeles Lakers basketball team: here was a man who gave his star player Shaquille O'Neal a copy of Nietzsche's *Ecce Homo* to get his neurons firing. But that was pretty much where the story ended. It seemed that organized sport, that frivolous diversion, didn't concern itself with philosophy any more than philosophy, presumably, cared for sport.

Yet paradoxically, in North America, especially in the United States, religion plays an important role in sports. We see it every day. The baseball player touching his foot to home plate after hitting a home run, as he points his finger heavenward in homage to the supernatural being who pushed the ball out of the park. The

---

1.   Ken Peters, "Goalie Bryzgalov Marches to Different Drum," *Washington Post*, May 6, 2006.

basketball player who openly thanks his Creator on national TV for the victory he has just achieved. The imposing NFL players who, after 60 minutes of intense combat, form a circle on the field, members of opposing teams mixed in with each other, to kneel in prayer. You could dismiss this as the faith of the simpleton and laugh that God must be seriously conflicted with all these different players to pay attention to, but still the phenomenon is deeply entrenched.

Philosophy's role in sports, on the other hand, is less obvious. When it *does* come up, it's most often in the most mundane sense of the word, as in "the general manager's philosophy on trading" or "the coach's philosophy about how to use his fourth line." Mere perspective or opinion passes for philosophy. We believe that both sport and philosophy deserve more credit than that, and this book is a first step in recognizing this.

One could chuckle that hockey has attained the status of a religion in this country. *Hockey Night in Canada* as Saturday night mass. Montreal, the Mecca of hockey. The Montreal Forum, the Temple on Saint Catherine Street. The Canadiens are known in French as la *Sainte-Flanelle*, the "Holy Flannel." And if we had Stanley Cup parades a bit more often, we could certainly talk of religious processions. Therefore, like all religious expression, and like all human endeavour (rational or otherwise) to explain one's mortality, to express one's allegiances, or to find one's place in a seemingly absurd universe, hockey is deserving of philosophical study. You could even say it has a duty to be held up to the light and taken seriously, to transcend its frivolous and playful identity.

A few years ago, in one of my columns in *Le Devoir*, I wrote of an imaginary philosophical review named after a mediocre attempt at wordplay: *Pense et compte* (after the Québec TV series *Lance et compte*, which translates as *He Shoots, He Scores*). As Victor Hugo said, "the pun is the droppings of the spirit on the wing." The review had articles about Kierkegaarding the net, the semiology of the "mitt" of Sisyphus, and the phenomenology of collecting hockey Descartes. The texts in this book will of course be much less facetious and a good deal more instructive. They also strengthen my resolve to create a new periodical: *Nietzsche's Corner*. Once a punster, always a punster.

Introduction

The Greek historian Diogenes Laërtius reports that Thales of Miletus (circa late seventh century to early sixth century BCE), who is generally credited as the first true philosopher, fell into a well while he was looking at the stars one night, for which he was mocked by his family. This image has persisted for centuries: absorbed in the affairs of the mind, philosophers are sometimes oblivious to the world around them. Even today, people still associate philosophers and philosophy with the cliché image of the bespectacled nerd, with his nose in a book and his head in the clouds.

Amusing though the image may be, it is a caricature. After all, philosophers have no monopoly on pondering—or absentmindedness, for that matter! This caricature denies the fact that philosophers have always been interested in the physical world, material reality, moral and political life, the relationship between body and mind, and many other subjects besides—which provides evidence (as though evidence were needed) that they do indeed have their feet on the ground.

This book is dedicated to hockey and serves as further evidence of philosophical groundedness. However, it does belong to a genre, the philosophy of sport, which is fairly recent on the scene—scarcely half a century old. Considering most *traditional* disciplines of philosophy have been around for two and a half millennia or so, the new kid on the block deserves a closer look.

∼

As we know, it was the Greeks who basically invented Western philosophy. Like the Romans after them, the Greeks placed a lot of importance on sport and saw physical activity—their famous gymnastics—as an indispensible part of a proper education. *Mens sana in corpore sano*, or "a healthy mind in a healthy body," as the Romans put it, is in reference to the words of the poet Juvenal.

So the philosophers of the ancient world belonged to cultures that very much valued the body and physical activity. And yes, some of them even actively practised various sports. Did you know that Aristocles, whom history remembers as Plato (from *platús*, "broad, wide"), was so named by his gymnastics teacher, Ariston, because of his robust physique? Or that Pythagoras, the figure who actually coined the word "philosophy," was a formidable athlete who participated in many Olympiads and won every boxing competition in the year 552 BCE?[1] That Cleanthes was a boxer before succeeding Zeno as the head of the Stoic school? That Thales himself was passionate about gymnastics and died while attending a sporting competition? Closer to home, Russell's passion for walking, Heidegger's for skiing, Umberto Eco's for soccer, and Derrida's for exercise biking are widely known.

Yet surprisingly, sport is largely absent from the history of philosophy. We find a smattering of references to sport, of course, but these are mainly incidental, used merely to illustrate an idea or to support a thesis. Why is this the case? There are any number of reasons. One could be forgiven for thinking that philosophers see sport as a trifling, even superfluous, activity, and therefore unworthy of formal study. And perhaps the disregard for the body imposed by the major monotheistic religions—or at least the body's secondary importance in those traditions—has contributed to this trend and long prevented philosophers from taking a good hard look at sport. This shameful situation was to change radically in 1969 with the publication of *Sport: A Philosophic Inquiry* by American philosopher

---

1. When it comes to Pythagoras of Samos, there may be a classic confusion between the mathematician and a gymnast who attained a certain celebrity in the sixth century BCE.

Paul Weiss. The book is widely considered to have made sport a legitimate object of philosophical study and made "philosophy of sport," a branch of philosophy in its own right, one that is now thriving.[2] But what exactly do we mean by the term?

The philosophy of sport

Quick refresher: philosophy is divided into disciplines (epistemology, ethics, aesthetics, and so on), each with its own general concepts, theories, and methods that it applies to given topics such as education, the environment, or, in this case, sport. The philosophy of sport attempts to clarify the highly complex notions that sport brings into relief (competition, justice, etc., not to mention the notion of sport itself) and addresses the many problems and questions that the practice brings up.

Drawing on **aesthetics**, the philosophical discipline dedicated to art and to judgments involving the concept of beauty, the philosophy of sport attempts to understand the sense in which a sport may be considered an art form, its practitioners artists, and its spectators appreciators. It also seeks to understand the nature of the aesthetic emotion that we can be said to feel when witnessing an athletic performance. Philosophical analyses of aesthetic judgments shed valuable light on the subjective or non-subjective nature of evaluations by judges in competitions where an artistic dimension is present.

Ethics, the philosophical discipline dedicated to the critical study of moral values, considers the implications of, for instance, potential genetic modification designed to produce athletes with qualities that are specifically sought after. It also considers the meaning of fair competition (the issue of disparities between Formula One racing teams is one telling example) as well as the role of competition in sport. The ethicist touches on other delicate questions as well: it is morally acceptable for an athlete to take performance-enhancing substances? Are certain sports, such as

---

2. I would be remiss if I did not acknowledge the important preliminary work of Dutch historian Johan Huizinga (1872–1945). *Homo Ludens*, his 1938 work dedicated to the role of play in European culture, contributed significantly to making sport a respectable object of study and research.

boxing, defensible from a moral point of view? Why? Sport is said to inculcate values and virtues. Is this plausible? If so, which ones? And how does sport actually accomplish this?

Sport is a fascinating playground for **social and political philosophy** too. What role does sport (in general) and do specific sports (in particular) play in a given society? What role might they play in identity construction? Why does sport rouse such passion in people, sometimes to the point of violence and even death? We know there are many conceptions of social and economic justice: how do we use these as lenses through which to view the salaries of professional athletes? Various forms of discrimination that exist in a society are manifestly reflected in sport, but is it typically something that exacerbates discrimination or, on the contrary, could it be used to mitigate it? And if so, how and why?

In the same vein, the tools of **epistemology**, **philosophy of mind**, **philosophy of language**, **logic**, and other philosophical disciplines have been used for the past 40 years to examine sport. This demonstrates the fertility of this vast yet largely untapped domain. Also, as far as we know, this book is one of the first works containing a philosophical treatment of the sport that is closest to Québécois' hearts: hockey.

A philosophical examination of hockey

The decision to publish a philosophy book on hockey was doubly appropriate for us as we begin a collection of philosophical works dedicated to popular culture. For many years, in fact, philosophers have been carefully considering this area of culture in which each one of us participates, at least to some degree, but which is neither high culture nor inherited traditional culture. The French series in which this book originally appeared deals with the culture we call popular and that is intentionally produced for mass consumption.

A number of philosophical reviews and books on pop culture have been published in recent years. Not only does this demonstrate the interest that members of the philosophical community have in pop culture, but it also raises the public's interest in philosophy—which is reflected in the fact that many of these works have been surprisingly successful in the book market. Such titles include *The Beatles and Philosophy*, *The Simpsons and Philosophy*, *The Sopranos and Philosophy*, *Hitchcock as Philosopher*, *Philosophy Explained Through Science Fiction Films*, and a host of other works on, say, Hollywood movies, Bob Dylan, or poker. . . *and Philosophy*.

The intent of this new collection is to celebrate Québec philosophy's place in this movement by examining various pop culture phenomena, particularly those that are native to Québec. Our goal is to combine accessibility and humour in characterizing the aspects of the human condition that this culture reveals. And what better place to start than hockey, which is such an emblematic part of Québec culture and plays such a defining role in its identity?

So, to this end, we have invited our colleagues and friends to join us in this philosophical examination of hockey. We thank them for their enthusiastic response and for their texts, which provide a wonderful taste not just of the philosophy of popular culture but also of the philosophy of sport. There's a ticket with your name on it too. Here's the game plan.

First period is dedicated to social and political philosophy. First off, **Tony Patoine** asks whether hockey can be a window into the differences between Québec and Canadian nationalism. He passes the puck to **Jean-Claude Simard**, who seeks to determine the fundamental similarities between the hockey arena and the political arena. Finally, **Mario Jodoin** shows how philosophy and economics can give us insight into the controversial matter of salaries in professional hockey.

As has been known to happen, we see a shift in the **second period**, which starts out in a mythological vein and then takes a decidedly metaphysical turn. The period starts with an account by **Julie Perrone** of how Maurice Richard became a true hero of the Québécois. Next, **Anouk Bélanger** and **Fannie Valois-Nadeau** look at spectator sport in their reflections on the myth of the *Sainte-Flanelle*. The period ends with a play by **Jean Grondin**, who proposes a new view of hockey based on the metaphysics of the north.

Third period is packed with ethical and aesthetic topics. It opens with a goal by **Daniel Weinstock**, explaining how the elimination of tie games in hockey constitutes a substantial loss for society. Next, **Christian Boissinot** unpacks the anthropological, historical, and economic data and slams hockey fights with a moral KO. **Normand Baillargeon** first turns his attention towards a possible aesthetics of hockey before examining the persuasive arguments in favour of banning performance-enhancing drugs from professional hockey. Full disclosure: Baillargeon tested negative in an anti-doping test conducted immediately after the completion of this text.

With the game still tied after the three regulation periods, we're into **overtime**. But first, we get the opportunity to visit the philosophers' dressing room with **Jon Paquin** as our guide. The period resumes with a goal by **Chantal Santerre** (assisted by Immanuel Kant). And that wraps up the period. But wait! This just in! In a surprising move, Santerre and Kant declare themselves offside to the referee, who hadn't noticed. They insist that the goal be cancelled on the grounds that it was against the rules!

And so the game resumes. Drawing inspiration from Søren Kierkegaard, **Charles Le Blanc** invites us to meditate on goalies: are they just a bunch of guys consumed by angst, or is there more to the story? Even through this meditation, the author doesn't let any shots through, and the overtime concludes with a draw. That's right, folks, the game will ultimately be decided by **shootout**! And it's Haitian player **Rodney Saint-Éloi** who will determine the fate of the match.

Will philosophy and hockey emerge victorious from the game? It's up to the armchair experts and managers to give the final verdict.

From our point of view as players, we can definitely tell you it was a good game and we gave it 110 percent.

Happy reading!

Normand Baillargeon
Christian Boissinot

Bibliography

On the philosophy of sport

BEST, David, *Philosophy and Human Movement*, London, Allen and Unwin, 1978.

DREWE, S.B., *Socrates, Sport, and Students: A Philosophical Inquiry into Physical Education and Sport*, Lanham, University Press of America, 2001.

EHRENBERG, Alain, *Le culte de la performance*, Paris, Hachette, 2001.

GODBOUT, Louis, *Du golf*, Montréal, Liber, 2007.

HYLAND, Drew, *Philosophy of Sport*, New York, Paragon House, 1990.

KRETCHMAR, R.S., *Practical Philosophy of Sport*, Illinois, Human Kinetics, Champaign, 1994.

MORGAN, W. and K.V. MEIER, *Philosophic Inquiry in Sport*, Champaign, Human Kinetics Publishers, 1988.

REDEKER, Robert, *Le Sport contre les peuples*, Paris, Berg International, 2002.

RIOUX, Jocelyne, *Petit exercice philosophique à l'usage des amateurs de sport et de leurs proches*, Montréal: Héliotrope, 2007.

SCHAFFHAUSER, Philipp, *Football et Philosophie: Ou comment joue-t-on au ballon rond ici et ailleurs?*, Paris, L'Harmattan, 2008.

SCHIFFTER, Frédéric, *Petite philosophie du surf*, Toulouse, Milan, 2005.

VARGAS, Yves, *Sur le sport*, Paris, PUF, 1992; *Sport et philosophie*, Pantin, Le Temps des Cerises, 1997.

Weiss, Paul, *Sport: A Philosophic Inquiry*, Carbondale, Southern Illinois University Press, 1969.

Two journals devoted to the philosophy of sport:

Journal of the Philosophy of Sport. Available online at: [http://www.humankinetics.com/JPS/journalAbout.cfm]

Journal of the British Philosophy of Sport Association. Available online at: [http://www.tandf.co.uk/journals/titles/17511321.asp]

On hockey

Guay, Donald, *L'histoire du hockey au Québec*, Montmagny: JCL, 1990.

Davidson, John, *Hockey for Dummies*, Foster City, IDG Books Worldwide, 1997.

Dryden, Ken and Roy MacGregor, *Home Game: Hockey and Life in Canada*, Toronto, McClelland and Stewart, 1989.

Robitaille, Marc and Gilles Archambault (eds.), *Une enfance bleu-blanc-rouge*, Montréal, 400 coups, 2000.

Websites

Backcheck: a Hockey Retrospective (http://www.collectionscanada.gc.ca/hockey/index-e.html)

Fous de hockey! (http://archives.radio-canada.ca/sports/hockey/dossiers/1545/). [In French]

1st period

Social and political philosophy

"On est Canayen ou ben on l'est pas":[1] Hockey, Nationalism, and Identity in Québec and Canada

Tony Patoine

Two nations: Québec and Canada. One national sport: hockey. In this chapter, we'll attempt to pin down the key features of Québécois and Canadian nationalism through the lens of this shared passion. We'll use sports to dissect national imaginations.

No matter where you are in Canada, there's no denying it. The Canadian media are incurably fixated on it, and the fever it gives us during the Winter Olympics proves the point further: more than almost any other part of our culture, hockey binds Canadians together *a mari usque ad mare*. Despite what some public opinion surveys say about the importance of certain symbols with respect to Canadian identity,[2] hockey sparks our passion and unites us much more powerfully than the Queen, the RCMP, or universal health care. Only snow, ice, cold,[3] and the Tim Hortons that dot our highways come close to competing with the sport. In a very

---

1. Meaning "Either you're Canayen or you're not." This title is inspired by the song of the same title by Eugène Daignault (1930) that speaks of the way of life of the Francophones of the era, who were called *"Canayens"* (*Canadiens*) at the time. You can hear this song by Daignault accompanied by La Bolduc at the following address: http://www.collectionscanada.gc.ca/obj/m2/f11/m2-4008-f.xml
2. For example, the *Focus Canada 2012* survey (by the Environics Institute) ranks hockey as ninth after symbols such as multiculturalism, Aboriginal peoples, and the Canadian Charter of Rights and Freedoms.
3. Note that a vast outreach campaign to unite Canadian athletes with the rest of the nation was conducted for the Sochi Olympics under the slogan "We Are Winter."

visceral way, hockey is linked to what it means to be "truly" Canadian.

Molson Canadian beer commercials have been capitalizing on this for years. The same is true of many other companies that, in the run-up to the Sochi Olympics, for example, opted to use nationalistic marketing tactics. Nike showed us that Canadian athletes, both men and women, will never be intimidated playing abroad because all Canadians are born with skates on their feet like the fabled Drew Doughty: "all ice is home ice." Canadian Tire fed us images of Jonathan Toews asking Canadians (seated in a maple leaf configuration) to help him score a goal because "we all play for Canada." And finally, the ubiquitous Tim Hortons invited Canadians to join Sidney Crosby on the ice because "nothing brings Canadians together like a good ol' hockey game."

We're also well aware that our politicians love to toss around hockey metaphors, especially during election campaigns.[4] It's good cred; it makes them easier to relate to. Prime Minister Stephen Harper took this a step further: he recently published a detailed academic-level book on an obscure bit of hockey history![5]

So, to sum up, hockey is synonymous with Canadian identity.

But this chapter is supposed to be about two nations. Where does Québec fit in all this? Can hockey be used to distinguish Québec from the rest of Canada, or does hockey instead assimilate the province into the Canadian monolith? Can hockey be used to serve Québec's nationalism as much as it serves Canada's? Could the sport be a key ingredient in building the national unity and identity needed for Québec's sovereigntist ambitions to be realized? And finally, could the Montréal Canadiens, the team widely seen as the province's flagship identity marker, serve as the catalyst for such a project, or would the much-touted Team Québec be a more promising option instead?

---

4. For example, Bloc Québécois leader Gilles Duceppe told Jack Layton the televised French debate in 2011 that "the NDP has never had as many players on the ice as we have." You know the rest.

5. Stephen J. Harper. *A Great Game: The Forgotten Leafs and the Rise of Professional Hockey* (Toronto: Simon & Shuster, 2013), p. 352.

In the pages ahead, these questions will allow us to see how hockey, beyond the sport itself, readily mixes with politics (for better or for worse), especially when it comes to the national imagination. We will see in the current context that hockey (primarily in the form of the Montréal Canadiens) is less powerful as a nation-building tool for Québec than it is for Canada. In Canada, hockey behaves as a *multifaceted* ideological tool that participates *actively* and *positively* in nation building. It plays an integral role in affirming Canadian national identity on a daily basis—even despite Don Cherry's numerous ethnically charged faux pas! By contrast, in Québec, barring an extreme change to the political landscape, hockey appears doomed to contribute to a *reactive* and barren discourse on national identity. This observation, which is central to our considerations, bears an uncanny likeness to a more historical and general observation that sociologist Fernand Dumont makes in *Genèse de la société québécoise* (1993). In many ways, contemporary talk about the importance of a Francophone presence on the Montréal Canadiens feels like a continuation of what Dumont writes about the *Canadiens* at the turn of the nineteenth century in the wake of the constitutional failure of 1791. In both cases, "the rise of the nation occurred, in some sense, in a negative way, under pressure from the other society . . . Everything occurred as though the [French-Canadians/Québécois] were forced to recognize themselves as a nation"[6] (without ever getting the upper hand, one would like to add). Given the essentially *bottom-up*, reactive nature of this discourse, which often follows the current of the news headlines, the positive and affirmative exploitation of hockey for political purposes by the nationalist elite appears to have very limited power in Québec as compared to the rest of Canada. In other words, in the current socio-political framework, the chances of hockey playing a part in a real nation-building project and true identity affirmation are rather slim in *la belle province*.

---

6.   Geneviève Mathieu, *Qui est Québécois ?* (Montréal: VLB, 2001), p. 22.

Hockey and Canadian nationalism

Hockey is a force to be reckoned with in the Canadian media, and appeals to nationhood are commonplace. Let's stick to television here. Without question, no entity has done more to insert hockey into the national imagination than the CBC, the country's English-language public broadcaster, which produces the legendary show *Hockey Night in Canada* (HNIC).[7] For the CBC, *HNIC* is more than just a cash cow; it is the primary vehicle of Canadian nationalism. Recall that part of the CBC's mandate is to "contribute to shared national consciousness and identity."[8] *HNIC* specifically has played a significant role in staking out hockey's place as an integral part of Canadian culture and mythology.[9] In its journey from the arena to radio to television over the years, hockey has become more than just a simple pastime: it is a true Canadian tradition, a quasi-religion. For these reasons, it's tempting to present hockey in Canada as a "total social fact."[10] To paraphrase historian Jacques Barzun's famous quotation on baseball and the United States, whoever wants to know about the heart and mind of Canada had better learn hockey.

Hockey's immense potential with respect to the "shared national consciousness and identity" led the CBC to branch out into wider-reaching television productions intended to show that hockey is a part of our DNA, productions in which hockey and the "Canadian way of life" go together like pancakes and maple syrup. The series *Hockey: A People's History* (2006) comes to mind; this was translated by the French-language broadcaster, Radio-Canada,

---

7. It will be interesting to see what treatment Sportsnet—which recently acquired major broadcasting rights for NHL hockey, including Saturday night coverage—will reserve for the patriotic dimension of hockey in presenting its new star product. For its part, TSN is all too happy to play up the patriotism angle, particularly during the famous world junior hockey championship that airs every year over the holiday season, in which Hockey Canada's maple leaf logo is always present on screen.

8. See the "Broadcasting Policy for Canada" as concerns the CBC: http://laws-lois.justice.gc.ca/eng/acts/B-9.01/page-2.html.

9. And how could we not mention the nation-wide public outcry in spring 2008 when the contract expired between CBC and Dolores Claman, composer of the famous *Hockey Theme Song*? The song, which dates back to 1968, is Canada's second national anthem in the eyes of many. The rights were ultimately purchased by CTV.

10. According to sociologist Marcel Mauss, the "total social fact" concerns all members of a given society and tells us something about all its members.

as *Hockey: la fierté d'un peuple*. There's so much we could say about the importance the show places on hockey in the Canadian national imagination, but let's limit the discussion to the English and French titles. On the English side, "*Hockey*" simply and unsubtly replaced the word "*Canada*" that was used a few years earlier in the celebrated series *Canada: A People's History* (2000). The message is clear: *hockey* and *Canada* are cut from the same cloth, ergo Canada is hockey. The French title, *Hockey: la fierté d'un peuple*, is noticeably different and, in our view, this is no mistake. This title was less likely to shock Québécois (especially the most nationalist ones) than did *Le Canada: une histoire populaire*, the slightly awkward translation of *Canada: A People's History*. With this new series on hockey, everyday Québec viewers were free to associate the word "*peuple*" with the people they identify with first and foremost, which is generally Québecois as opposed to Canadian. They could also feel a sense of *fierté* in the exploits of their own Richards, Béliveaus, Lafleurs, and Roys and with the Canadiens' 24 Stanley Cup victories. So the *hockey*, *fierté*, and *peuple* referred to in the French title are in fact seen through the lens of the Canadiens, and therefore speak to viewers as Québécois first.

Still in the realm of television, there's also the famous *Hockey Day in Canada* (HDIC), another CBC production. The show is a sort of "super-*HNIC*" that, every winter since 2001, has brought viewers over 12 consecutive hours of programming dedicated to *our* national sport. It features three NHL hockey games involving as many Canadian teams as possible. However, the most interesting part of the show in terms of nationalism is actually the rest of the *HDIC* coverage. Between the games—and the usual shots of Canadian military troops playing pick-up hockey on mission in some far-flung part of the globe, thus underscoring the age-old association between sport and war—*HDIC* presents short segments depicting the "Canadian way of life." We see images of ordinary people from Everywheresville, Canada: people serving tacos in a bag at the canteen in the local arena, those good-hearted souls who build outdoor rinks for the whole neighbourhood to enjoy, families from every province schlepping from tournament to tournament, immigrants who integrated into Canadian society through their

involvement in hockey, and last but not least the thousands of tire-
less volunteers who work to ensure a good time is had by all. It goes
without saying that these fine people all do their bit in carrying on
the quintessential Canadian tradition: hockey and everything surrounding it. In a nutshell, this is both the magic and the power of
HDIC: presenting the whole affair as "just another a day in Canada,"
showing how hockey shapes our daily lives and knits together
Canadians of all ages, places, and origins. It is through the ordinariness of hockey that the CBC gives us a snapshot of Canada at its
best, united in its purest tradition (or, should we say, in its best fab-
ricated tradition). As English author Michael Billig writes in *Banal
Nationalism* (1995), the appeal of nationhood is always stronger
when it is presented as the most ordinary thing in the world.

In a different vein, it is fairly common nowadays—and the
uproar surrounding the famous Québec Charter of Values has
done nothing to quiet this—to hear and to read, especially in
English Canada, that Québec nationalism is largely based on
ethnicity,[11] namely that of the French-Canadian majority, and that
Canadian nationalism, being an extension of multiculturalism, is
fundamentally civic. But is it as simple as that? Is this a popular
misconception? Can hockey help us question this hygienic view of
Canadian nationalism?

The CBC may have ditched the theme song to *HNIC*, but it
kept Don Cherry.[12] A "cultural icon," the network's star commentator is of English and Scottish extraction and has always flaunted his
allegiance to Great Britain. So it's possible to suppose, with certain
reservations, that hockey in Canada contributes to a form of "civic
collectivist nationalism,"[13] with Don Cherry serving as a fitting representative of British ethnic nationalism that still persists in English
Canada. In an interesting article, Raymond Breton takes stock of
nationalism among English Canadians that has its origins in (*quelle*

---

11.   Mathieu Bock-Côté (2007) nevertheless laments that this ethnic component
        of Québec nationalism has been blotted out by the Québec elite since the 1995
        referendum, thereby leading to a profound "quiet denationalization."
12.   It remains to be seen what Sportsnet will do with him next season.
13.   In a nutshell, this means that it is part of the national fabric for all who live in
        Canada regardless of ethnicity, an idea that is very much conveyed through
        Hockey Day in Canada and *Hockey: A People's History.*

surprise!) ethnic nationalism: "The society this collectivity was trying to build would be British." One of the defining features of this
British nationalism was the supposed superiority of Anglo-Saxons
over all other ethnicities: "The Anglo-Saxon, religious, and secular
values and the corresponding way of life were considered superior."
As Breton goes on to mention, this nationalism "still exists today to
a certain degree." [14] In the same vein, it is interesting to note that in
his book on hockey, dedicated to "Canada's military families, past
and present," Stephen Harper provides an example of this British
nationalism at work. In recounting the story of hockey's beginnings
in Toronto, Harper pays extra-special attention to the character of
John Ross Robertson,[15] whose words he cites at the outset of the
book: "We have a great game, a great country, and a great empire—
if you gentlemen are as great as the possibilities of the O.H.A., if we
Canadians are as great as the possibilities of Canada, and if we
Britons are as great as the glory of our Empire—the flag of amateur-
ism in your hands will be as safe from harm as the Union Jack was
in the hands of your fathers and mine!"[16]

Not once but twice in the space of a few pages, we find this
other telling quotation from Robertson in the Prime Minister's
book: "The Ontario Hockey Association is a patriotic organization,
not in name exactly, but in nature most assuredly. A force we stand
for is fair play in sport, and sport is one of the elements in the work
of building up the character of a young nation. . . We have tried to
live up to the ideals which are part of our birthright as Canadian
sons of the greatest of countries, and as British citizens of the
grandest of empires."[17]

14. Raymond Breton, "From Ethnic to Civic Nationalism: English Canada and
Quebec," *Nationalism: Critical Concepts in Political Science*, Vol. V, John
Hutchinson and Anthony Smith (eds.) (London: Routledge, 1988), pp. 1847–
1865.
15. Robertson was an influential Toronto press baron who was proud of his
British roots and who fought tooth and nail for the English-aristocrat-style
vision of amateur sport in his capacilty as president of the Ontario Hockey
League at the turn of the last century. This pure and healthy vision of sport
nicely complemented the Victorian Protestant and Puritan morals that
guided the conscience of "The Queen City" in that era.
16. Harper, *A Great Game*, p. vii.
17. Ibid., pp. 23 and 28.

Despite having chosen the very British figure of John Ross Robertson as the "hero" of his book, Harper cannot be accused of systematically promoting the ethnically British vision of the Canadian nation. However, it's worth acknowledging that Harper's book aligns neatly with his "passion" for reintegrating the British colonial tradition into the Canadian myth.[18]

Closer to home, Don Cherry's discriminatory remarks about European and Francophone players (accusing them of lack of toughness, impugning the courage of those who wear visors, saying European captains never win the Stanley Cup,[19] etc.), together with his deep love of the "good Canadian boys" playing for various NHL teams, have a whiff of this supposed moral superiority of WASPs. The "right" way to play, according to Cherry, involves a mix of virility, a sense of honour, and gentlemanly modesty; it requires strength of character, hard work, and self-sacrifice. These values are implicitly associated with the Protestant morality of a bygone era, and this moral system formed one of the main pillars of British nationalism, as evidenced by Harper's recent book on the birth of hockey in the Toronto area. It's hard to look past the ethnic component of the nation. But as old Don would say, "Anyhow. . ."!

We see that hockey contributes to Canadian nation building at all levels: it participates in creating Canada's identity, unity, and national myth. Accordingly, it is a keystone of Canadian lore and ideology. All people who live in Canada, regardless of ethnicity, age, or gender, are Canadian and identify as Canadian at least partly because they like, watch, listen to, or play hockey, or because they hear about it every day. This means that hockey unites them

---

18. This "passion" also led him to replace a work by Québec painter Alfred Pellan with a portrait of the Queen at Parliament in Ottawa, to return to the names Royal Canadian Navy and Royal Canadian Air Force within the Canadian Armed Forces, and to remove the maple leaf from Canadian military uniforms and replace them with the British "stars" that hadn't been used since 1968. According to the *Focus Canada 2012* survey by the Environics Institute, only 15 percent of Canadians, mostly in the most elderly age bracket, see the Queen as an important Canadian identity symbol.

19. An argument that is all the more fallacious since Nicklas Lidström, the Swedish captain of the Detroit Red Wings, snagged the coveted trophy in spring 2008. Note that there were very few Europeans in the NHL before the 1980s and, perforce, even fewer captains.

regardless of the regional boundaries and petty feuds that divide them. Don Cherry and Stephen Harper remind us that Canadian nationalism is not simply a pure construction *ex nihilo*. Like most forms of nationalism—for better or for worse—Canadian nationalism both preserves and relies on an ethno-cultural component that can't be overlooked.

Hockey and Québec nationalism

Since the departure of the Québec Nordiques,[20] Québec nationalism with respect to hockey has revolved around two major facets: the presence of the Montréal Canadiens and the absence of a truly national Québec team, a "Team Québec." The Montréal Canadiens can be viewed as a barometer or a mirror indicating the sense of identity and vision of the Québec nation as historically expressed by the Francophone majority. As we will see, it is important to question if not the power then at least the true value and depth of these feelings of identity within Québec nationalism. In conclusion, we will note that the absence of a senior Team Québec, which Hockey Canada wishes to maintain, deprives Québecois of an important source of national affirmation.

The Montréal Canadiens: mirror of the Québec nation

From its inception, the *Club Canadien* or *Club de Hockey Canadien* (from which the famous "CH" is derived) has represented the *Canadiens* of that era, namely not Canadian citizens of all origins, but exclusively the descendants of French settlers.[21] As evidenced

---

20. In the minds of many, the 1980s saw the Nordiques steal the "identity torch" that until then had been held high by the Montréal Canadiens. Will the Nordiques one day rise from the ashes?

21. Ironically, it was an Ontario investor by the name of John Ambrose O'Brien who founded the team in 1909. In a sense, he wanted the Francophone aspect of the team to be its primary selling point, which is why, from its inception, the team has been made up of almost exclusively of Francophone players. The team would earn nickname after nickname: the *Tricolore* and the *Bleu, blanc, rouge* symbolizing the link with France; the *Sainte-Flanelle* to refer to the sacredness that the jersey has taken on, which incidentally is not without reference to the profound cultural influence that religion had in Québec for so many years; the *Habs*, the most commonly used epithet in the English-language media and by spectators at games, refers to the *habitants*, i.e., the French settlers who settled in New France—our first Francophone farmers!

by its creation, its history, and the epithets it has earned in the last hundred years, the team has always been associated with the French-Canadian, New French, Francophone majority. This has made it Québec's national team by default.[22]

This raises the question of what the history and popular discussion surrounding the Montréal Canadiens can teach us about Québec nationalism. In the absence of clear definitions, what sort of images of the nation does it portray? Are the Canadiens still today considered a strong ethnic symbol? Or is the modern, globalized, multi-ethnic team morphing into the symbol of a Québec-style multicultural nation? And if so, does this speak to the acceptance of an increasingly liberal and civic vision of the nation in the hearts of Québécois? Perhaps the reality is somewhere in between: especially considering the emphasis often placed on the sensitive issue of language, what if the Habs, the great national mirror of Québec, are the outward sign of the uneasy gestation of a Francophone socio-political nation that may or may not see birth as a sovereign state?

It is true that the ever-loyal fan base of the Montréal Canadiens is still mostly Québécois of "pure" French-Canadian, New French, Francophone origin—in other words, the same "majority" that Jean-François Lisée (2007) refers to as *nous*. For this base, there is no question that *their* team will always be able to count on at least some "*indigènes*" (natives), to borrow a term from the celebrated sports columnist Réjean Tremblay. It's often the journalists with nationalist tendencies, such as Tremblay, who say that the Canadiens are the team of Francophone Québécois. Seen from this

---

Finally, there is the name of the *Glorieux*, which appeared over the course of the team's many wins.

22.   The Québec rap group Loco Locass sings in its song "*Le But*": "*Les Canadiens de Montréal: notre équipe nationale.*" The group also emphasizes the unifying character of this team for Québec: "*Anglo, Franco, peu importe la couleur de ta peau, si tu détestes Toronto, le sang qui bouge dans tes artères est aussi rouge, mon frère, que le chandail de nos vingt cœurs de vainqueurs qui luttent avec honneur, les Canadiens, pour une fois, rallient tous les Québécois.*" (Anglo, Franco, no matter the colour of your skin, if you hate Toronto, the blood that flows through your veins is just as red, my brother, as the jersey of our twenty champions who fight with honour, the Canadiens, for once unite all Québécois.")

perspective, scouting and drafting from Québec is a sign of respect from the CH organization to the most faithful of the faithful. Francophone players, provided that they are skilled and would not hurt the team's chances at winning, would be preferred.[23] Since Québec is one of hockey's ancestral lands, it would seem a moral duty for the organization to draw from the Québec talent pool.[24] As we will see, the presence or absence of Québécois/Francophone players and managers on the team is central to all issues of identity that have historically surrounded the happenings of the team. And in this regard, no figure has spilled more ink or made more of an impression than Maurice Richard.

We could easily have written this chapter solely on Maurice "Rocket" Richard, the popular idol so often associated with the birth of the Québec nationalist movement. The riot of March 17, 1955, in response to Richard's suspension for the remainder of the season and from the playoffs, deserves a closer look. A frequently cited article by André Laurendeau in the March 21, 1955, issue of *Le Devoir*, a few days after the Riot (with a capital R),[25] is a powerful testament to the Rocket's national importance: "French-Canadian nationalism seems to have taken refuge in hockey. The crowd that raised its head in anger last Thursday night was not driven solely by the love of sport or a sense that its idol had suffered an injustice. It was a frustrated people, who were protesting against their fate. On Thursday, their fate was Mr. Campbell; he embodied all the enemies, real or imagined, of this small people."

Here, Laurendeau speaks of the Riot as a phenomenon with an ancient and latent mythological origin that the sport, with its new

23. Historian Emmanuel Lapierre (*Globe: revue internationale d'études québécoises*, Vol. 15, no. 1–2, 2012, pp. 317–335) even says, cautiously but with statistics to back it up, that a French-Canadian/Québécois form of ethnocultural nationalism, which arose at a time when 50 percent of the players were Francophone, seems, in all likelihood, to have had a positive impact on the performance of the Montréal Canadiens in the playoffs between the 1926–1927 and 2011–2012 seasons.

24. Especially since the famous rule giving the Canadiens first dibs on the best players from Québec was repealed over 40 years ago.

25. The capital comes from Benoît Melançon, *The Rocket: A Cultural History of Maurice Richard* (Montréal: Fides, 2006).

whipping boy, had just brought back to life.[26] So already in 1955, and even a bit before, Maurice Richard was seen as an affirmative symbol of French-Canadian identity, an ethnic political symbol, a comrade in arms. Richard was already recognized as a great French Canadian, and the Riot "canonized" him. It's fascinating to note the extent to which the Québec nationalist movement, beginning in the 1960s, gradually began reappropriating Richard, who was, for what little he shared about his personal politics, a federalist-autonomist.

Yet this episode, which had just reactivated the very mythology of the French-Canadian people, set a definite precedent to be used by generations of Québécois who will always be ready to defend the cause of having Francophones on the Montréal Canadiens—which is, again, Québécois's national team *by default*.

And so, every summer, the amateur NHL draft once again reopens the classic debate on Québec/Francophone representation on the team. The 1980 draft—which fell just three weeks after the "No" victory in the referendum on sovereignty-association—saw one of the most controversial decisions in Habs history. The organization chose Doug Wickenheiser, a big guy from the West rather than Denis Savard, a little guy who grew up in Verdun, a stone's throw from the Montréal Forum. You know the rest. The Canadiens, regardless of whether the team was seen as an ethno-cultural symbol or as a symbol of this "new" nation of Québec (a product of the 1960s, and much more socio-political and zealous about its language), had no right to snub the "p'tit gars de chez nous" (little guy from back home).[27] More recently, in the June 2007 draft, which unfolded against the backdrop of the reasonable accommodations crisis—and which many feel was mainly an *identity* crisis—the non-hiring of Angelo Esposito (a Montréaler of

26. Note that the very title of Laurendeau's article, "On a tué mon frère Richard" (my brother Richard was killed) was in reference to a famous speech dating back to 1885 by Parti National leader Honoré Mercier: "Riel, notre frère, est mort" (Riel, our brother, is dead). Richard, like Riel, is depicted here as a brother in combat and a national martyr.

27. Following a brilliant career in Chicago, Denis Savard, who was just past his peak, was finally repatriated in 1990 in exchange for star defenceman Chris Chelios, a dubious exchange for the Canadians in terms of hockey.

Italian origin who expressed himself well in French) and David Perron (a player hailing from nearby Sherbrooke) provoked similar reactions. Two Americans, Ryan McDonagh and Max Pacioretty, were chosen in their place.[28]

That summer, there was no rest for our beloved Canadiens on the identity front. If you didn't hear anything about Daniel Brière that summer, you probably didn't make it this far in the book![29] Brière, at the peak of his career, was the one player that fans had been desperately hoping to snag since April. But he decided to sign a multi-season contract with Philadelphia. For so many people, the Habs were the most potent symbol of the Québec nation—and the climate of identity politics was, shall we say, somewhat livelier than usual at the time—so Brière's decision definitely went beyond mere sport and struck a nerve with the nation itself.

Many people felt that Brière wordlessly but nevertheless clearly refused to play the national hero. Looking at the situation from this angle, it's obvious that "Brière the Québécois" should have sided with Montréal and is guilty of treason. But in order to be a *traitor*, you must have first been a *comrade*. In this particular case, one could even say you must first have been an identity symbol with a strong ethnic component. Liah Greenfeld, another expert on nationalism-related issues, may help us understand why Brière's decision left so many with a bad taste in their mouths: "One's nationality determines one's interests and sentiments and is expected to project itself naturally in one's sense of attachment and commitment to the nation. Conduct that fails to answer such expectations is perceived as unnatural and perverse, and provokes extreme revulsion and condemnation."[30]

---

28. Esposito, on whose shoulders the greatest hopes and dreams were placed, is currently struggling to play in an obscure league in Austria, while the other three players involved in this controversy have become established players, or even star players, in the NHL.
29. Interesting phenomenon: six years later, in summer 2013, after upheaval in his personal life and after having his impressive contract bought out by the Philadelphia Flyers, Brière finally decided to sign with Montréal! The fans' reaction to this announcement was fairly tepid.
30. Liah Greenfeld, *Nationalism and the Mind: Essays on Modern Culture* (Oxford: Oneworld, 2006), p. 107.

In other words, in many people's minds, Brière was regarded as a soldier who failed to answer the call of his brothers-in-arms, a child who disowned his family, a pariah who disobeyed the "nation god," a born Québécois who spat in the face of his ancestors. In summary, his decision was not normal. It defied the logic that Greenfeld calls ethnic-collectivistic nationalism. And all of this came into play at a time when the identity of the majority very much needed a Québec hero to calm its nerves a bit. . .

And after all that, who knew what to make of what eventually became the annual fuss surrounding the Finnish captain of the Montréal Canadiens, Saku Koivu, a.k.a. Mr. Neverspeakfrench? In October 2007, the Canadiens organization unleashed a bombshell by failing to obligate Koivu to speak French on the scoreboard! In the wake of the Bouchard-Taylor commission and the reasonable accommodations crisis, Parti Québécois leader Pauline Marois, who had just introduced a bill on Québec identity, was called to speak on the issue. Marois declared that "Effectively, it could be an avenue, to help the players speak French." Nothing more. That's all that was needed to stir up a media maelstrom the very same day. It's no surprise that opinions were extremely divided on the subject. The nationalist camp asserted that the Canadiens were still a very powerful identity symbol and therefore had a duty toward the majority *nous*. The other camp included people like *La Presse*'s Jean-François Bégin, who no longer believed that the team held the same symbolic value in modern Québec society. Bégin, reluctant to politicize sports, and sick and tired of hearing the nationalist "broken record," established a clear dichotomy between the ancestral, traditional Québec and modern, post-Quiet Revolution Québec in his piece on November 2, 2007:

> What's that you say? The Canadiens have a symbolic value in our society? And this forces the captain into having extra duties? Nonsense. Back when French Canadians (and I use the term expressly) were a people that was more or less subservient in the old Anglo Canada of the '40s and '50s, yes, the Canadiens were more than just a team. They were a vehicle for the nationalistic aspirations of a people that dreamed of one day having its place

in the sun. A captain or a star player who spoke French, that meant something—something like "Attaboy, Maurice, you show those *maudits Anglais*!"

But today? Thirty years after the adoption of Bill 101, Québec is no longer the society on the verge of "Louisianization" that it perhaps was. Québec is a confident society that doesn't need a few "bonjours" and "mercis" from a hockey player to ensure its long-term survival.

My own estimation of Québec society's level of confidence in its own identity is perhaps less optimistic than Bégin's. While Québec is no longer viewed as a society on the verge of "Louisianization," Québec identity nevertheless remains very sensitive, especially when it comes to language. The recurring phenomenon surrounding Saku Koivu is just one example among many of this hypersensitivity associated with more modern, socio-political,[31] and Francophone[32] visions of the nation.

The hiring of the unilingual Anglophone coach Randy Cunneyworth in the middle of the 2011–2012 season was another example, and just as significant a one, of the eternal powder keg of linguistic issues surrounding the Canadiens. Once again, the debate made its way to the National Assembly, where every last one of the people's representatives felt that the coach of the Canadiens had a duty to speak French.[33] Obviously, the symbol was under threat. The Canadiens had no idea how sensitive its fans and the general

---

31.   To get past the barren dichotomy of the ethnic vision and civic vision of the nation, Michel Seymour developed his concept of socio-political nationalism in a number of books and articles. Generally speaking, socio-political nationalism is an inclusive form of nationalism characterized by emphasis placed on the history, culture, and language of a people objectively forming a national majority occupying a recognized territory, often alongside national minorities, and by the fact that this people subjectively perceives itself as forming a national political community.

32.   It was Gérard Bouchard who gave us the conception of the Québécois nation as a "North American Francophonie." The French language is seen as an acceptable ethnic criterion in a modern and open form of nation building, as languages (unlike races and religions) are not exclusive; they can be acquired and shared by anyone.

33.   At the press briefing announcing Cunneyworth's nomination, general manager Pierre Gauthier's famous and rather dry comment "you can learn a language," in response to a tricky question from a journalist, didn't make matters

population were about language before making this important decision. Experience has taught us that people see the Montréal Canadiens as more than just a private company; it has become a veritable Québec institution in everyone's eyes. Therefore, as a major identity symbol, it found itself bound to uphold a specific vision of the nation that inspires the majority of people who live in the society. And the French language is ever-present in this vision. It's at play even behind the bench![34]

To sum up: the Montréal Canadiens team is perceived by the general public as a pregnant symbol of our history, both as a people and as a nation. Whether it wants to or not, the team mirrors Québec society in public life; it helps the society see itself better. Accordingly, the media frenzy surrounding the Canadiens often gives us insight into the variations and nuances of the national conception.[35] If hockey has indeed supplanted religion in this country and the Canadiens have replaced the Holy Family, then the various media platforms and websites devoted solely to the Canadiens[36] are now the church steps. And what do we hear spoken on these virtual church steps? The ongoing debate between different visions of the nation—couched in debates about politics and sports between die-hard fans.

A Team Québec?

When all is said and done, the political influence of the Montréal Canadiens, the national team of Québécois by default, appears rather limited. While the Habs regularly push us into debates of politics and identity nationalism, these debates are so often reactionary and contingent on the news. Add to this the fact that from the very beginning, the Canadiens organization and its star players,

---

any calmer. The immediate support for Gauthier's decision by Geoff Molson, president and owner of the team, added another layer to this.

34. The Canadiens hockey team has given players and coaches the opportunity to take French courses since 2013.

35. For readers wishing to get a handle on the different conceptions of the Québec nation, I strongly recommend Geneviève Mathieu's enlightening book *Qui est Québécois?* (2001).

36. Fannie Valois-Nadeau and Anouk Bélanger deal with this phenomenon in greater detail in a later chapter of this book.

in playing the *political neutrality* card, have always leaned towards the federalist side, and you have a fairly accurate picture of the team's limited power when it comes to Québec nationalism.[37] While often forced to react, the Habs remain lukewarm on the idea of beating Québec's nationalist drum.[38] Even the Rocket himself, the greatest of the greats, asked the people on the day after the Riot to stop causing "trouble."[39]

For these reasons, there is no doubt that a Team Québec, a politically legitimate project that 72 percent of Québécois support,[40] would do much more for Québec nationalism than the Montréal Canadiens can. In fact, it's safe to say that such a team would probably do much more to bolster Québec national identity than any other strategy Québec nationalists could ever dream up. In our opinion, it would be a one of the strongest tools in the sovereigntist's toolkit. Just as Team Canada has done since 1972, a Team Québec would inspire more than just reactions to the news; it would create a sustainable and renewable sense of collective identity; it would contribute to a concrete and positive national *affirmation* and breathe energy into a disembodied nationalism that is too abstract in the eyes of the average Québécois, a nationalism that even artists struggle to keep alive these days. And, no matter how well it does internationally, a Team Québec would be a source of pride across Québec, a symbol of success, our very own "Yes We Can"! The 20 players on its roster would symbolize a Québécois *nous*, one that's as civic, socio-political, inclusive, and pluralistic as "we" have become. A Québécois *nous*, which, one fine evening,

37. Recall the former coach Jacques Demers, who became a Canadian senator; the great federalist Jean Béliveau, who for personal reasons refused several offers of a Senate post; Richard and Lafleur, who never personally associated themselves with the Québec nationalists; and finally the various owners of the team who never took up the nationalist cause.
38. Major media action and pressure were needed before the song "*Le But*",could be played in the Bell Centre. The song is by the nationalist band Loco Locass and is an in-your-face celebration of the glorious past and the Canadiens' status as the national team. It has recently become the official goal song.
39. As some readers will remember, Pierre Boivin, the president of the Montréal Canadiens, reacted similarly to journalists in an attempt to put and end to the "Brière saga" in summer 2007.
40. At least, this is what was suggested by a survey by Léger Marketing led by Guy Bertrand in October 2006.

could go head to head with the Canadian *us*, a duel that would arouse as least as much passion as that famous game against the USSR did in 1972. And who knows what could come out of an emotional game? A memorable goal? Fights? Insults? Disputed calls by the referees? Stifled inside its Canadian (and Canadien) cocoon, the gentle sound of the frogs could become something more than just. . . babble. Those frogs could roar—with joy or with anger!

But there isn't a level playing field when it comes to using hockey for nationalistic purposes. It certainly seems that, for Canada and for the Hockey Canada organization, it is too much of a risk to create a Team Québec, made up of our best players, that would participate in major competitions.[41] It might be the spark that lights the powder keg. After all, in the words of Stephen Harper, shouldn't this province remain "a nation within a **united** Canada"?

Further reading

Kymlicka, Will. *Multicultural Citizenship: A Liberal Theory of Minority Rights*. Oxford: Oxford University Press, 1995.

> For a far-reaching study of minority rights, particularly enlightening in the Canadian context.

Lisée, Jean-François. *Nous*. Montréal: Boréal, 2007.

> For a text that looks at the relationships between the Québécois majority and minorities and that lays the groundwork for a proposed Québec citizenship.

Mathieu, Geneviève. *Qui est Québécois ? Synthèse du débat sur la redéfinition de la nation*. Montréal: VLB Éditeur, 2001.

> For a highly accessible synthesis of the main conceptions of the Québec nation.

Melançon, Benoît. *The Rocket: A Cultural History of Maurice Richard*. Montréal: Fides, 2006.

> For everything there is humanly possible to know about the cultural history of the "Rocket."

---

41. Hockey Canada has jealously managed this matter for many years. Bertrand noted with regret that his efforts in favour of a Team Québec as part of the world championship in 2008, a one-shot deal to mark the 400th anniversary of Québec City, which hosted the tournament, were in vain.

SEYMOUR, Michel. *Le pari de la démesure*. Montréal: l'Hexagone, 2001.

> For a committed and inspired perspective on intransigence towards Québec, potentially inspiring for proponents of a Team Québec.

This is what happens when the French meddle with hockey...

People in France just love their English words. Their business and media jargons are peppered with terms like *cross-merchandising supply chain, top fifty, hit, mail, buzz,* and other *happy few.* Are these examples of silliness? Snobbishness? Thoughtlessness? Eager globalization? Let's leave that debate to them. In any event, the English influence is something the world of sport is powerless to resist. Just look at these artifacts from a piece on golf, taken from the very serious French sports publication *L'Équipe.* It would shock the average Québec reader:

"Ernie Els jouait le premier et plaçait son fer au milieu du *fairway* tandis que Thomas Levet sortait une nouvelle fois le *driver.* Ayant atteint le *rough* à droite avec ce *club* lors du premier barrage, le Français compensait trop à gauche et attrapait un *bunker* de parcours... Jouant le drive ... il trouvait donc le *rough* à droite puis le *bunker* devant le *green...* Après un mauvais *tee-shot* à gauche, il ratait son approche et ressortait du *green* avant de faire approche-deux *putts* pour un *double bogey.*"

Honourable mention goes to those responsible for Frenchifying ice hockey terms. The following is a short list of terms that were popularized in Québec by the likes of René Lecavalier and Jean-Maurice Bailly, along with the equivalents used in France.

Québec	France
rondelle, disque, la puck	palet (le puck)
hockey, bâton de hockey	crosse
banc de pénalité ou de punition	prison, box
tirs de barrage	tirs au but
lancers	shoots
séries éliminatoires	play-off
marqueur, compteur	buteur
la LNH	la NHL
Match (partie) des étoiles	All-Star Game
mise au jeu	engagement
lancer de pénalité (de punition)	penalty
lancer frappé (slapshot)	tir frappé
jambières ou pads	bottes ou guêtres
arrêt	parade
mitaine	gant d'attrape
prolongation	mort subite

(C.B.)

Hockey and Politics, Same Battle!¹

Jean-Claude Simard

Can the findings of anthropology teach us anything about today's world? Can examining the primitive origins of sport bring us to a deeper understanding of contemporary rituals, specifically hockey rituals? And can we take a serious look at our national sport and still have fun doing it? In this chapter, we'll take a stab at these questions plus a few more.

Prior to European contact, several Central American peoples practiced a rather unusual game called *ullamaliztli* in the Nahuatl language. The *tlachtli*, or playing surface, was delineated by two high walls facing each other. At the top of each wall was a stone ring. The players were divided into two opposing teams, and the object of the game was to shoot a heavy rubber ball through these rings (rubber, as we know, is a material that originated in the Americas).

There's something familiar about this description; the whole affair looks a lot like a contemporary sport. Certain people even see *ullamaliztli* as a distant ancestor of modern-day basketball. There were a few key differences back then, however. For one thing, after the game was over, the captain of the losing team was generally decapitated with a knife made of obsidian in a planned ceremony! The walls were sometimes adorned with sculptures of animal

1. This text has been revised for publication in English; it differs markedly from the original French version. The examples in the text have also been updated.

rituals or human sacrifices. Also, in Aztec cultures, the heavy ball often contained a human skull. The spectators were compulsive gamblers who wagered their possessions, their harvests, and even their property on the outcome of the match. Some even went so far as to put their children, their freedom, or their own lives on the line. (I'm reluctant to admit that this puts Loto-Québec, with its casinos and 12,000 slot machines, in a more favourable light.) The K'iche' Maya, who called the game *pitz*, used it as a way to recount an origin myth. Here's how the story goes in their sacred text, *Popol Vuh*: in the very first *pitz* game, the sovereigns of Xibalba, the kingdom of the dead, battled a pair of twins, who were vanquished and sacrificed. It so happened that one of the twins was the maize god; his skull germinated and grew into a woman, who gave birth to a second set of twins. This was the redemption that had been so hoped for, for the twins ultimately went on to vanquish the cruel rulers of Xibalba. The second pair of twins rose into the heavens, where they are embodied by the Sun and the Moon. But before they left the infernal kingdom, they brought the maize god back to life. Ever since, the underworld has remained in order: the sacred plant has nourished humans and, to the delight of all, the two celestial orbs illuminate the Earth. The trajectory of the rubber ball retraces their path across the sky, while the struggle between the two teams replays the initial battle between good and evil, symbolized by day and night.

How does this retelling of the origin myth relate to sport? What were *ullamaliztli* and *pitz*, those fascinating Mesoamerican reformulations of the cosmic tale? In acting out the changeless cycle of death and rebirth, and the alternation between day and night regulated by the periodic return of the twin brothers, were the Mesoamericans simply playing a cruel game or an especially gruesome sport? Or was the practice more in the vein of a religious ritual, or even a political myth? The answer is both none of the above and all of the above. Lumping together recreation with religion and melding sport with politics is at odds with our usual categories. Our minds automatically separate and compartmentalize sport, politics, religion, myth, and play. But is it possible that modern sport has retained something of its mytho-religious roots—an intrinsic link with political life, for instance? Could both these activities be, to turn Clausewitz's famous formula on its head, the continuation of war by other means? Let's unpack this question and attempt to grasp the meaning of contemporary sport by visiting a more familiar past. We'll start with a trip to Ancient Greece.

We know that it was the Ancient Greeks who created both sport and politics in the modern sense of these terms, which is to say as fully distinct and secular activities. Following a process of secularization that gradually freed them from their religious shackles, the Olympic Games appeared in the year 776 BCE. Democracy followed less than two centuries later. But even after this necessary journey from divine rule to the human order was complete, sport and politics long retained something of their original symbiosis throughout Antiquity. Obviously, our current separation between these spheres precludes a Mesoamerican-style fusion of the two. But taking a step back, we can still spot fragments of their common origin and cut to the heart of this curious homology. Let's see what an impartial, quasi-anthropological perspective can teach us about Québec's two national sports: hockey and politics.

~

Looking in on the situation as impartial observers, we are first struck by the observation that both practices unfold in highly ritualized spaces, namely Parliament and the hockey rink. Only certain people are granted entry into these confines, which abound in special rules and conventions that differ significantly from those found in other institutional spaces. Because of this, the players in these arenas enjoy a kind of immunity, despite the inherent combativeness of their exchanges. Indeed, politicians are masters of insinuation, subtext, verbal attack, challenging people's integrity, and more. And in sport, crosschecking is an obvious example of combativeness. Some instances of the practice, which is becoming more common in hockey, have been covered extensively in the media and are still fresh in our minds. As I write this, ten retired hockey players are filing a lawsuit against the NHL with the federal court in Washington DC, including Rick Vaive and Gary Leeman, formerly of the Toronto Maple Leafs. They allege that the league promotes a "culture of violence" and fails to provide adequate protection for players. They contend that the league effectively refuses to prohibit underhanded body checking and violent blows to the head, which are obviously the cause of repeated concussions, all in the name of profit and dubious tradition. They attribute their brain injuries and other injuries directly to their NHL careers. QED.

Are they right? Unquestionably. Think of it this way: outside the confines of hockey, these common displays of aggression (veritable *casus belli*) would be grounds for criminal proceedings for assault, either with or without causing bodily harm. Yet most often the transgressors are excused or, in the most serious cases, suspended—a slap on the wrist considering the seriousness of these acts. Butting heads has always been part of hockey and politics; the former is a full-on contact sport, and the latter certainly qualifies as an adversarial pursuit. The public always enjoys a good old bout of fisticuffs on the ice, which of course translates into tidy sums at the box office. When controlled and refereed in this fashion, violence becomes ritualized: a hockey game just isn't complete until somebody throws down the gloves, in the same way that a parliamentary session is inconceivable without a virile debate or a lively row. But in the case of hockey, it's important to distinguish between fighting and intent to injure, virility and unsportsmanlike conduct, toughness and wanton violence. If wild acts of aggression are rarely punished, it's because the justice of the Wild West prevails in this peculiar precinct; the normal standards are, well, out of bounds. But how much longer can symbolism fulfil its ceremonial purpose in this lawless arena? O virtue of impunity!

These two precincts also exhibit a symmetrical division of space. The opposing camps are arranged to be literally facing each other, which clarifies their positioning and bolsters team spirit. War essentially boils down to an effort to conquer new territory. This is also true of team sports in which the playing surface is usually symbolically divided into two equal-sized areas, with each team aiming to occupy and control the opponent's zone. Just as politics wages war by other means, sport acts as a civilized and ritualized

The hockey stick blues

It's my job to get the puck from A to B. To serve as an extension of the player's arm, to allow him to show what he's made of, to demonstrate his talent to the fullest: that's my *raison d'être*. Ah! To act according to one's nature will always be, as Spinoza said, the ultimate pleasure of all reasonable beings. And I fully appreciate my lucky lot in life. Still, I must admit I find some recent trends disturbing. Like, was it really necessary to give me this accentuated curve? For such a manly sport, it strikes me as kind of girly. And what about hooking? Using me to fend off other players, honestly! I'm not one for underhanded violence. Hooking is one thing. But spearing players from the other team, or even clubbing them with both hands, that just goes against every fibre of my being. It tears me up inside. . . If somebody back in the workshop had told me that I could be used a weapon, I definitely would have considered another career. Maybe it's not too late. Apparently, I can be recycled in the Canadian Armed Forces. There's plenty of work in Afghanistan and, if recent reports are to be believed, the pay isn't bad. I'm not sure I'd want to be carried in a bandolier, though.

battle. This sanitization of war is also found in archery, equestrian events, pentathlon, fencing, biathlon, and of course, martial arts. It is less obvious but still present in hockey, which is a form of *agonistic* duel (think *protagonist*, *antagonist*). The concept of *agon* is used by the French sociologist and writer Roger Caillois, who in turn borrowed it from Nietzschean philosophy. The term originally comes from the Greeks, who used it to name an activity in which opponents struggle against one another but still abide by the established rules—much like knightly jousting, with its code of honour. So it is with sports and politics, in which adherence to this original spirit still shines through their apparent ordinariness. For example, loyalty to the leader, team spirit, and the English concept of fair

play are found in both. Attack and defence strategies are indispensable to both. Finally, and most importantly, both contain forms of
violence that are circumscribed and channelled.

Having said this, we must also note two important differences
between sport and politics. The first difference is that sport requires
an alternate timescale, a game clock that is superimposed over the
normal clock time. And, with the notorious exceptions of baseball
and cricket, this parallel dimension of time is bounded; for example,
hockey games are capped at 60 minutes. Game time is also special
in that it can be paused; the ticking of the clock can be suspended,
and certain actions can even be done over again. In other words,
the symbolic space of the field is undergirded by ahistorical time.
(It would be very interesting to discuss the various rituals imposed
by this singular space-time.) This rare privilege obviously does not
carry over into daily life in Parliament. The second difference is
that, in politics, one of the two entities governs while the other
obstructs it or, in the best-case scenario, opposes it. (Parliament
theoretically involves organized opposition.) So, the camps are not
equal as they are in team sports. This is an important feature. In
addition, both sport and politics have delegated representatives of
the people who are chosen, among other reasons, for their skills.
(The notion of representative democracy is the second pillar in the
modern political establishment.) But while in the one case leaders
must survive the test of the ballot box, in the other they must display hard work and talent, sometimes even garnering public adulation. Simply put, politics is governed by democracy while sport is a
form of meritocracy, theoretically impervious to the privileges of
wealth or birth. But both fields have their popular heroes, who are
chosen by the public. This fact is what allowed Roland Barthes, the
rebel semiologist, to decipher the remnants of ancient beliefs in
various activities of contemporary life. His celebrated work
Mythologies (1957) represents a model of the genre. For example,
in his analysis of the Tour de France and the people who compete
in it, he compared the epic efforts of the cyclists who brave the high
passes of the Alps and the Pyrenees to the battles of Homeric
heroes. Commenting on this text in an interview a few years ago,
the great German philosopher Sloterdijk, a follower of ancient

Cynicism, noted that the thirst for heroism engendered a paradox-
ical attitude.[2] On the one hand, we want to believe in something,
and the need to admire is resilient in the face of all odds. On the
other hand, doping corrodes professional cycling (the Lance
Armstrong affair is a familiar case). In Sloterdijk's view, the result
is simple: despite the scourge of doping, the competitors still retain
something of their sacred aura. And, I would add, even if deeply
tainted, superhuman effort still represents the path to glory:
through sacrifice, the athlete is sanctified, cleansed of doubt, and
redeemed.

There is another unique feature that unites sport and politics
for the Greeks: both have a game-like dimension. Consider the
concept of isonomy, equality before the law, which translates into
hockey either as the impartiality of the referee (who is bound to
apply the rules of the game across the board) or as equal odds of
winning (without which the game would have no point). Let's also
note just how fine the line between sports and games can be. First
of all, unlike work, neither produces anything useful. This is still
true for contemporary professional sport, handsomely paid though
it is. Of course, games involve little training or physical effort and
are more up to random chance. (The unknowns of sport are too
numerous to completely ignore, however.) One is of course practiced more by adults, while the other is mainly associated with
childhood. Yet adults still do enjoy many games, from board games
to the lottery to the countless game shows and video games that
have enjoyed such phenomenal popularity in recent years. So we
see that the dimension of playfulness, present in both politics and
in sport, sometimes makes it difficult to distinguish sport from a
simple organized game.

Let's note one last feature that's common to both practices. As
public activities, sports and politics both involve a form of spectacle. It is certainly no accident that the Greeks also invented theatre, another form of civic and agonistic expression. Going into
specifics would be beyond the scope of this chapter, however.

---

2.   Lothar Gorris, Dirk Kurbjuweit, and Peter Sloterdijk, "Entretien. 'Même
      dopés, ils sont sacrés,'" *Courrier international* No. 924, July 17, 2008, pp. 7–9.

Suffice it to say that, far from diminishing the spectacle, the modern media (especially television) are in fact the pinnacle of the theatrical creation that the Romans, despite the the extravagance of their circuses, never dreamed of. Extensive media coverage, made possible by the rise of screens and the ubiquity of images, has altered how we view sports as much as we do politics. Since that time, we haven't stopped talking about, as Guy Debord phrased it in 1967, the society of the spectacle.

Up to this point, most of our attention has been focused on the homologous relationship between sport and politics. This exercise has highlighted a complicit duality stemming from their shared origin of long ago. But our anthropological considerations can take us on a still deeper journey, which we will undertake presently.

Let's start by looking at one of Lévi-Strauss's first works, *The Elementary Structures of Kinship* (1949). The ethnography of traditional societies teaches us that men have always sought to tame Nature. For this purpose, they created Culture, which is primarily predicated on the establishment of rules. And the very first rule was exchange. It is spoken of in myths; it is borne out in the various systems of kinship. So, then, how do men communicate; what are the two main channels of exchange? One way is through the words of language, and the other is through women, the objects of desire. Words are signs, women are signs and value; words constitute the source of all symbolic thought, women constitute the promise of all social life. Thus, men communicate both through discourse and through matrimonial alliances. (For Lévi-Strauss, the two systems of signs, language and culture, are unified by the phonological model, but that is beyond the scope of this discussion.) This is why anthropologists posit that the prohibition of incest and exogamy are absolutely fundamental to human relations. These norms effectively cordon off the mechanism of forging alliances, while at the same time ensuring the necessary circulation of women. This dual process thus establishes a new human order, that of acculturation. The establishment and regulation of the order push brute nature to a distance and keep it there. In this way, against all expectations, "the savage mind," to use Lévi-Strauss's famous expression, is shown to be closely related, if not identical, to our own.

So, we have a system of relations that conditions human existence, with exchange being the most elementary form of social relation. Let's expand on this principle, which Lévi-Strauss consciously limits to superstructures. Economic infrastructure—to use the register of Marxist terminology—represents another clear case in which the exchange of objects, services, and various forms of money (which obviously stand in for objects and services) plays the central role. It is hard to imagine how wealth could be distributed any other way. When it comes to politics, we know that verbal exchange plays a major role, if only through the related modes of discourse and dialogue, two features that are essential to democracy. (Both these modes were analyzed extensively by the ancient Greeks, who created politics in the first place.) But can the same be said of sport? This is a much more difficult problem, one that seems not to have been investigated fully. We know that Lévi-Strauss barely considered the issue, given that sport as a secular activity is conspicuously absent from traditional societies, as clearly seen in the Aztec and Mayan cases that we discussed at the beginning of this chapter. Does this mean that sport is a system of exchange analogous to language, economy, politics, and systems of kinship? In my opinion, the answer has to be yes. Here's why.

First, let's disregard sports in which the goal is to bring down an opponent, such as boxing and wrestling (although it is true that boxers do exchange blows). Let's also exclude the two main forms of individual races, swimming and track. We'll also leave out jumping events, weight lifting, gymnastics, golf, and so on. What does that leave? Sports like tennis and badminton, plus team sports: basketball, handball, soccer, football, and hockey. What do these sports have in common? Plenty, as it turns out, including the fact that each involves a travelling object. In individual games, the object is exchanged with the opponent. In group sports, it is passed around among teammates. Let's unpack this key point a bit further.

Group sports differ fundamentally from individual games, either with or without objects. In the former, the individual is effectively fused into the group, in a kind of tribalism. The mechanism by which this fusion is achieved is the circulation of the object within the team. During the game, the circulation is what binds the individuals together and activates the team. Thus, the moving link becomes the true engine of the game, and this "object of the game" (pardon the pun), assumes an exalted status. In a famous passage of Gaston Bachelard's *The Philosophy of No*, the author proposes the notion of the "super-object" and calls it the modern-day atom, for it is the result of a critical objectification, the output of the sophisticated machinery of technoscience. The same can be said of the travelling object in group sports. It is the intermediary that creates the game; it ensures collective cohesion, the link between teammates, or friendly competition between opponents. Thus, in transcending the thing itself, which is inherently static and meaningless, the super-object engenders a dynamic sublimation and transforms the players. For as long as it is not in their possession, as long as it is not circulating among them, they are mere subjects-in-waiting, their roles potential, their abilities virtual. But the instant the connection is made, they become agents and sources of creative freedom. Thus the game is unleashed, and the completion of this action can engender the collective magic through which each player transcends his condition of being a mere mortal to attain the status of hero. After all, what hockey player hasn't dreamed of scoring the winning goal in Game 7 of the Stanley Cup finals?

Let's note in passing that, in order to activate the game, most team sports use a round object, often a ball. As always, there is an exception to this: rugby. Honestly, you really need a people as eccentric as the English to invent an oval ball. (Football, in both its Canadian and American variants, also uses this "oddball.") Their excuse: it's not meant to roll on the ground. Now, without trying to be chauvinistic, let's take a moment to appreciate the rather singular shape of the puck: circular, yes, but not spherical. After all, it is a creature of its habitat. Instead of rolling it must, like the skate blade, glide.

The fate of the puck

Those humans make my family and me laugh. To think that they are the driving force of hockey. Ha! They do deserve some credit, of course. But honestly, where would they be without us? If we decided to stop letting ourselves be constantly pushed around, slapped by sticks, and passed between players, could the game even happen at all? We're the ones who create team sports, and we're also what keeps them together. After all, who else shows the skaters' speed and skill? Let's say it without vanity: the sport owes its beauty to our lightning-quick movement. And for the record, I find it a bit insulting being relegated to the level of a simple inanimate object. You think it's easy defying gravity? Think of the hours of training you need to glide as we do, almost frictionless, across the ice.

Despite the lack of praise, it's pretty decent work if you can stand the constant crashing, the stick constantly on your backside, and the violent smashes against the boards. In fact, there's only one thing that worries us. Actually, it terrifies us: sudden disappearance. Sometimes we talk about it in hushed whispers after the game. We don't like to cower in the face of danger, but... Rarely do members of our family ever go out of sight. Even if we've been to the back of the net, we can always get back in the game. But if one of us chances to fly above the glass and land in the crowd, it's game over. We never see them again. What happens to them? Nobody knows. And so it's with fear and trembling that we speak of that "undiscover'd country," as Hamlet said in his famous monologue, "from whose bourn no traveller returns."

To recap. A group sport is an activity in which subjects-in-waiting circulate a super-object. This makes it a powerful metaphor for human society. We all believe ourselves to be autonomous beings, full and complete subjects, but this is an illusion. In reality, as potential agents, we exist only through the intermediary of various fetish objects, and especially through the intermediary our fellow subjects-in-waiting. Without this double mediation, it would be impossible to create the linkages that are necessary for life, whether these be words in a language, discourse, goods and services, or alliances; it would be impossible to experience cohesion with kinship, the market, the state, or existence itself. So does team sport differ all that much from the supposedly nobler domains of family, economics, politics, and society? And if not, is it time to revisit this age-old rift in which high culture is prized and pop culture is devalued?

We have already discussed a few of the important differences between sport and politics, one being that the latter requires elections. Another key distinction arises from their shared relational aspect: political life is highly complex, especially in our postmodern era. The issues are diverse, the world is multipolar, bureaucracy is rampant, power is diffuse, lobbying is excessive, multinationals are destructive, the economy is globalized—all in all, the world around us is anything but easy to comprehend. But not so with team sports. By limiting the action to just a handful of players, by placing them under the authority of a leader (the captain), by limiting the laws to a few basic rules, by circulating a single clearly identified object, by polarizing the two camps, and finally by allowing for a clear victory, we simplify this microcosm of society. You could even say we stylize it. The clarity of the game clears away the grey areas, the maybes of daily life. This metaphor for community even has its own system of aesthetics that reinforces the timeless grace of the perfect play. Nuance be damned! Team sport, this clear distillation of human relations, is a form of social refinement, a sort of existential concentrate.

The stylization of sport has some notable effects. The first is stardom. Heroes like Maurice Richard, Bobby Hull, and Guy Lafleur are *stars*; they are *idols*. Terms like these paint them as demigods, supernatural beings boiled down to their pure essence who transcend the human condition: we speak of *rockets*, *jets*, and *demons*. I think this is one of the reasons behind the exorbitant salaries of the elite players. I'll be the first to admit that they help their team win, which in turn allows the owner to reap a profit. But that's not where the fans get their enjoyment: for them, the players are the supreme embodiment of the act; they graze artistic perfection. Sports heroes elevate us; they give us something to dream about—and that dream necessarily has its price.

The second effect of this purification process is even more deserving of the attention we fail to give it. The complexities of economic and political life may turn people off, but when it comes to sports, everybody believes himself to be competent, if not an expert. Just tune in to a call-in show or observe the extraordinary appeal of hockey pools: there's no shortage of "armchair managers." In my opinion, this has to be one of the reasons why team sports are so popular, why they have such exceptional rallying power. How would we ever run a country if there were no sports to help us channel a significant amount of human aggression? In fact, it's as if the stylization of team sport, the microcosm, reflects back on crowd, reducing the complexity of the human heart to one powerful emotion after another: tension, agitation, disappointment, overflowing joy. This tribal range of emotions, as intense as it is limited, can easily overcome the barriers of countries, eras, and various political systems. This is as true for the fans as it is for states. Politicizing sport by controlling the veneer of emotion is easily done. We allow Olympic athletes to compete under the flag of their country, we play the national anthem if they win, and so on. What an incredible vector of identity! Unfortunately, politicization easily spills over into exploitation if it is abused. We saw this with the Berlin Olympics in 1936, which ultimately were used to champion the racial supremacy of the German people. And for half a century, we scoffed when athletes were reduced to vaunting the superiority of Communist regimes. Recently, we saw this with China, which shamelessly used the 2008 Olympics to serve its new global ambitions.

The Clamour of Being

There is a peculiar theory that team sports consist of quasi-subjects circulating a super-object. It may seem strange, but then why not? After all, I, the humble flag, have seen far stranger things in my time.

Take the Olympics, for example. When the crowds are excited, with their arms a-waving and their feet a-stomping, there's electricity in the air. And think of the emotions that get unleashed when a goal is scored or when a fight breaks out! From way up here, the spectacle is just incredible. The fans are supercharged, they do the wave by the thousands, they jump up and cheer with one voice; the building shakes on its foundation. The deafening clamour, the convulsing tide of synchronized human bodies—it's all so surreal. Is this monstrous being that appears a superior Being or a subhuman Beast? It's hard to say. Its arrival is so unpredictable, its disappearance so sudden.

But what astounds me the most is how this behemoth reacts to things. I'll never understand how a simple piece of fabric can unleash such violent passions. Is it my instantly identifiable design? Maybe it's my vivid primary colours. I don't know, but regardless, I symbolize the nation in its own eyes for some reason or another. Just how I manage to do this is beyond me. I can remember a certain Good Friday in Québec. . . But no, it would be best to forget that.

You'll notice that it's even worse for my cousins in the crowd. The things they tell me about what it's like among the fans—ridiculous! They get all bent out of shape over it. At least here atop the flagpole, I'm out of reach; I never get pulled in all directions, or bent, or torn. I shudder to think of it. Must be the wind.

We've just looked at a few areas of overlap between sport and politics. I would be remiss if I closed without examining hockey in

Québec, onto which nationalistic fervour so easily latches. One case stands out above the rest: the legendary rivalry between the Canadiens and the Nordiques. This rivalry is still fresh in many people's memories, and some would even like to see it live another day. It steamrolled over the boundaries of sport and healthy competition, and instead became one of the most extreme instances of the politicization of sport in Québec history. When hostilities were at their fiercest, the province was rent asunder. People would refuse to speak to their own flesh and blood. They would go out in the middle of the night to show their hatred for the opposing team.

Of course, the imbroglio that this became was no accident. The flames were actively fanned by the media. In addition, the coaches of the two organizations engaged in psychological warfare at all levels. And the whole affair was magnified by an intense battle of the breweries, with Molson (allied with the Canadiens) on one side and O'Keefe (allied with the Nordiques) on the other, each looking to increase its respective market share.

This perfect storm stirred the fans' sense of pride and inflated the players' spirits. It was only a matter of time before these appalling excesses erupted, as they did one famous Good Friday. But what made this politicization possible in the first place?

From its inception, the Canadiens had always borne the aspirations of the French Canadian people. But in the wake of the Quiet Revolution, Québécois soon found themselves with two irreconcilable ways of seeing their role in the federation: Trudeau's and Lévesque's. And the arrival of the Nordiques accompanied this rift between the two allegiances: one federalist, the other separatist. We can therefore advance a simple hypothesis: the two hockey teams furthered this schism of loyalties and cast a political hue over the entire sport. Overnight, the Canadiens, which had always represented the Québécois, especially in the era of Richard and Béliveau, saw the Nordiques challenge them for this role and take up the sovereigntist cause. Consider the following as evidence:

- The predominant colour of the Canadiens and the Nordiques, red and blue respectively, neatly corresponded to those of the two main political parties, as do the Canadian and Québec flags.

- The managers' politics reinforced this divide, with Serge Savard being conspicuously federalist and Marcel Aubut clearly sovereigntist.
- The Nordiques had more Francophone players, while the Canadiens were dominated by Anglophones.
- The home cities of the two teams also underscored the split, Montréal being much more multi-ethnic and Québec City being almost exclusively Francophone.
- Even the choice and personalities of the coaches mirrored this dualism, Lemaire exhibiting a decidedly British arrogance and aloofness, while Bergeron, "The Tiger," had an eminently Latin temper. (He later suffered from serious heart problems. . .)

On top of all this, there was one final major factor: sociologically, Montréal's meteoric rise over the course of the twentieth century gradually gave it the status of an international city down the road from an oversized village, Québec City. In other words, the old unilingual capital was now to the multicultural metropolis what the province of Québec was to Canada.

This pernicious political symbolism was fed for years and years. With so many destructive ingredients reacting with one another, the situation was bound to spiral out of control. In light of our discussion of the primitive origins of sport—the idea that team sport is a watered-down and ritualized version of war and therefore fires emotions that are as primal as they are powerful—is it any wonder?

∾

What can we conclude from this? Team sport—and hockey is no exception—is a crystal-clear metaphor for community, a microcosm of society. Even in the absence of any politicization (or of its caricaturized form, instrumentalization), team sport still flirts with politics. In ancient societies, such as the Aztecs and the Mayas, the two were inseparable. Does this spontaneous marriage explain the separate but near-simultaneous birth of the two practices in Ancient Greece? And can this homology be expected to disappear any time soon? Unlikely. Given that it is practiced in its own special arena and regulated on its own special timescale with its own special rules, and given that it feeds a passion not seen anywhere else, sport is above common time. A supreme form of popular spectacle, yet at the same time a distillation of the act, an emotional veneer, and a social stylization, sport inspires dreams and creates heroes. Given its free-entry nature, a trait that makes it somewhat less like politics and more like a game, it is an eminently mimetic activity. Therefore it will undoubtedly continue to mirror society, now and in future. How can you resist a beautiful image? Especially when this embellished reflection offers to free us from our worries and cares. After all, isn't sport's greatest virtue exactly that: to lift us out of the dullness of everyday life?

Further reading

CAILLOIS, Roger. *Les jeux et les hommes: le masque et le vertige*. Paris: Gallimard, 1958.

> To learn more in-depth about the four cateogies of games identified by Caillois, including agon.

HANDKE, Peter. *L'angoisse du gardien de but au moment du penalty*. Paris: Gallimard, 1982. [*Die Angst des Tormanns beim Elfmeter*] Trad. de l'allemand (Autriche) par Anne Gaudu.

> Just for laughs.

VERNANT, Jean-Pierre. *Les origines de la pensée grecque*. Paris: PUF, 1981.

> To learn about ancient Greek thought and the role of speeches in the city.

Hockey Salaries: Scandal or Fair Pay?

Mario Jodoin

Daniel Brière, Scott Gomez, and Thomas Vanek rake in $10 million a year. Jaromír Jágr had to settle for a paltry $8.36 million in 2007–2008, down from $11 million in 2003–2004.[1] Astronomical, mind-boggling, staggering—there's no shortage of descriptors when it comes to hockey salaries. And yet, as we saw in Jágr's case, they actually decreased overall by 24 percent in 2005 with the NHL's new collective bargaining agreement. What's more, in a jaw-dropping burst of social democracy, the players saw the minimum salary raised from a meagre $185,000 to a more respectable $450,000 in exchange for this. And none of these figures includes goodies on the side, like income from advertising campaigns.

Is this situation fair, or is it scandalous? To answer this question, first we must ask how salaries are traditionally established on the labour market and why certain jobs and professions are more highly paid than others in the first place.

1 Salary determination

"How much does it pay?" Much to the disappointment of guidance counsellors everywhere, this is often the first question a young person will ask about a potential job. The question itself illustrates one of the great myths in common circulation, which is that the salary

---

1. According to http://fr.wikipedia.org/wiki/Salaires_des_joueurs_de_la_LNH; all links mentioned in this article were checked on December 7, 2008.

in a given profession conforms to a specific pay scale. This is rarely the case. As in hockey, where those at the top of the ladder make 20 times as much as those at the bottom, salaries vary considerably in almost all professions. What are the factors affecting this variation?

1.1 Living wage and the Iron Law of Wages

Adam Smith, who is widely considered to be the first modern economist, first advanced the idea that the equilibrium wage is the one that allows a person to subsist and to raise a family.[2] He was followed by David Ricardo, another influential economist of the era, with his concept of the natural wage[3] (pretty much the same thing) and, about a century later, by none other than Karl Marx, the icon of Communism! In one of his critiques of capitalism entitled *Value, Price and Profit*, Marx denounced the fact that the worker, in renting out his "labour power" to his employer (which Marx of course referred to as the "capitalist"), couldn't obtain a wage greater than the cost of reproduction of his labour power, which was equivalent to the subsistence wage for him and his family.

In the same era, Ferdinand Lassalle, a much less well-known figure, "refined" the thinking of Smith and Ricardo by comparing labour costs to the costs of production. According to him, just as one must provide a machine with fuel and save up money to cover the expense of replacing it at a later time, so too must one feed the worker so that he can work and also provide him with the means to raise children in order to replace old workers that have become "defective." Without a hint of humour, and utterly convinced of the soundness of his thinking, he named his theory the Iron Law of Wages.

We have reason to believe that this "law" fell out of practice well before the turn of the twentieth century. In the early part of that century, even here in Québec, people still justified the lower wages that women made on the grounds that they didn't have to

---

2. Adam Smith, *The Wealth of Nations* (London: W. Strahan and T. Cadell, 1776).

3. David Ricardo, *On the Principles of Political Economy and Taxation* (London: John Murray, 1817).

provide for their families. In fact, the reasons behind this practice were not economic but moral (or rather immoral, as we might say today): a woman's place was at home, especially if she was married. From 1921 to 1955, the federal government placed restrictions on the hiring of women and actually forced them to resign when they got married[4] because they now had a man to provide for them and their families!

This makes us more sympathetic to the hockey player who, with a tear in his eye, sighs that he's being forced to accept a higher-paying contract with a different team because he's got his family's security to think about. Clearly.

1.2 Supply and demand

The law of supply and demand obviously plays an important role in salary determination. But is it really a law? Many economists assume it's as immutable as the law of gravity.[5] Others, who consider economics a social science, say it's more a principle than a law, or even that it's a theory used to rationalize and justify certain political choices.[6]

1.2.1 Derivatives markets

In analyzing salary determination, the first thing to understand is that the labour market functions as a derivatives market. It's influenced by the market for the goods and services produced by labour. So, hockey salaries are determined on the basis of supply and demand for players, which in turn depends on the supply and demand for hockey games.

---

4. See the year 1920 at http://www.psc-cfp.gc.ca/abt-aps/tpsc-hcfp/index-fra.htm.
5. For a recent example, see Guy Sorman, *L'économie ne ment pas* (Paris: Fayard, 2008).
6. See, among others, Jacques Généreux, *Les Vraies Lois de l'économie* (Paris: Seuil: 2001, and the declaration *Pour une autre vision de l'économie* (*Towards a different vision of economics*) by a group of Québec economists in http://economieautrement.org/files/Pour%20une%20autre%20vision%20de%20l%27economie.pdf.

1.2.2 Maximizing utility and profit

The law of supply and demand is predicated on the idea that demanders want to maximize their utility (or economic well-being) while suppliers want to maximize their profits. To maximize her utility, a fan who buys a hockey ticket must have previously evaluated all other purchases that she could have made with this money and concluded that no other expense of the same magnitude could have brought her more economic well-being. For his part, the supplier maximizes profits by investing in the market that will allow him to extract the highest possible profit, having rejected all other investment options.

1.2.3 Economic rationality

To maximize their utility and profit, respectively, demanders and suppliers must behave like good *Homo economicus*, which is to say in an economically rational fashion. But do humans always act rationally?

Bertrand Russell clearly demonstrates that humans often make decisions, economic or otherwise, in reaction to uncontrollable impulses rather than rational analysis.[7] Similarly, Kahneman and Tversky, psychologists of cognitive biases, have conducted dozens of studies showing major cognitive biases on the part of participants,[8] especially when it comes to evaluating numbers and probabilities. In any event, is it rational to suppose that a human can evaluate every single possibility in every single purchase and investment decision?

As economically rational suppliers, the workers are supposed to make career decisions and choose their jobs based solely on maximization of profit, therefore on their pay. In reality, however, they consider several other factors. If they are to be satisfied with their jobs, for example, they must consider their interests. And many hockey players have accepted less lucrative contracts in order to

---

7. Bertrand Russell, *Principles of Social Reconstruction* (London: Allen & Unwin, 1924).

8. These studies have been amply cited in Gérald Bronner's *L'empire de l'erreur* (Paris: Presses universitaires de France, 2007); some cases are presented in http://www.cess.paris4.sorbonne.fr/CR261103/CR261103Bronner.htm.

increase their chances of playing with winning teams or to settle in a city that their partner would rather live in. These are completely rational things for a person to do, just not as a *Homo economicus*.

Similarly, some owners are prepared to run teams at a loss in order to win. This behaviour isn't irrational in the common sense of the term, but it is irrational in economic terms. The reason why professional sports leagues adopted salary caps and the NHL declared a lockout in 2004–2005 was to discipline the "less rational" owners as much as it was to protect themselves from the players' salary demands.

Jim Balsillie, former owner of Research In Motion and inventor of the BlackBerry, has tried to purchase the Pittsburgh Penguins and the Nashville Predators, and possibly even the Buffalo Sabres and the Atlanta Thrashers, in order to move the team to Hamilton, it would seem. According to a more recent rumour, he wants to purchase the Montréal Canadiens! Whatever Balsillie's true motives are, his behaviour in no way matches that of an economically rational investor who wants to maximize profits. He looks more like a consumer who wants to make a dream come true. Is this man an investor or a consumer? Can someone be a supplier and a consumer at the same time? If so, is he rational?

1.2.4 Perfect competition and its conditions
Even for fans of the law of supply and demand (who aren't necessarily Canadiens fans), the law applies only in situations of perfect competition. In order for a market to have perfect competition, it must meet five conditions that aren't found anywhere in the real world.

1.2.4.1 Homogeneity of products
It's almost a given: all products on a given market must be very similar if not identical.

This criterion is not met in hockey because ability varies greatly from one player to the next. Teams hire scouts who rigorously evaluate players from a very young age. So it's no surprise that the players' association has never moved to adopt a pay schedule based on seniority!

1.2.4.2 Atomicity

No, we're not talking about the number of atoms in a molecule. We use this image to indicate that perfect competition can operate only in instances where there is a large number of suppliers and demanders (number of atoms), and in which each of these suppliers and demanders is of such a small (atom-like) size that they exert no influence on the functioning of the market.

But the number of demanders is small in hockey: just 30 teams. Also, a single player or team can indeed influence the behaviour of the market. The signing of a major contract changes the playing field entirely and causes the other players to become more demanding. That said, the adoption of salary caps has greatly reduced the impact of this condition.

1.2.4.3 Transparency

We're pretty much into an alternate reality at this point. All the agents in the market, demanders and suppliers alike, must have access to all available information.

But rather than advertising their Achilles heels, teams purposely use vague terms like "lower-body" injuries. Also, while the information on players' salaries is widely distributed, this is not true of the teams' financial standings. In fact, one of the main stumbling blocks in the labour dispute that led to the cancellation of the 2004–2005 season was the teams' refusal to "open their books" to the players' association to substantiate the claim that they had accrued $300 million worth of debt.

1.2.4.4 Free entry and exit

This condition pushes us even further into that alternate reality. The market must be free of all barriers (regulations, tariffs, protectionism, etc.). No market meets this condition, least of all the labour market, with its labour standards, workplace health and safety regulations, employment insurance, professional bodies, unions, employers' associations, etc.

Access to the NHL is very difficult for investors, as any purchase or creation of a new team must be approved by the league. Also, the salary cap and the regulations governing drafting and free agent status greatly restrict the players' freedom.

1.2.4.5 Perfect mobility of factors

Did I mention an alternate reality? If the factors were perfectly mobile, all agents (demanders and suppliers) could, instantaneously and with zero cost, leave one market for another. Demand for tomatoes is falling? Let's make computers! Accounting is in a slump? Why not play hockey?!

Because of the low mobility of factors on the labour market, one must often go back to school to change careers, unless previously acquired skills carry over and meet the requirements of the new job. Because their skills are transferrable to only a limited number of professions, many retired hockey players become coaches (some coach their own children) or sports journalists. That, or they open breweries.

1.2.5 Elasticity

While the conditions for perfect competition do not exist anywhere in the real world, it can't be denied that supply and demand still play an essential role in the functioning of markets and that all human beings, despite their limited rationality, still try to maximize their well-being. For instance, we know that consumers generally purchase less of a good when the price goes up. But how much will they trim their consumption in response to a given price hike? That's where the notion of elasticity comes in. Generally speaking, the quantity of essential needs sold (food, housing, etc.) does not vary when prices increase. You always need food in your belly and a roof over your head, so elasticity is low for these goods. The opposite is usually (but not always) true when it comes to less necessary goods, such as meals in restaurants.

Even when we take this categorization into account, elasticity is almost impossible to evaluate or predict. For example, the spike in gas prices we saw in 2007 should have reduced gas consumption considerably, but that didn't happen (Canadian consumption actually increased by 2.5 percent from 2006 to 2007). Economic theory may tell us that the consumption of gas would eventually decrease if prices remained high or continued to increase, but it cannot tell us how much it would decrease based on a given price level. In other words, it cannot quantify the elasticity of demand for gas.

When it comes to NHL hockey, demand varies considerably based on how good the teams are, how high the stakes are, and where the teams are located. Demand in Montréal is not very elastic, considering the supply (one team, about 21,300 seats, and 50 games a year). Despite the increase in supply generated by the construction of the Molson Centre (now the Bell Centre) in 1996, the team's uneven track record, and the steep price increase in recent years, the Canadiens have no trouble selling tickets, even for exhibition games.

1.2.6 Salary rigidity

On the labour market, salaries are fairly elastic to go up, but not to go down. Salaries usually increase in times of labour shortage, but they rarely ever decrease, even in times of labour surplus. The concept of salary rigidity comes to us from John Maynard Keynes, probably the most influential economist of the twentieth century. Keynes said that while employees may ultimately agree to a salary freeze (effectively a pay cut, given inflation), they react vociferously to a drop in nominal salary. We saw this in the 2004–2005 hockey lockout; it took a year for players to agree to a 24 percent drop in nominal salary.

1.3 Productivity

No single factor explains differences among salaries for the different professions better than productivity. In the usual sense of the term, to be more productive is to be more efficient, to work faster. But in economics, "Labour productivity is measured as gross domestic product (GDP) per hour worked."[9] So, being more productive isn't necessarily a matter of just working harder and faster, but rather of producing goods and services with a higher monetary value. The level of hockey salaries and the differences between them reflect the revenue the teams generate from spectators, TV networks, and purchases of derivative products (jerseys, hats, etc.)

---

9. John R. Baldwin and Wulong Gu, *Productivity: What Is It? How Is It Measured? What Has Canada's Performance Been?*, The Canadian Productivity Review, No. 017 (Ottawa: Statistics Canada, 2008), p. 7. http://www.statcan.gc.ca/pub/15-206-x/15-206-x2008017-eng.pdf.

thanks to the performance of their players. This means hockey players are in fact paid based on their productivity.

Also, hockey players don't work any less hard than players of other team sports, but because their sport is less popular (in lower demand), they are less "productive." In 2007, the highest hockey salary ($10 million) was in fact much lower than the top salaries in basketball (Shaquille O'Neal, $26 million), baseball (Roger Clemens, $28 million), football (Dwight Freeney, $30.75 million), and soccer (Ronaldinho, about $35 million).

The collective bargaining agreement between the NHL and the players' association clearly illustrates the relationship between salaries and productivity. They agreed to a variable salary cap based on the owners' revenue, and therefore on the players' collective productivity. As a consequence of the increase in owners' revenues, the salary cap increased by 45 percent in only three years, from US $39 million in 2005–2006 to $56 million in 2008–2009. In light of the economic crisis in swing at the time of writing, it would not be surprising if the cap were to drop next year.

1.4 Other factors in salary determination

Despite its dominant influence, work productivity doesn't explain everything. For example, salaries have increased very little in the United States since the 1980s, even though there has been strong growth in productivity. Some authors attribute this wage stagnation to the effects of outsourcing, relocation of operations to lower-wage countries, new modes of organization and the consequences of growth in the "new economy." Paul Krugman, winner of the 2008 Nobel Prize in Economics, doesn't deny that these factors play a role, but he attributes wage stagnation mainly to the appropriation of productivity gains by corporate managers and to the inegalitarian Republican policies implemented since Ronald Reagan came into office in the early 1980s.[10]

Below is a brief discussion of a few more factors affecting salaries and salary trends.

---

10. Paul Krugman, *L'Amérique que nous voulons*, trans. by Paul Chemla (Paris: Flammarion, 2008) [Paul Krugman, *The Conscience of a Liberal* (New York: W.W. Norton & Co., 2007)].

1.4.1 History and values

Because the first daycares in Québec were established through job creation programs in the 1970s and 1980s, remuneration of daycare educators has remained much lower over the years than that of professions requiring similar skill levels. It took worker unionization, a series of protest movements, and the adoption of the *Pay Equity Act* in 1996 (the outcome of changing societal values), for the situation to be rectified somewhat. Also, Curt Flood's refusal to be traded to another baseball team in 1969, which was appealed all the way up to the Supreme Court of the United States, was ultimately unsuccessful but set the stage for free agent status and the meteoric rise of salaries in professional sports.

1.4.2 Compensating differentials

Salaries tend to compensate for how hard a job is (mining, construction, etc.) and how inconvenient the hours are (nights, weekends, prolonged time away from home, etc.). Hockey players certainly benefit from these compensating differentials given the amount of travelling they do and especially the brevity of their careers.

1.4.3 The efficiency wage

Employers offer a higher wage than productivity would otherwise dictate in order to create incentives for their employees to engage more in their work. For example, a French senator, Yvon Collin, observed in 2004 that soccer teams paid their players more in order to increase their attachment to the team. Teams like these are essentially just encouraging the players to "give it 110 percent."

1.4.4. Other factors

Salary levels also depend on other factors that we will not analyze here: education, experience, skills, power dynamics (i.e., individual or collective through unionization), company size, talent, attitude, good looks (you better believe it![11]), luck, etc.

---

11. Sceptics will be astounded by this article: Jean Dion, "Et puis euh – La vie est injuste," *Le Devoir* (October 23, 2008). http://www.ledevoir.com/sports/actualites-sportives/212084/et-puis-euh-la-vie-est-injuste.

2. Salary and justice

The above analysis certainly gives us a better grasp on the factors that push hockey players' salaries so high. But even so, are they just?

2.1 The just salary

Back in 1891, Pope Leo XIII attempted to define a just salary in his encyclical *Rerum novarum* ("Of revolutionary change"): ". . . wages ought not to be insufficient to support a frugal and well-behaved wage-earner." This statement is basically a step down from the Iron Law of Wages, as the Pope sets out two conditions under which workers would make a subsistence wage! Given all the juicy tidbits fed to us by the sports media about performance-enhancing drugs and the unsavoury beverage-inspired acts our heroes commit at parties, it's not clear that all of them are sober and honest workers deserving of a subsistence salary.

In another piece tinged with religious morality, Louis Dutheillet de Lamothe[12] claimed that a just salary had to satisfy two forms of justice that Aristotle talked about, namely commutative justice and distributive justice. In this view, a salary must correspond to the value of the work performed; it can't be too high or too low. The minimum salary must allow for more than just subsistence—it must provide a decent life—whereas the maximum salary cannot exceed the social utility of the work performed. People's general good humour the morning after an important win suggests that hockey players' salary is fully justified by the social utility of what they provide. On the other hand, the general frustration we see the morning after a humiliating defeat might make people want to rail against the grossly overpaid schmucks from the rooftops. So take your pick.

---

12.   Louis Dutheillet de Lamothe, *Le juste salaire* (2005). http://www.eleves.ens.fr/aumonerie/en_ligne/paques05/seneve004.html.

2.2 Justice and egalitarianism

For John Rawls, the famous American liberal philosopher, justice doesn't mean egalitarianism;[13] rather, it's based on two principles that must apply to all members of society. The *liberty principle* covers most charter rights: the right to vote, freedom of expression, the right to property and protection, etc. The *difference principle* allows for economic and social inequalities, but only if people with equal talent and skill are given equal opportunity. Recognizing that individuals are not responsible for the talent they do or do not possess, he adds to his difference principle the obligation that the most affluent members of society share some of their wealth with the most disadvantaged. Applying these principles, we can say that all those who are talented at hockey have a roughly equal chance of making it into the NHL. Given that the taxes they pay help distribute some of their fortune to benefit their poorer fellow citizens, their salaries can be said to be just. Having said this, they would be more just in Canada than in the United States, and more just in Québec than in Alberta—but less just in Russia, where players pay very little in the way of tax (a flat rate of 13 percent)![14]

The French philosopher Patrick Savidan vehemently rejects the notion of equality of opportunity for equally talented people because of the enormous barriers to social success experienced by youth in disadvantaged neighbourhoods, people with disabilities, ethnic minorities, women, and so on.[15] While underscoring the importance of Rawls's contribution, the humanist economist Amartya Sen, recipient of the 1998 Nobel Prize in Economics and one of the people who created the Human Development Index, criticizes the difference principle on the grounds that it conflates means with ends by associating justice solely with the possession of goods, without accounting for the individuals' specific "capabilities" to convert these goods into liberty, the true indicator of

---

13.   John Rawls, *A Theory of Justice* (Cambridge: Belknap Press of Harvard University Press, 1971).
14.   See, among others: Frédérik Lavoie, "Une ligue russe aux ambitions continentals," *La Presse*, September 12, 2008. http://www.lapresse.ca/sports/200809/19/01-671518-une-ligue-russe-aux-ambitions-continentales.php.
15.   Patrick Savidan, *Repenser l'égalité des chances* (Paris : Grasset, 2007).

human justice.[16] Conversely, libertarian philosopher Robert Nozick, who believes that individuals do deserve their innate assets, rejects the obligation imposed by the difference principle to spread people's wealth without giving them a say in the matter, as this deprives them of pleasures to which they are entitled in compensation for their work.[17]

Almost as if he wanted to help us on this chapter, Nozick applied his notion of justice to the disproportionate salaries seen in the world of sports.[18] He did so by considering the case of Wilt Chamberlain, the most highly paid basketball player in 1974 ($250,000 per year). He began by estimating that the price a spectator should pay to admire this exceptional athlete was 25¢ per game. In Nozick's view, it is completely ridiculous to call the situation of consenting adults willingly paying 25¢ to enjoy moments of happiness they would not otherwise have enjoyed an "injustice" based solely on the fact that Chamberlain earned such a high salary as a result. In this case, an egalitarian approach would decrease happiness for spectators and for Chamberlain. A number of authors have attempted to refute this reasoning. For example, they have claimed that Chamberlain was so successful not just because of his talent alone, but because he benefited from the organization of society by the state through education, health, and security. Others wondered whether Chamberlain would have agreed to play for a lower salary anyway.

When it comes to hockey, we can always quibble and say that the minimum salary of $450,000 per year means that spectators pay a premium to admire not just the exceptional athletes who are working hard but also the "plumbers" in the corner who are hardly working!

---

16. Amartya Sen, *L'économie est une science morale* (Paris : La découverte, 1999).
17. Robert Nozick, *Anarchy, State, and Utopia* (New York: Basic Books, 1974); see also Jean-Jacques Sarfati, *La critique de John Rawls par Robert Nozick* at http://www.catallaxia.org/wiki/Robert_Nozick:La_critique_de_John_Rawls_par_Robert_Nozick_dans_%C2%ABAnarchie,_%C3%89tat_et_utopie%C2%BB.
18. Joseph Heath, *The Efficient Society: Why Canada Is as Close to Utopia as it Gets* (Toronto: Viking, 2001); an excerpt of the French translation can be read athttp://policyoptions.irpp.org/issues/bank-mergers/la-societe-efficiente-book-excerpt/.

2.3 Exceptional incomes
Hockey players and other athletes are not the only people who earn extraordinary incomes. For example, the heads of the largest American corporations currently earn almost 400 times what their employees earn on average, whereas in the 1960s and 1970s those at the top earned only 30 times as much.[19] And in show business, we can point to many artists, singers, and comedians who make even more than the most highly paid hockey and ball players. How just is this?

2.3.1 The body/mind relationship
In 2001, Jean-François Doré, a Québec philosopher of sport and former radio host, asked why so many people got their dander up about salaries in sports but didn't seem to care that people like Céline Dion and Mel Gibson were raking in tens of millions.[20] He attributed this to the "body/mind relationship." Citing numerous philosophers, he arrived at the conclusion that people generally respect intellectual professions more than they do hands-on professions.

His analysis contains many good points and is based on plenty of observations. Training in manual trades (mechanics, construction, etc.) is increasingly unpopular among young people and also looked down on by their parents, despite excellent employment rates and relatively high pay. Perhaps also because of their own class, editorialists and other opinion-makers, who are all highly educated, are more sympathetic to the claims of those working in the liberal professions than manual labourers. In 2006, many such people in Québec called for the incomes of medical specialists to be brought into line with those of doctors in other provinces, even though their annual income (after office expenses) was already the

19. Paul Krugman, "Incentives for the Dead," *The New York Times* (October 20, 2006), p. A23. http://select.nytimes.com/2006/10/20/opinion/20krugman.html.
20. Jean-François Doré, "L'argent et le problème de la relation corps/esprit: Une explication philosophique du ressentiment à l'égard du salaire d'Alex Rodriguez" (Université du Québec à Montréal, 2001). http://www.unites.uqam.ca/philo/pdf/doretxt.pdf.

highest among the 520 professions in Québec[21] and, in 2005, was almost double that of university professors, who had the same level of education. Conversely, the same opinion-makers overlooked the fact that consultants at the Liquor Control Board of Ontario (LCBO) were paid 30 percent more than consultants at the Société des alcools du Québec (SAQ). Why? Because their salaries were still higher than those of "associates" at Walmart!

But, as Doré himself concedes, his analysis is incomplete, as it is much less applicable to millionaires in individual sports, such as the golfer Tiger Woods ($83 million in 2007), who get much less flak for their lavish salaries.

2.3.2 Merit

If Tiger Woods stopped winning, his revenue would plummet and his stream of lucrative advertising contracts would dry up. The same is true for singers and other stars in the arts and entertainment world: these people are freelancers, not employees. While sometimes reluctant to do so,[22] society generally accepts inequality of income based on merit. But it still condemns inequalities in salary that are due to factors other than merit: sex, ethnicity, family (nepotism), etc. Salaries in hockey and other team sports are not tied to the players' performance when they reach their salary level (as is the case in individual disciplines), but rather to their past performance.

2.3.3 The relationship with salary

Whether a singer sells 10 albums or 10 million albums, it doesn't cost me any more or less to buy a copy—but this drastically changes the artist's income. Therefore, the relationship between my purchase and the singer's income is very weak. However, even though the Bell Centre is always full, it has a limited number of spaces. And with beer priced at $10 a glass, hockey fans can't help feeling that they are downing some of the players' salary with every sip.

---

21.   Average annual income in 2005, according to Statistics Canada's 2006 census.
22.   Patrick Savidan, "Le mérite individuel peut-il justifier les inégalités sociales?" *Observatoire des inégalités* (August 24, 2004). http://www.inegalites.fr/article. php3?id_article=251.

Similarly, our relationship with the princely incomes of corporate CEOs is much less direct. Even if such a sum is only possible
through a loss in profit for the shareholders (including our private
and public pension plans), a reduction in the salary paid to the
employees, or an increase in the price paid by consumers, members
of the general public are less likely to feel that it comes directly out
of their pockets.

Conclusion: Scandal or fair pay?

This little tour of economic and philosophical concepts, while wonderfully illuminating, doesn't settle this question beyond a reasonable doubt. If those who cry scandal over high salaries in hockey
were really consistent, they should also be railing against the
incomes of other stars and corporate leaders or questioning the
fundamentals of capitalism and the market economy. And it
doesn't appear that these people will jump on the bandwagon of the
proletarian revolution anytime soon.

At the end of the day, our adherence to the concepts of justice
proposed by liberals (such as Rawls), humanists (such as Sen), or
libertarians (such as Nozick) depends much more on our personal
values than on the quality of their arguments. Arguments certainly
help us think about the issue and better stake out our position, but
rarely do they succeed in changing our minds. The French philosophy teacher Sylvain Reboul sums up the relationship between our
values and our vision of justice very well: "There is no such thing
as justice in and of itself, as the idea of justice is relative to basic
political positions."[23]

Having said this, the extreme salaries of stars and hockey players make most people at least a little uncomfortable, no matter
what their personal values are. As French philosopher Ludivine
Thiaw-Po-Une so eloquently put it: "Are the outrageous salaries of
stars not a symptom of the real difficulty our society has in determining the conditions under which inequality is just?"[24]

23. Sylvain Reboul, "Aristote et la justice." http://sylvainreboul.free.fr/etu.htm.
24. Ludivine Thiaw-Po-Une. "Le salaire des stars" (June 4, 2006) http://www.
philo.fr/?c=blog&path=2006/06/04/28-le-salaire-des-stars.

Mythology and metaphysics

The Rocket: The Making of a Hero

Julie Perrone

Introduction

For Montréal Canadiens fans, autumn is always a time of great hopefulness. It's the start of the new hockey season, pregnant with possibility, dreams, and memories of victories past. Each year, the fans are pulled into the hysteria of the season, gradually becoming convinced that this is the year their boys in red, white, and blue will bring home the Stanley Cup. They've been disappointed every year since 1993, but Montréal fans have never abandoned their legendary team. Nothing could ever diminish their devotion and loyalty to the Canadiens, the Habs, the *Sainte-Flanelle*. And Maurice "Rocket" Richard has long been and continues to be the object of their devotion and loyalty.

Maurice Richard

We need not discuss Maurice Richard the man at length here. He is an important part of our cultural heritage, a hockey player whose renown has outgrown the walls of the Forum, extending beyond the borders of Canada and transcending generations. The reader may easily refer to any one of the panoply of biographies published since he hung up his skates. Suffice it to note simply that the Rocket began his career with the Canadiens in 1942, scored his first goal in his third game, and didn't stop scoring them until he retired in 1960. He won 8 Stanley Cups, played in 14 all-star games, and scored a total of 626 goals. He broke all existing records and still holds some of them, even after the coming and going of both Mario Lemieux and Wayne Gretzky. He still ranks as one of the NHL's top scorers. In his retirement, he remained directly and indirectly active in the hockey world and lent his name to a number of products, associations, and messages. He received many honours, fought a courageous battle with cancer, and finally succumbed on May 27, 2000, at age 78.

Everyone agrees that Maurice Richard was an exceptional player; but his status in Québec is far grander than most hockey players could ever expect. Few Canadiens alumni can claim to have received both the Order of Québec and the Order of Canada, or have been named Companion of the Order of Canada and member of the Queen's Privy Council for Canada—not to mention having an arena, a junior hockey team, and (almost) a highway named after them. This red-carpet treatment is reserved for our heroes, and Maurice Richard is without question one of Québec's absolute greatest.

Maurice Richard, hero

Maurice Richard, Québec's hero, is a sacred being: his soul is pure, his behaviour blameless. Even today we view the Rocket only in the most positive light, and we use his example to epitomize important values. It's important to understand that we're the ones who create our heroes, that we fashion them according to our needs and most deeply held values. A hero with no admirer would simply not exist, because no one would be there to glorify his existence, whether through celebrations, monuments, literature, or photographs. The individuals we choose as heroes and heroines, however, are not exactly who we tell ourselves they are; Maurice Richard, the man who lived, is a slightly different beast from Maurice Richard, the hero who has been constructed. First we will explore the definition of hero to ascertain whether Rocket is indeed a bona fide hero.

What makes a hero?

Many authors have delved into this complex question and come up with many answers as to what makes a hero, but we can easily extract some of the common features. For example, heroes are often said to come from a relatively low social class: it is well known that the Rocket was a "little guy from Bordeaux" and that he opted to continue living in that neighbourhood his whole life. In fact, everyone knew where he lived: when he died, the sidewalk in front of his house in Ahuntsic became a site of pilgrimage for his admirers in mourning.

Next on the list in the hero's "job description" is an impressive suite of performances that are admired by the public. Maurice Richard meets this criterion handily. The events that marked Rocket's career are the stuff of legend: he once scored a goal while half conscious; another time he scored one with a defenceman hanging from his shoulders. He was the first player to score 50 goals in 50 games, and the only player ever to earn all three stars.

A hero is also someone whose exploits are interpreted in a mythical fashion. The narrative of the riot triggered by the suspension of Richard in 1955 became loaded with meaning long after the fact. The day after the riot broke out, people spoke of furious fans and enraged Montréalers, but this story would soon be adjusted and gradually transformed from a sports riot into a politically motivated revolt. The events of March 1955 are now depicted as the first stirs of the Quiet Revolution, a precursor to the flood of social changes that lay in waiting.

Finally, a hero is defined in relation to an enemy, an obstacle, a villain. Rocket's enemy was any player who stood between him and the other team's net, or any blabbermouth who shouted at him. Richard also had his nemesis: Clarence Campbell, the NHL president who suspended him on several occasions and slapped him with several heavy fines. Campbell was the ideal nemesis because he was different from Richard in every way: he was Anglophone, from a well-to-do family, educated, with a military background—virtually the polar opposite of Richard, and perhaps also the most fitting image that Richard's contemporaries had of Anglophones at the time.

A hero in the making

Humble beginnings? Check. Impressive performance? Check. Mythical interpretation? Check. Note how the necessary ingredients for making a hero also seem to coincide with stages in time. Hero figures, it seems, are not born, they emerge gradually. In my research on Maurice Richard, I noted three distinct stages in his creation as a hero.

The first stage was the construction of the hero image from 1942 to 1955, the period in which Richard racked up so many impressive performances and distinguished himself from his peers. Scoring five goals in one night after moving furniture all day, showing a thug nicknamed "Killer" who's boss, scoring 50 goals in 50 games—these are just a few examples of Richard's exploits during this fabled period. This stage ended with the riot of 1955, a time of widespread fury caused by the Rocket's suspension from both the regular season and the playoffs. This riot, which doubtlessly cost the team the Stanley Cup and cost Richard the Hart Trophy, would later be reinterpreted as a French-Canadian revolt. This is an instance of the mythical reinterpretation we referred to above. The riot birthed Richard's image as a knight in shining armour or as a torch-bearer for the Francophone people, although in reality he never wanted to be associated with any cause.

Richard showed his mettle during this period, but this didn't mean his star status was guaranteed. After one game in which he scored eight goals, the morning papers shrugged his performance off, explaining that it was either because his opponents had not been on top of their game or because Richard had received perfect passes from Elmer Lach and Toe Blake every time. There was a certain reluctance to credit Richard, but this reluctance would vanish by the time Richard was mythologized by the riot.

During this stage, Richard's image in the media was full of contradictions (and this is understandable because that's where people's immediate reactions are recorded). Richard was seen by some as something of a choirboy, someone who rarely lashed out. Yet there's no shortage of stories that are at odds with this image. This kind of inconsistency is well illustrated in the following story: Richard was suspended from a game for being aggressive with a linesman and insulting the referee. One sports journalist reported that the Rocket simply pushed a linesman and explained the situation to the referee in an un-diplomatic fashion. Another told the story a bit differently, saying that Richard actually broke his stick over the linesman's back and hurled outright abuse at the referee. Contradictions of this kind simply show that, at this stage, Richard was not immune to criticism and that there wasn't unanimous agreement as to what he actually did on the ice.

The second stage, the hero legitimization stage, was from 1960 to 1996. Certain aspects of Maurice Richard's image became more sharply defined during this period, during which his importance as a hero was justified and his special status in society was affirmed. For Richard, this legitimacy came in the form of two biographies and three honours bestowed upon him by the Canadian and Québec governments. This was a stage of legitimization, yes, but also confirmation; actions were taken to cement and justify Richard's position at the peak of his celebrity, which he attained in the riot. It was between 1960 and 1996 that Richard would receive most of his recognition and honours. Here we see if not the emergence of a static narrative then at least a smoothing over of the negative parts of Maurice Richard's image. The honours the Rocket received strengthened the recognition of his status by the Canadian and Québec governments, which both used the symbol to their own ends. Here, the person being celebrated seems less important than the people doing the celebrating; the focus was not on Richard himself so much as on the honours he received. The Rocket was feted as a Canadian hero at the hundredth anniversary of Confederation (Order of Canada, 1967), then later decorated with a prize that is distinct from the rest of Canada (National Order of Québec, 1985), and again honoured when there was an attempt to seduce Québécois with a new constitutional agreement (Queen's Counsel, 1992). His image is that of an extraordinary hockey player, but he also represents a group that the Canadian nation is constantly trying to appease. To recognize his importance is to honour all the Québécois, albeit indirectly.

In the wake of these honours, the image of Maurice Richard has been institutionalized and appropriated, the third stage in the heroization process and one that continues today. The living memory of Richard has been glossed over somewhat; the idea now is to bolster his story to create an idealized portrait of the hero that aligns with the values we want to present and that we hope the consumers of the image will internalize. This stage began with the closing ceremony of the Forum in 1996, where the ovation the Rocket received famously eclipsed the other celebrations and marked the beginning of the final stage in the making of a hero. On this occasion, the image of Maurice Richard was used as a symbol of hockey and of a particular era. This was done first to legitimize the Molson Centre (now the Bell Centre) as the new home of the Montréal Canadiens, and second to soften the emotional blow the fans would feel at the closing of the Forum. It is now clear that the image of Maurice Richard adds value to the Forum's closing by association. At this point in history, Richard's significance no longer requires outside confirmation or effort; it has taken on a life of its own. A concrete example of this is the fact that Maurice Richard became a trophy in 1998. His death in 2000 marked a new era in the strengthening of his image, for it was then that he truly entered the domain of the sacred. Everything he had touched in life became an artifact enshrined in folklore, and his personal belongings were displayed for all to see in the media. The newspapers were flooded with memories in May 2000, and everything took on a special import: a guide tells us about how he once cooked a trout that the Rocket had caught; an administrator introduces his young son named Rocket; every one of the Rocket's visits to Québec City are listed along with his family tree. In other words, our Rocket became a great man and everything connected with him was revered as much as he was.

Hero and philosophy

That's all well and good, you may be saying, but what does the idea of the hero have to do with philosophy? Much is written of the great man in philosophy, a concept that Friedrich Nietzsche called the *Übermensch*, which translates into English as the "overman" or the "superman." This expression refers to a person whose qualities are superior to those of the human race. In Nietzschean philosophy, this figure represents a perfected state of human nature, transformed to such a point that no examples exist and we forever await its incarnation. This quasi-religious description may seem a bit far-fetched in relation to the Rocket, but perhaps not as much as all that. In my opinion, we should keep two parts of this concept in mind. The first is that Nietzsche's superman, humanity's hero, does not exist. We'll come to the second in the conclusion.

The Greek term *heros* refers to a figure with the charisma of a sacred and religious being. The hero is someone who serves as an inspiration and symbolizes the ideal of the group who venerates him. This gives him something in common with the superman: the hero is not real because we admire him for what he represents—what he ought to be, not what he really is. This quotation from Georges Minois neatly sums up this word of warning: "The great man whom we revere is never the man as he lived, with his flaws, his pettiness, his trivialities. What we revere is his image, the one he created with the help of his social circle and that is accepted by society."[1]

We must immediately acknowledge that Maurice Richard did actually exist, and that he is admired for feats that he actually achieved. True. But how do we remember this man who was the Rocket?

The making of Maurice Richard as a hero began with journalistic accounts of Richard's actions and deeds, which sometimes differ from or even contradict one another. In the later stages, these contradictory accounts coalesce into a single narrative that constantly feeds into the essentially positive image of the Rocket.

One notorious change in the Rocket's image was that he became less violent and more passive over time. He went from being a player who was known to attack his enemies and be on the front line in every fight, to being a man whose only dream was just to play hockey but who was reluctantly forced into being a fighter. At one game in 1945 in New York, there was a memorable fist fight on the ice between Maurice Richard and Bob "Killer" Dill, a notorious brute from the New York Rangers. Reports the following day stated that Richard had knocked Dill out twice in a row, once on the ice and once when they were beside each other on the penalty

---

1. Georges Minois, *Le culte des grands hommes: des héros homériques au star system* (Paris: Louis Audibert, 2005), p. 9.

bench. This violent outburst perplexed many journalists of the day. By 1998, however, this action had been justified because Dill reportedly called Richard a "goddam [sic] Canuck."[2] Richard was pushed to the boiling point because he didn't have the word power to talk back and tell Dill what he thought of him. The Rocket was muzzled by his lack of ability in English, therefore he had no choice but to speak with his fists. This interpretation first appeared about fifty years after the fact.

One biography of the Rocket tells the story of a game in which the Rocket and John Mariucci of the Chicago Blackhawks were slapped with two different penalties for being in the same fight: Richard got five minutes while Mariucci got just two. Seeing the injustice in this, Richard decided to continue his skirmish with Mariucci on the bench. In the author's telling of the story, Richard was forced to take justice into his own hands.[3] But in reality, this sounds more like the behaviour of a player who not only lashed out in violence but also blamed the wrong guy: it was the referee, not Mariucci, who had given the penalties.

The best-known example of such a shift in perspective has to be the event that triggered the Rocket's famous suspension in 1955. One of the arguments raised in the months following the suspension—but less and less over the years—was that Maurice Richard had intentionally punched a referee in the face. Several journalists said Campbell was obligated to be heavy-handed so that violence in the NHL would be punished and eventually abolished. But since that time, it's been argued that Richard's transgression was one of pure instinct. In this revised version of the story, Richard struck the linesman by accident, and the imagery of a boxing match or car accident is used to explain his almost unconscious state of mind and to justify the actions he took in the heat of the moment. These are two rather different depictions of the Rocket.

From the time of the riot (which made Richard one of society's hallowed heroes) to his retirement (in which his actions were

---

2. Jean-Marie Pellerin, *Maurice Richard: l'idole d'un peuple* (Montréal: Édition l'Homme, 1976), p. 49.
3. Roch Carrier, *Le Rocket* (Montréal: Les Éditions internationales Alain Stanké, 2000), p. 96.

crystallized), we've seen the construction of collective memory and the mythological interpretation of his actions. This collective memory is shaped by the media, which continue to praise the Rocket for his courage; this is what nudges the original story further and further away from the one reported in the headlines.

For example, defenceman Earl Seibert undergoes significant weight gain from one biography to the next; this further serves to illustrate the kind of shifts that occur and are eventually internalized into personal and collective memory. The day after the Rocket scored a goal with a player on his shoulders, nobody said a word about Earl Seibert. In 1960, Andy O'Brien reported that Seibert weighed 145 pounds, which makes Richard's feat more spectacular. By 1998, Seibert had ballooned to a supposed weight of 225 pounds in Jean-Marie Pellerin's book, and a 2005 article in *Le Devoir* pegs the figure even higher at 250 pounds. This again shows how Richard's feats behave like fish stories as the years go by. It points to the conclusion that there are two versions of the Richard story: the original version, whose content is simple but still extraordinary, and the revised version, which is constantly being updated to reflect the passing years, in step with the society's changing values and needs. A rift emerges between story and legend, just as the hero diverges from the man on which he is based. Nietzsche's superman will never appear because he does not exist. Each one of us has our own superman that symbolizes what we'd like to project about ourselves—but to a degree of perfection that is ever out of reach.

Conclusion

This leads us to the second thing to keep in mind about that philosophical concept of the superman, and the conclusion of this chapter: the superman is an invitation for us to do better, to always expect more of ourselves. Instead of focusing on the negatives and saying that heroes don't exist, or dismissing the people we call heroes as frauds, let's focus on the fact that these heroes are people just like us who decided to make something more of themselves. The Rocket had a level of tenacity and motivation that few of us can hope to live up to. He should be admired for this, rather than for the fact—or fiction—that he carried another player on his shoulders.

Further reading

BUTLER, Bill. *The Myth of the Hero*. London: Rider, 1979.

CARRIER, Roch. *Le Rocket*. Montréal: Les Éditions internationales Alain Stanké, 2000.

GOSSELIN, Gérard. *Monsieur Hockey*. Montréal: Les Éditions de l'Homme, 1960.

GRUNEAU, Richard and David WHITSON. *Hockey Night in Canada: Sport, Identities and Cultural Politics*. Toronto: Garamond Press, 1993.

MINOIS, Georges. *Le culte des grands hommes. Des héros homériques au star system*. Paris: Louis Audibert, 2005.

O'BRIEN, Andy. *Rocket Richard*. Toronto: Ryerson Press, 1961.

PELLERIN, Jean-Marie. *Maurice Richard. L'idole d'un peuple*. Montréal: Trustar, 1998.

From the Shinny Pond to the Bell Centre: Reweaving the Myth of the *Sainte-Flanelle*

Anouk Bélanger and Fannie Valois-Nadeau

When people talk hockey in Québec, one of the things they love to discuss the most is the commercialization of the sport and its insidious effects. The corruption of hockey's soul provides endless fodder for sports blogs, radio call-in shows, newspapers, and essays about hockey (specifically the Montréal Canadiens). Commercialization, runs the argument, is a disfigurement of "real hockey" and perversion of a "pure" national symbol.

But what is the nature of this "True hockey," both outwardly and deep within its soul? Again and again in books and documentaries on the history of the sport, a persistent image is used to portray the sport in its purest state: a little boy wearing leather skates playing shinny on a frozen pond.

Hockey has always enjoyed a special place in the collective memory and imagination of Québécois and Canadians. Hockey is intrinsically linked to our frosty climate: it is the quintessential winter sport. Because we're the ones who created it, "our" national sport is often presented as a natural outgrowth of our relationship with climate: ice became the natural playing surface; wood, the raw material of our country, became the instrument; and the sports technique that brings ice and wood together clearly speaks to our connection to the Canadian landscape and its people's adaptability to harsh conditions. The image of the child reinforces this conception of purity: untainted by aspirations of salary and upward mobility, the child plays just for the fun of it, with his whole heart, and to defend the honour and pride of his team and village.

This popular depiction of the little boy on the frozen pond—which even made it onto the $5 bill at one time—is a far cry from how we portray professional NHL hockey on TV (from *La Soirée du hockey* on Radio-Canada to *Hockey 360* on RDS). And yet both images play a role in the social construction of the Montréal Canadiens that speaks to its fans and to Québécois in general.

This rift between the symbolic story of hockey in Québec and the actual history of NHL hockey as a spectator sport has been cemented in place over the last century by means of a construct that posits hockey as a "pure" national symbol. To understand this naturalized link propagated in social discourse, and the cultural constructs that underlie our emotional attachment to the sport and, more specifically, to the Montréal Canadiens, we must look back at history—not just the team's history, but also that of amateur and professional hockey. The Montréal Canadiens symbolize both this naturalization and this perversion of hockey: through the different images and narratives associated with the team, the Canadiens become an expression that is shaped and refined through history by investors, promoters, and fans.

There is a paradox here. It's the same paradox that crops up in any mythical construction as soon as we start to question the transcending image of a changeless past that lies behind the myth in question and the "real" story it conceals. Historically speaking, there is no direct, linear evolution from the folk practices we associate with hockey to the institutionalization of the spectator sport we know today. This direct evolution only becomes necessary to feed the myth that hockey has become for Québécois, and it is even more necessary to feed the symbol of the Montréal Canadiens. The myth represents the "ideal understanding of things; it is the euphoria of men raised for a while above the constitutive ambiguity of everyday situations and placed before the panoramic view of a univocal Nature, in which signs at last correspond to causes, without obstacle, without evasion, without contradiction."[1] This

---

1.   Roland Barthes, *Mythologies*. (Paris: Seuil, 1957), p. 23.

representation, which has been used ever since the Montréal Canadiens first came into existence, is the work of three entities: the market, the media, and the fans. The myth of hockey is not simply constructed for the interests of one of these entities while taking advantage of the others. Rather, it emerges from a collective momentum that inevitably flows through the spectacle it brings us and the relationship we have with its form and content.

In this chapter, we'll tease apart these naturalized links between hockey and Canadians, and between the Montréal Canadiens and Québécois. We'll visit various points throughout history and look at a number of actors (such as team owners, NHL managers, and fans) and spheres (spectator sport and sports media) in order to understand their participation in the emergence and construction of this myth. By following this historical thread from the team's very inception right up to comments from fans in the 2006–2007 season, we endeavour to show the many faces of this myth and highlight the various social contexts of the eras in which they have appeared.

From the logic of the commercial spectacle to the genesis of the Montréal Canadiens

> From the original Olympics in Ancient Greece and the chariot races and gladiator fights in Ancient Rome, sports have long been a major site of entertainment and spectacle.[2]

The story of amateur hockey is mainly one of ethnic and local rivalries, and of capitalizing on the sport's entertainment value. The Montréal Canadiens weren't born of any natural process, but rather of a calculation in the context of the development of organized professional hockey and the need to increase revenue by expanding audiences.[3]

---

2. Douglas Kellner, *Media Spectacle* (London, New York: Routledge, 2003), p. 65.
3. There is an ambiguity that must be raised here: the double historical construction of this myth. This myth is just as strong in English Canada as it is in Québec. It is directed towards the same sport and often towards the same

Ever since the commercialization of hockey began at the turn of the twentieth century, it has been the object of moral judgment. Commercialization, it is argued, pushes the sport in the direction of sensationalism (rather than the game) and towards heated or even violent passions (rather than moral discipline and the motivation to play the sport "fairly and for its own sake").[4] But this idea of playing the sport for pleasure came under threat the instant hockey teams began to stand in as representatives of different social and geographical communities. Once that shift occurred, organized amateur sport showed its potential as the theatre of local and ethnic tensions, as a show of identity with all the attendant passions this supplies and demands. The moral judgment that was passed on amateur sport at the turn of the twentieth century, embedded as it was in Victorian ideals of amateur sport, dictated that the market was fundamentally responsible for a dangerous and irrevocable change. However, the commercialization of the sport is just one of the factors that together created the market of modern professional sports.

On one hand, "A longstanding taste for spectacle in popular culture, a desire for competitive teams in communities that lacked the populations and resources of the major cities, the articulation of individual and collective identities in sporting competition, and the impulse towards civic boosterism in a competitive market society: all of these elements combined to create markets for professional hockey."[5] And on the other hand, "most working-class Canadians embraced an inclusive, innovative, urban popular culture that welcomed into its ambit a vast repository of commercial and semi-commercial entertainments. This culture was imbued with a tolerance for commercial spectacle, and a sense of popular rights to pleasure, that resonated more closely with the rapidly expanding world of American popular entertainment than the

---

symbol (the Montréal Canadiens), but only evoked in the context of different or even opposite identities than those that appear in the historical construction of this myth for Francophone Québécois! There are a number of books on hockey in English Canada that deal with this issue.

4.   Richard Gruneau and David Whitson, *Hockey Night in Canada: Sports, Identities and Cultural Politics* (Toronto: Garamond Press, 1993), p. 69.

5.   Ibid., p. 69.

Illustration of the hockey's lucrative potential from its very beginnings

- 1893–1903: "Hockey is proving quite lucrative for amateur sports teams in large cities. From 1893 to 1903, Montréal's club reports a comfortable annual yearly profit of $2,000, with the bulk of its revenue coming from rental fees and ticket sales."
- 1901: A year of disputes between teams over ticket revenues: visiting teams claim 33 to 40 percent of revenues.
- 1902: At the final game between Montréal and Winnipeg, the major economic spinoffs are obvious to the owners. It is almost impossible to get good seats. Tickets sell for $20 and for $25 before the game (more than double the cost of the finest men's overcoats).

(Michael McKinley, *Un toit pour le hockey: du sport au spectacle, un siècle d'histoire*, Montréal: Hurtubise, 2001, pp. 54–56.)

dour world of property and seriousness promoted by cultural leaders within the dominant classes in Canada."[6]

During the period of industrialization, spectator sport quickly became one of the most lucrative forms of popular entertainment in urban settings: it offered folks an organized, professional, and entertaining version of their traditional pastimes that they could identify with. This form of spectator sport, however, presented them with a leisure activity in which participants had much less agency: chiefly influenced by an emerging network of promoters and owners from across Canada and the United States, it was predicated upon the consumption of "products," and symbolic attachment served as the driving force behind the nascent sports industry. Like the threads of an arrowed sash tightly woven together

6.   Ibid., p. 65.

by the market, the ties between the Montréal Canadiens and its fans were primarily symbolic.

Representing French Canada and Montréal: Birth of a symbol

While some would claim that the Montréal Canadiens were once the team of the Francophones (the NHL gave it a monopoly on drafting players from the province of Québec), it's important to note that the person responsible for founding and commercializing the team was an Anglophone. The Canadiens were founded in an era when teams were commonly formed along ethnic lines, although they did not represent any particular political program.

Indeed, from the earliest beginnings of sport (and therefore of hockey in its "organized" form in Canada, which is to say at the beginning of the nineteenth century), "it was common to form teams based on ethnicity."[7] In this historical context, the ethnic rivalry that was "omnipresent in the Québec society of the Conquest of 1760 extended into hockey. Since it was the Anglo-Saxons who dominated the sport until the beginning of the twentieth century, the French Canadians pursued the objective of forming a team that could compete with the best."[8] And so, the very end of nineteenth century saw the formation of the first two Francophone teams: the Nationals[9] and the Montagnards. The Nationals were the first French-Canadian team admitted into the senior leagues; it attained professional status at the same time as the leagues, which were stirring up excitement among spectators. It was in 1903 that the Nationals entered the Federal Amateur Hockey League; then in 1909, after a few years of controversy and precariousness, the team returned to the ice as part of the Canadian Hockey Association (CHA) on two conditions, one of which was that it be made up exclusively of French-Canadians. "The CHA managers understand how important it is for their league

---

7.   François Black, *Habitants et Glorieux: les Canadiens de 1909 à 1960* (Laval: Mille-Îles, 1997), p. 17.

8.   Ibid., p. 21.

9.   This name would be brought back in our collective imagination some 80 years later, as part of the hit series *Lance et compte*.

to have a Francophone team if they want to attract the interest of the many French-Canadian fans."[10]

In 1909, the Montréal Canadiens saw the light of day thanks to financing from Ambrose O'Brien, a rich Anglophone mine owner. O'Brien wanted to win the loyalty of a vast audience not represented by the other teams in the Montréal league, so he ordered that the Montréal Canadiens be made up of Francophone players. By playing to the fans' nationalist sentiment, partly with a uniform design that alluded to the colonies of New France (Go Habs Go!), he aimed to monopolize a large portion of Montréalers who were not yet interested in the Stanley Cup.[11] An immediate attachment between the fans and the team was expressed in the local press: "Oh, what wonderful things you can do with the homegrown talent."[12]

The beginnings of the Canadiens were fairly modest; Francophone Montréalers were somewhat reluctant to support a team that was not managed by one of their own, and it wasn't until the mid-1920s that they saw the team as a true flag-bearer of the nation. By that time, the team had come under the ownership of a Francophone, Léo Dandurand. From 1924 to 1938, the Montréal Canadiens saw an increase in popularity that has never been equalled since. This sudden appeal of the Montréal Canadiens is partly attributable to the arrival of the Maroons, an Anglophone team from Montréal: competition from that team built a firm sense of belonging among Canadiens fans. Fuelled by the socio-economic tensions of the day, the on-ice rivalries reverberated all the way into the stands: it was not unusual for fights to break out among the spectators, who were now coming out in larger numbers—11,000 per game on average—to see the cultural phenomenon first-hand.[13] The spectacle sport of the Montréal Canadiens converged to become primarily the spectacle of a Francophone nation, which it remained from then on. Although the team wasn't 100 percent made up of Francophone players, its image was seen

10.   Ibid., p. 26.
11.   Ibid.
12.   *Le Devoir*, January 9, 1911). Quoted in Black, *Habitants et Glorieux*, p. 5.
13.   Black, *Habitants et Glorieux*.

all over North America and strengthened the French-speaking population's sense of pride. The arrival of the "Flying Frenchmen Line," an explosive trio of French-Canadian players, also helped export this image of talent that the people could feel proud of. The team was seen as a true object of national promotion: a certain Mr. Beaudry, chairman of the board of the Union Saint-Jean-Baptiste d'Amérique, even recognized "that the players on the Montréal Canadiens hockey team are the most solid and profitable publicity that the province of Québec could have in the United States."[14] In the end, the slowing Montréal economy would seal the Maroons' fate: the division of the Montréal market coupled with the Francophone majority in the city drained the team dry. With a few disappointing seasons on the books as well, there was nothing for the Maroons to do but disband, and its strongest players went on to join the ranks of the Montréal Canadiens. From that point on, Francophone Montréalers had to "share" the emblem of their national pride with the rest of the island. To gain the support of former rival fans, the owners and managers made it a priority to recruit local players. They promoted pride of place: the focus was now on belonging to a land rather than a language group. In emphasizing the bilingual character of the team, the managers obscured the Francophone face that the Montréal Canadiens had worn for the previous three decades, and instead focused on being a Montréal and a Québec team—which isn't to say that ethnicity was any less prevalent in the press, however:

> It's because of the Vézinas, the Lalondes, the Laviolettes, and the Pitres that the Canadiens carved out the personality that we still know today. "They have a certain Latin charm," observed Peter Gzowski, then managing editor of Maclean's magazine and one of the one of the keenest observers in the North American press. "The way they devote themselves to the game has made them the national team of French Canada; no team has ever represented all of Canada, a country where ethnic origins still remain entirely

14. François Black, *Évolution de l'image projetée par le Club de hockey Canadien depuis ses origines jusqu'au mythe de la tradition glorieuse*, Master's thesis (University of Montréal, 1992), p. 50.

distinct; I have sometimes wondered if their rallying cry "Les
Canadiens sont là" is a better motto for the national spirit of
French Canada than "Je me souviens."[15]

The last time the team had a majority of players with
Francophone roots was 1937–1938, and their presence has declined
since then.[16] Yet paradoxically, the Francophone audience has
grown exponentially with advances in information technology.
With the first games broadcast on the radio in 1938, and later on
television, the Habs expanded their Francophone fan base, thereby
"provincializing the phenomenon of the Canadiens."[17] This turned
the spectacle into a narrative told through the eyes of the commentator, and the collective event saw the rise of a much more familial,
social, and individualized form of fanhood. Broadcasting now
allowed the whole province to watch its team compete in real time,
to follow its developments "up close," and to feel a sense of ownership and even participation. The collective imagination in which
the Canadiens became a national emblem expanded to include
Francophones (and non-Francophones) right across the province,
thereby fortifying its rallying power. Some years later, the Montréal
Canadiens' legendary success on the ice would elevate the team to
the status of a dynasty and obviously amplify the symbolic attachment required to build and sustain the myth. In 1946, under the
direction of manager Frank Selke, the team developed a farm struc-
ture for the junior ranks that, in the years that followed, became a
gold mine of talent.[18] As the emerging glorious team saw its name
engraved on the Stanley Cup year after year, it benefitted from the
advent of televised games and the (now defunct) *La Soirée du
hockey* to further develop the deep sense of attachment on which
the myth rests. Indeed, the team's successes, in combination with
the arrival of a visual format that generated more widespread identification with the team, made the Montréal Canadiens a symbol of

15. Stan Fisher and Maurice Richard, *Les Canadiens sont là! La plus grande
dynastie du hockey* (Scarborough: Prentice-Hall of Canada, 1971), p. 16.
16. Black, *Évolution de l'image.*
17. Ibid., p. 85.
18. Ibid., p. 63.

The "Rocket Power" Affair and the Watson Affair

What came to be known as the "Rocket Power" Affair sullied the team's pure image. It saw the recruitment of a player whose value was unquestionable but whose ethnic origin posed a problem. "The fans criticized the team's managers of false representation, of claiming to offer the public a uniquely French-Canadian product when this was not the case" (Black, *Habitants et Glorieux*, p. 39.) just for the sake of maintaining its patriotic cachet. This event eventually led to an official agreement that gave the Canadiens "ethnic" rights.

This affair is interesting in terms of the origin of the nicknames given to "Rocket Richard" in the 1950s and "Flower Power" in the 1970s.

The Watson Affair would once again expose the difficulty of enforcing the agreement that gave the Montréal Canadiens first dibs on all players of French-Canadian origin. Phil Watson was of "mixed" origin (a Francophone mother and an Anglophone father). These cases are significant because they led to the granting, and finally to the rescission, of the Canadiens' French-Canadian hiring and recruitment rule. These ethnic rights, which were in force from 1910 to 1935, remain symbolic rights that still today are invoked by fans and considered by recruiters and managers in selecting players and nominating captains (the Watson page can be consulted on the Hockey Hall of Fame website, but the affair itself is recounted in Black's works.).

glory and victory recognized by all. The phenomenon also gained momentum from the presence of star Francophone players with the calibre of Richard, Bouchard, Geoffrion, and Béliveau (to name just a few) who both embodied and inspired national pride, and contributed to the emergence of a wider audience—now numbering almost a million spectators.

As teams that aspired to ethnic representation were being formed, the development and expansion of the NHL network took shape across the major urban centres. Beyond the popularity of hockey among locals, the size of the potential fan base was the decisive factor in locating teams. Already between 1925 and 1928, many small Canadian cities such as Hamilton saw their teams disappear because they were too small to compete with nearby metropolises.[19] In order to survive within a market-driven logic and withstand pressure from media outlets, which were now stakeholders in both the financing and the broadcasting of hockey, NHL amphitheatres had to be able to hold as many spectators as possible and accommodate new information technologies.

This trend continued and marked the history of all major sports teams, including NHL teams like the Montréal Canadiens. Decades later, vestiges of this development mentality are seen in the ways in which spectator sports are produced, sold, and experienced. In 1996, the team moved from the Montréal Forum to the Molson Centre, a larger sports and entertainment complex that could hold 5,000 additional spectators plus more corporate boxes, in addition to having more impressive technical capacities. The Montréal Forum, until then the Mecca of Montréal culture (both Francophone and Anglophone) was truly an institution that was home to a slice of the city's history, or even the province's: "The Forum had emerged as a vital public space in Montréal, the argument ran. It was a commercial space, of course, but the building had been claimed symbolically over the years by 'the people.' Not only had the Forum provided a home for legendary hockey games, but also concerts and political rallies that were significant in the development of Québec's pre- and post-war popular cultures."[20] The announcement of the move sent a shockwave through the Montréal community. To ease tensions and ensure the new

19.   Jean Harvey, "Whose Sweater is it? The Changing Meanings of Hockey in Quebec," *Artificial Ice: Hockey, Culture, and Commerce*, edited by David Whitson and Richard Gruneau (Peterborough: Broadview Press, 2006).

20.   Anouk Bélanger, "Sports Venues and the Spectacularization of Urban Spaces in North America: The Case of the Molson Centre in Montreal," *International Review for the Sociology of Sport*, Sage 3, 3 (September 2000), p. 402.

amphitheatre would be viable, the Molson family (which owned both the team and the arena) orchestrated a marketing campaign based on a series of planned events to ensure that the myth would live on. A "dramatic marketing" approach was used to transfer the symbol from one location to the other: people associated the new building with a sense of belonging through the appropriation of the spirit of the Forum and of the Montréal Canadiens. This was made tangible through a public auction (in which almost all the goods accumulated over the course of nearly a century were liquidated), a parade (using symbols related to the mythology of the place, such as the Olympic flame and the Ghosts of the Forum), and a family-friendly open house at the Molson Centre.

These events were orchestrated on the basis of a narrative that swept away all controversy, legitimized the move, and steered the collective memory where it was meant to go; they served to build up a glorious, unifying image. The moments of tension, conflict, and significance that had made the building an icon of Montréal culture were surgically removed from the official discourse and hidden; they would have yielded more ruffled feathers than ticket sales.[21] In the end, Molson's sensational stunt of collective memory succeeded in keeping the myth intact: the fans seem just as interested and loyal as ever. And as various speeches planned by the Canadiens were delivered and ample commentary from the Montréal public was shared, the Forum itself also passed into myth, which in turn magnified the myth of the team.

Professional hockey as media spectacle

Sport, whether professional or amateur, is one of the most media-oriented spectacles in the world. As we alluded to earlier, the media are central to the alliance, or even the symbiosis, between institutionalized sport and the market, without which the myth could not exist. The media serve as a financial go-between, granting sports teams access to the general public while paying them for broadcasting rights. They also serve to grow the audience, as their reach extends beyond the physical and geographic limits of the venue. No

21.   Harvey, "Whose Sweater is it?"

myth can be sustained without a massive rallying of the troops, and the myth we discuss in this chapter was constructed at a time when modern mass culture and its media were rising to prominence. The necessary interactions between the Montréal Canadiens and the fans have all taken place through newspapers, radio, television, and the Internet. Accordingly, the media account for a large portion of sport's ability to articulate the ". . . spectacles of race and nationalism, celebrity and star power, and transgression and scandal, elevating its icons to Godlike status, and then sometimes bringing them down into the depths of scandal and disgrace."[22]

It was from a journalist's description of the first Montréal hockey game, played in front of an audience in an indoor arena, that sports historians have been able to pinpoint the birth of the sport: modern professional hockey as we know it today was born on March 3, 1875.[23] It is interesting to note that even the very first game was joined by an umbilical cord to the public and the media: without the combined presence of the many spectators and the *Montreal Gazette*, modern hockey would never have had this game as its founding moment. The first modern hockey game wasn't played by little boys on a frozen pond: it was in an indoor arena, with an audience there taking it all in. The presence of the crowd and the indoor environment in which hockey evolved also influenced how the game was played: "because this game had to be played for the first time on an indoor rink, they decided to use a wooden block in place of a lacrosse ball. Because there were windows all along the length of the building and no boards along the surface of the ice, they had to find an object that wouldn't injure the spectators or break the windows."[24] There are lots of examples of hockey being adapted to a spectacle format, and already on its official (or at least agreed-upon) birthdate, hockey took shape through its ability to entertain.[25] In addition to the media description that

22. Kellner, *Media Spectacle*, p. 65.
23. Michel Vigneault, "Les débuts du hockey montréalais, 1875-1917," *La culture du sport au Québec*, edited by Jean-Pierre Augustin and Claude Sorbets (Talence: Maison des Sciences de l'Homme d'Aquitaine, 1996).
24. Ibid., p. 188.
25. Richard Gruneau and David Whitson (eds.), *Artificial Ice: Hockey, Culture, and Commerce* (Peterborough: Broadview Press, 2006).

was important in the discovery and publicization of the sport, Vigneault reminds us that hockey's popularity and expansion can also be attributed to another spectacle: the Montréal Winter Carnival. Hockey was presented at this major North American gathering from 1883 to 1886, which is also where the first tournaments were played. It was also at this carnival (whose purpose was to promote the city of Montréal across North America) that "the coming of a more structured organization was announced, along with games to be held all throughout the season."[26] The event attracted scores of spectators. Several hockey leagues grew out of it, including the senior leagues that gave us hockey as we know it today. The rapid standardization of rules and game calendars, which show games being held on holidays, speaks to the owners' desire to attract spectators.

Technological advances, like the creation of an icy playing surface that lasts for months at a time, are also considered key factors in fostering hockey's institutional development in North America. Artificial ice, on which NHL hockey has been played since the early 1920s, made it possible to plan a regular calendar far in advance and thereby extend hockey's reach into otherwise unviable seasons and regions. These technological aspects fly in the face of depictions of hockey based on "happy naturalism,"[27] as if the spectacle of hockey were somehow a direct expression of our ability to survive harsh conditions and hold fast in adversity. Hockey, like the ice on which it is played, is not natural; it is a human and social construct.

Generally speaking, hockey's development in Québec was a function of its entertainment value. Had it not been played in an arena (with all the technology this requires), had there been no radio play-by-play, had there been no television coverage, hockey could never have infiltrated the daily lives of millions of Québécois. And without these entertainment platforms there to fuel the pride of an entire people and galvanize it in support of the Montréal Canadiens, the team could never have grown into the national

26.   Vigneault, "Les débuts du hockey montréalais," p. 190.
27.   Richard Gruneau and David Whitson (eds.), *Artificial Ice*, pp. 29–52.

Illustration of the commercialization of a symbol
- *Authentic gear for authentic fans!* At the Montréal Canadiens' official shop, you can buy Canadiens-brand clothing and other products designed for babies, children, and (imagine!) women.
  (http://shop.nhl.com/Montreal_Canadiens_Gear)
- *The Montréal Canadiens flag: consumer product or symbol of belonging?*
- While total sales figures are unavailable, the sale of Habs flags is a telling feature of the spectacle of hockey. According to certain fans on the rds.ca forum, an estimated one in ten inhabitants of the city of Longueuil proudly displays the flag in their car window, and this phenomenon is seen all across the province. It is also interesting to note that Radio NRJ organized a sale of 20,000 flags, with a portion of the proceeds going to Opération Enfant Soleil, one of Québec's best-loved charities. Putting one's sports patriotism on display adds to the joy of belonging to a group of supporters, thereby drawing interest to the team.

emblem it is today. In fact, the spectacle of media coverage for Canadiens games, not to mention certain events and ceremonies surrounding the team, taps into this myth so deeply that the team sometimes drowns in it.

Fast forward to the 1990s, and we see that media entertainment, sport, and the market all became more closely intertwined through the strategic alliances that hockey teams form with the media. One example of this is Molson Brewery's expertly choreographed dance between beer and hockey: as owner of the Montréal Canadiens team, the Bell Centre, and Molstar Productions (which rebroadcasts games), the company places beer at the centre of this synergy to boost consumption in the temple, in bars and taverns, and even in little cottages.

Where myth meets money: The stars of hockey

Hockey (and the Montréal Canadiens in particular) has gone through a process of commercialization as well as identification and belonging in relation to the people of Québec. At the heart of these processes, the hockey player—specifically the star player— feeds the mania surrounding his team and hockey in general through his achievements, statements, and public appearances. Not only does the team need the Howie Morenzes, the Maurice Richards, the Jean Béliveaus, the Guy Lafleurs, and their colleagues to win on the ice, but it also needs them off the ice to promote the team and to garner popular favour, which is based on a strong sense of attachment and identification.

This correlation between myth and money, between national idols and merchandise, is neither fortuitous nor con- tradictory. Player-as-star and player-as-merchandise "are two sides of the same coin: human needs in the era of twentieth- century capitalist civilization."[28] The need for unifying symbols to build national identities is just as real for the nation it is for the citizenry, and mass media have been the conduit for these symbols. Nationhood is always constructed through the use of symbols and idols, and sport is a special incubator of these. Through the spectacle of media, sport quickly became an incred- ibly profitable base of recruitment in North America; as Whitson and Gruneau say of hockey and its mythology in Canada, "like it or not, profiting from the game has been as Canadian as the beaver"![29]

The Canadiens and its stars are idols, icons, and national emblems; the public makes this so. But it's the hockey industry that readies them, moulds them, shapes them, presents them, and manufactures them—for the public to reappropriate. The Canadiens meet an emotional or mythological need that the hockey industry doesn't create, but without the industry this need "would lose its shape, its supports, its aphrodisiacs."[30]

---

28. Edgar Morin, *Les stars* (Paris: Seuil, 1972), p. 102.
29. Richard Gruneau and David Whitson, *Hockey Night in Canada: Sports, Identities and Cultural Politics* (Toronto: Garamond Press, 1993), p. 27.
30. Edgar Morin, *Les stars*, p. 98.

Obviously, history is an important variable in this equation. If Maurice Richard's career had unfolded in the 1920s or the 1980s, he would not have benefitted from the "era" in which he represented not just an exceptionally talented hockey player competing for "his" local team, but actually the embodiment of the entire French-Canadian people (especially Québec's working class) in the midst of emancipating itself and affirming its identity. Where myth meets money, we also see a confluence with history.

Generally speaking, the stars of the Canadiens, like the Ghosts of the Forum, are symbols as much as they are consumer products and deities. The hockey gods have the power not only to promote the team, preserve the aura of the myth, and boost sales in the boutique, but moreover to sell innumerable products.

Obvious effort goes into preserving the iconic and sacred quality of these stars even after they retire. Just look at the numbers we retire and the jerseys we hang in the temple so that their flame will continue to flicker in our memory (there are 17 in the Bell Centre).[31] And in the old Forum gift shop, which is located in the Bell Centre, you can find portraits of old players, bronzed skates, autographed sticks, and other memorabilia presented and preserved as sacred relics; there are also biographies, documentaries, and exhibits on idols like Maurice Richard, "Butch" Bouchard, and Guy Lafleur.

As fans, we're given a chance to own these symbols by buying from the extensive merchandise of the team and its idols: in so doing, not only do we promote the team to sell tickets, but we also gain access to items from baby pyjamas (so the little darlings will have CH imprinted on their hearts before they're out of diapers), to scarves (those markers of style and team loyalty in the schoolyard), to the coffee mugs that grown-up fans tote with them to the office, to the team jerseys that, as we know from the famous book *The Hockey Sweater*,[32] are a must-have on the neighbourhood rink and in the tavern on game night. We are even "lucky" enough to be able to enjoy the symbol or blessing of our idols with the purchase

---

31.   http://canadiens.nhl.com/team/app/l_fr/?service=page&page=NHLPage&id =16628.

32.   Roch Carrier, *The Hockey Sweater* (Montréal: Toundra Books, 1979).

Advertising with the stars!

- Over the course of his career and even into retirement,
  Québec's star player Maurice Richard attached his
  name to brands including Bovril, Quaker Oatmeal,
  Campbell's Tomato Soup, Kellogg's cereals, Grecian
  Formula, Ultramar heating oil, and two life insurance
  companies, just to name a few (Benoît Melançon, *The
  Rocket: A Cultural History of Maurice Richard*,
  Montréal: Fides, 2006).

- Guy Lafleur lent his name to the Hairfax hair trans-
  plant company, a televised message on erectile dys-
  function by the maker of Viagra, Yoplait yogurt,
  Lafleur products, his Flower Power energy drink, his
  Guy Lafleur No. 10 cologne, and his 1979 disco album
  Lafleur!

- In 1993, Patrick Roy held the newly won Stanley Cup
  high above his head yelling, "I'm going to Disneyland!"
  as per his pre-contract with the company as part of a
  future advertisement.

of certain household items, vehicles, and other consumer products—sometimes even into the most intimate aspects of our lives.

Spectacle of a myth. . . with a little help from the fans

There are various processes of rallying, articulation, and myth construction at play in hockey on TV. In the post-war period, the work
of solidifying, preserving, and readapting the myth of the authenticity of "real" hockey has intensified owing to three factors: (1) the
Canadiens' television spectacle has become more similar to that of
other sports and forms of popular entertainment, (2) multiple
expansions have resulted in the recruitment of players from other
continents, creating an increasingly heterogeneous player base, and
(3) the mobility of players has increased even within the NHL. We
see this process every day, and it's facilitated by fans who latch onto
the myth for different reasons than promoters and broadcasters do,

which primarily involve sales. As proof of this, consider recent efforts by the fans to incorporate new elements into the myth of what the Canadiens are, specifically when it comes to the values of honour and patriotism.

Canadiens fans are master critics, and they are more than happy to spout their opinions in everyday conversation and on media platforms like radio call-in shows. The lengthy and passionate comments about the Canadiens posted on the RDS website are a good example of the media's important role in sharing commentary, as well as the "debate" aspect that typifies many conversations about the Canadiens. These platforms, which are open to the public, become particularly important spaces for myth building, as evidenced by RDS.[33]

For example, the name "Special K" emerged over the course of the 2006–2007 season in reference to the successes of the star players Kovalev and Koivu, who sometimes appeared together in the same line. Then in 2007–2008, the expression resurfaced and took on the meaning it has today. First used to refer to the trio of Kovalev, Kostitsyn (Andrei), and Plekanec, (cf. "Special K, a line with depth"[34]) the term was used more broadly over the course of the season to ultimately encompass all players with a letter K in their name: Koivu, Kostitsyn (Sergei), Komisarek, Kostopoulos, Hamrlík, Markov, and others. Now synonymous with talent and excellence, the expression is most often used in good times, when people want to speak of the team's performance in terms of pride and success: "The CH has a stable line all year long. . . Special K, a line that will surely have made the difference compared to last year. Thanks to Special K."[35] So, this expression that marries "exoticism" (few players of Québécois, Canadian, and even American "stock" have a K in their name) and familiarity (Canadians have been starting their day with Kellogg's cereals for generations) speaks to an acceptance of, and perhaps even a pride in, foreign players in this

33.   Fannie Valois-Nadeau, *Quand le coeur a ses raisons: analyse de la construction mythique du club de hockey le Canadien de Montréal*, Master's research paper. (Montréal: Université du Québec à Montréal, 2009).
34.   Forum RDS, bobgoodnow January 15, 2007.
35.   Forum RDS, Oliver_doyle, April 2, 2008.

traditional sport. This special status is not guaranteed, however: in order to exist, it must be accompanied by spectacular performance and high rankings. These forums are sometimes coloured with racist and xenophobic remarks, thus preserving the myth of naturalness in a different way.

So, the inclusion and reappropriation of these successes, especially in the case of the "Special Ks," largely occurs against an ethnic and nationalist backdrop, which sparks discussions on the authenticity of the sport, how it ought to be played, and the perfect recipe for a win. The association of "naturalness" with players (based on shared ethnic or geographic origin) is diminishing due to market pressures on professional hockey and the globalization of the players' circuit. Because of this, the fans' work in creating a sense of belonging, familiarity, and pride is all the more obvious. They do this by rehashing the so-called "original" values of yesterday's good old boys and hybridizing them with ethnic characteristics (for some forum contributors, the fact of being strong, proud, brave, and ultimately victorious is mainly a characteristic of Francophone and Canadian players), via a fundamentally ethno-folkloric discourse. In other words, if fans note certain qualities in players from other countries (i.e., that they are strong, proud, brave, devoted, emotionally invested, and loyal), the foreign players' image can be conveniently woven into that of the little boy skating on the pond.

However, we must acknowledge the significant failure of the Montréal Canadiens in getting French-Canadian players on the roster, as well as its poor performance in the 1990s, when it was mostly made up of French-Canadians. Despite people's initial intentions, at no point has the Canadiens ever been 100 percent composed of French-Canadian players.[36] Nor have the fans ever 100 percent retained this ethnic dimension in proclaiming their greatest stars. Howie Morenz, the first Ghost of the Forum, is an obvious example. The work of preservation has been part of the Canadiens since the team began. However, it has never stood in the way of there being a powerful sense of identity and a multitude of

---

36. Black, *Habitants et Glorieux*.

Examples of popular works about and around hockey in Québec, the Montréal Canadiens, and its star players

- Exhibitions: Maurice Richard at the Château Ramezay; Butch Bouchard at the Écomusée du fier monde.
- Songs: "*Salut mon Ron*," Les Cowboy Fringants; "*Le But (Allez Montréal)*," Loco Locass; "*Bleu, Blanc, Rouge*" sung by Michel Como and Thierry Dubé; and all the incredible YouTube productions including the very prolific Gomartgo: "*Go Canadiens*," "*On veut faire les séries*," "*Je déteste les Flyers*," "*Ne prends pas pour Boston*." These songs were aired on CKOI and Radio NRJ.
- Books: *The Hockey Sweater* by Rock Carrier; *On a volé la coupe Stanley: les enquêtes de Berri et Demontigny* by Girerd and Arsène; *Rondel et Baton à la conquête du Saladier d'argent* by André Pijet and Michel Blanchard.
- Visual art: Serge Lemoyne and the *Bleu Blanc Rouge* series, including *Larouche, Mondou, Période supplémentaire, Le Masque, Trente-Trois Millions*.
- Art: Jean-Paul Riopelle, *Hommage à Duchamp (Hommage à Maurice Richard)*; *La Joute* is a sculpture originally located in the Parc Olympique in honour of the artist's childhood heroes; Henri Boivin, *Maurice Richard en Superman*.
- Television: *He Shoots, He Scores* created by Réjean Tremblay.
- Film: *Maurice Richard*, directed by Charles Binamé.

artistic expressions and institutional representations of the team's popularity.

Conclusion

Our daily lives are full of myths, including that of the Canadiens. We are attached to it symbolically, emotionally, and historically. But, in analyzing it, "we constantly drift between the object and its demystification, powerless to render its wholeness. For if we penetrate the object, we liberate it but we destroy it; and if we acknowledge its full weight, we respect it, but we restore it to a state which is still mystified."[37] The idea behind this chapter is not to further contribute to the naturalization of this myth or to its undoing, but rather to take a step back and consider the various factors that have fed it over time, along with the different social contexts and advances in technology and media. We also aim to give ourselves a space to enjoy the pleasures of spectacle, popular entertainment, and the emotions that the Canadiens bring us without this automatically being understood as appeasing either the ideology of modern mass culture or the professional sports industry that has succeeded in carving out an imposing presence within that space. As we have tried to present it here, the myth is discussed; it evolves and transforms. And each time it does so, it rearticulates images of the essence of hockey (and that of the Canadiens). For these reasons, we have presented a historical perspective on the active participation of the promoters, the fans, the stars, and the media in constructing, and further today in preserving, a symbol that is all too rarely critically examined.

Further reading

AUGUSTIN, Jean-Pierre and Christian POIRIER. "Les territoires symboliques du sport: le hockey comme élément identitaire du Québec." *Bulletin d'histoire politique*, vol. 9, no. 1 (Fall 2000), pp. 104–127.

BARTHES, Roland. *Mythologies*. Paris: Seuil, 2000.

BÉLANGER, Anouk. "Le hockey au Québec, bien plus qu'un jeu: analyse sociologique de la place centrale du hockey dans le projet identitaire des Québécois." *Loisirs et Société*, vol. 19, no. 2 (Fall 1996), pp. 539–557.

———. "Sports Venues and the Spectacularization of Urban Spaces in North America: The Case of the Molson Centre in Montreal." *International Review for the Sociology of Sport*, Sage, vol. 35, No. 3 (September 2000), pp. 378–397.

---

37. Roland Barthes, *Mythologies*, back cover.

BLACK, François. *Évolution de l'image projetée par le Club de Hockey Canadien depuis ses origines jusqu'au mythe de la tradition glorieuse*. Master's reasearch paper. Université de Montréal, 1992.

———. *Habitants et Glorieux. Les Canadiens de 1909 à 1960*. Laval: Mille-Îles, 1997.

FISHER, Stan and Maurice RICHARD. *Les Canadiens sont là ! La plus grande dynastie du hockey*. Scarborough: Prentice-Hall of Canada, 1971.

GRUNEAU, Richard. "Making Spectacle: A Case Study in Television Sports Production." *Media, Sports & Society*. Edited by Lawrence A. Wenner. London: Sage, 1989.

GRUNEAU, Richard and David WHITSON. "Upmarket continentalism: Major league sport, promotional culture, and corporate integration." *Continental order? Integrating North America for Cyber-Capital*. Edited by V. Mosco & D. Schiller. Lanham, MD: Roman & Littlefield, 2001.

———. "The (Real) Integrated Circus: Political Economy, Popular Culture, and Major league Sport." *Understanding Canada. Building on the New Canadian Political Economy*. Edited by Wallace Clement. Montréal, Kingston: McGill-Queen's University Press, pp. 359–385.

———. HOCKEY NIGHT IN CANADA. SPORT, IDENTITIES AND CULTURAL POLITICS. Toronto: Garamond Press, 1993.

GUAY, Donald. *La conquête du sport. Le sport et la société québécoise au XIXe siècle*. Outremont: Lanctôt éditeur, 1997.

———. *L'histoire du hockey au Québec: origine et développement d'un phénomène culturel avant 1917*. Chicoutimi: JCL, 1990.

HANNIGAN, John. "From the Maple Leaf Gardens to the Air Canada Centre: The Dowtown Entertainment Economy in 'World Class' Toronto." *Artificial Ice: Hockey, Culture and Commerce*. Edited by David Whitson and Richard Gruneau. Peterborough: Broadview Press, 2006, pp. 201–214.

HARVEY, Jean. "Whose Sweater is it? The Changing Meanings of Hockey in Quebec." *Artificial Ice: Hockey, Culture, and Commerce*. Edited by David Whitson and Richard Gruneau. Peterborough: Broadview Press, 2006. pp. 29–52.

JANSON, Gilles. *Emparons-nous du sport. Les Canadiens français et le sport au XIXᵉ siècle.* Montréal: Guérin, 1995.

JHALLY, Sut. "Cultural Studies and the Sport/Media Complex." *Media, Sports & Society.* Edited by Lawrence A. Wenner. London: Sage, 1989.

KELLNER, Douglas. *Media Spectacle.* London, New York: Routledge, 2003.

McKINLEY, Michael. *Un toit pour le hockey.* Montréal: Éditions Hurtubise, 2001.

MORIN, Edgard. *Les stars.* Paris: Seuil, 1972.

MOUTON, Claude. *Toute l'histoire illustre et merveilleuse du Canadien de Montréal.* Montréal: La Presse, 1986.

VIGNEAULT, Michel. "Les débuts du hockey montréalais, 1875–1917." *La culture du sport au Québec.* Edited by Jean-Pierre Augustin et Claude Sorbets. Talence: Éditions de la Maison des Sciences de l'Homme d'Aquitaine, 1996.

WHITSON, David and Richard GRUNEAU (eds.). *Artificial Ice: Hockey, Culture and Commerce.* Peterborough: Broadview Press, 2006.

Did you know?
When it first began in the 1870s, Canadian professional hockey was played on natural ice surfaces with snowbanks for boards and wooden posts for goals. Each team had nine players on the ice, and passing forward was against the rules!
(Source: *The Canadian Encyclopedia*)

Did you know?
Hockey Night in Canada, presented on CBC on Saturday night from 1952 to today, is the oldest TV show in North America. Its French counterpart, *La Soirée du hockey*, aired on Radio-Canada from 1952 to 2004.

Did you know?
The first broadcast of *Hockey Night in Canada* and *La Soirée du hockey*, on October 11, 1952, started around 9:00 p.m., at the beginning of the third period. At the time, it was feared that fans would desert the Montréal Forum and Maple Leaf Gardens in Toronto. . . It wasn't until October 12, 1968, that the game was broadcast in its entirety.
(Source: *Radio-Canada archives*)

Did you know?
Contrary to popular belief, neither Jacques Plante in 1959 nor Clint Benedict in the 1920s was the first to wear a goalie mask. This honour rightfully belongs to a woman, Elizabeth Graham, who wore a fencing mask during the 1927 season playing for Queen's University!
(Source: *Library and Archives Canada*)

Did you know?
It wasn't until 1994 that hockey officially became Canada's national winter sport. MP Nelson Riis introduced a bill to

replace lacrosse with hockey as "Canada's national sport."
After a debate, the *National Sports of Canada Act* received
royal assent, recognizing hockey as Canada's national
winter sport and lacrosse as the national summer sport.
(C.B.)

The Metaphysics of Hockey

Jean Grondin

> I don't think anybody really watches
> hockey any more.
>
> Tiger Woods (June 4, 2008)

Amidst the monotony of modern life, hockey affords us a breath of transcendence. In a world of disenchantment, devoid of miracles, it offers us something spectacular and creates moments of ecstasy. To borrow from Marx, hockey is a bit like "the heart of a heartless world, and the soul of soulless conditions." It gets our blood pumping and infuses our day-to-day lives with poetry and dream. Embodying as it does a rare (or perhaps not-so-rare) moment of celebration, it is, to borrow from Hegel this time, the "Sunday of life"—except we most often celebrate it on Saturday night (as dictated by its liturgy). The stadiums are its temples, and the playoffs and other important championships (including the Summit Series) are its holy days and times of revelry. Its elite athletes are venerated as saints and gods. We lap up even their most mundane comments after the game, or even between games. After all, that's all there is, isn't it? Time between games? The year is virtually defined by the hockey calendar, at least for the fans, just as it used to be defined by the Christian calendar (Christmas, Easter, Trinity Sunday, Michaelmas Day, what have you).

If we can speak of the metaphysics of hockey, it's because the game allows its participants and spectators (and it's not always necessary to distinguish between them) to experience a moment of transcendence that inspires them to do better than their best. But surely this is true of other sports as well. What distinguishes the metaphysics of hockey from other sports ontologies is its exclusively northern character.

A northern metaphysics

One of the sport's most memorable teams was named the "Nordiques," which hailed from the fine city of Québec. It wasn't lack of passion that killed the team—far from it. No, the Québec Nordiques was the casualty of the singularly cruel logic of economics ("too small a market" and other nonsense—as if the "market" in Phoenix, Columbus, Atlanta, or Nashville were somehow more suitable). In any event, the team's name did a good job of conveying the wintry essence of the sport, which is certainly not a game for the thin-skinned.

Hockey fans are aware that most of the world doesn't really "get" their sport. In fact, what we call hockey, everyone else calls "ice hockey." But sometimes we forget that the rest of the world plays the sport on grass, with sticks that to us would seem small and crude. The fact remains that infinitely more people play field hockey than ice hockey. In fact, the field kind is quite highly regarded in countries like Pakistan and India. The combined population of these countries is 30 times that of Canada but, like our country, both are former British colonies. And while we like to credit our French forebears (you know, the people who abandoned their colony), it was actually the English who gave us their superb sports ethic.

The world of ice hockey is limited to a handful of northern countries. In the so-called world hockey championship—not the most exciting event for the average fan—only five or six teams have a serious chance at bringing home the hardware: Canada, Russia, Sweden, Finland, the Czech Republic, and sometimes the United States (whose "miraculous" victory against the USSR in 1980 is still remembered around the world). True hockey aficionados can be found in this handful of countries—and perhaps only in these countries. And yet—and this is an aberration that grates on all fans north of the 49th parallel—while most NHL teams are located in the United States, hockey isn't all that popular there. Baseball, football, and basketball are infinitely more popular with the Yanks. . . as are golf, auto racing, boxing, tennis, soccer, and wrestling.

So, while most inhabitants of our planet are blind to hockey's existence and deaf to people's passion for it, they also don't know (for better or for worse) what it's like to live in a land where winter is king. Yes, soccer has infinitely more fans on a worldwide basis. But that sport is much less exhilarating to the average hockey fan for purely rational reasons: in soccer, the players are too many (22!), the goals too few, the nets hopelessly large, the penalties too easy, the hooligans insufferable, the offsides phenomenologically unverifiable, and the fouls less deserving of yellow or red cards than Oscars. (I happen to be a soccer fan, actually, but *sine ratione.*)

In hockey, the icy playing surface also makes things much livelier, much faster, and much more exciting. But this is deceptive: you might think the ice is easy enough to slide around on, but the effort it demands of the "being-for-the-heart-attack" (the *Sein-zum-Herzinfarkt*) is intense: after a two-minute burst of effort (if not less—"ice time" is now measured in seconds!), it's back to the bench for you. In soccer, you could stumble around the field for two hours straight without seeing any action at all.

Now an effort like that definitely shows the northern spirit: you need determination, courage, fire in the belly. That's because the northern spirit has to struggle against nature, while the Southern spirit has the luxury of working with it. When we tell South Americans we sometimes play our sport outdoors in −25°C weather, they look at us like we have two heads. But that's who we are: we're the screwballs who managed to conquer winter (and its conditions) by inventing the most rugged sports.

Mon pays, c'est le hockey

Our frosty white garden is the glue that holds our "collective identity" together. Sometimes we forget how true this can be. One of our most famous and most nationalistic singers said it best in a well-known song: "*Mon pays ce n'est pas un pays, c'est l'hiver*" (my country is not a country, it is winter). It would be a mistake to assume this song was intended to have a national flavour, however. On the contrary, it is an anti-national anthem: it says that our country, however we define it, is not so much this thing or that thing (say, Canada or Québec, with all the propaganda tearing them apart at the seams) as winter itself, a season imposed upon us by the nature of things. And winter is no less punishing in Chicoutimi as it is in Edmonton, Minsk, Helsinki, or Vladivostok. I insist on this point because I have always felt that we tend to over-glorify the linguistic part of our makeup (though this cannot be denied) and too often leave out climate, geography, and nature. What shapes us more, language or geography? Who would dispute the claim that Africans, Mexicans, or Indians are also defined by their climate, perhaps even chiefly so? Metaphysically speaking, this is what makes us a northern people. Our country is not primarily this thing or that thing; it is winter. And what is there to occupy our time with in winter, other than philosophy? Pretty much just three things: hockey, hockey, and hockey. Whether the nationalists like it or not, hockey is one of the most powerful facts of Canadian belonging; the passion is most assuredly the same *a mari usque ad mare*, from sea to sea. Besides—irony of ironies—Québec's best-loved team is called the "Canadiens," a name that no one, to my knowledge, has ever tried to change. It would be hard to imagine going to a "Montréal Québécois" game and seeing uniforms that were more blue than red. Yes, Germany may have her thinkers and poets, but Canada is defined by her hockey personalities: Maurice Richard, Bobby Orr, René Lecavalier, and so many other masters of metaphysics.

Make no mistake: hockey is politically divisive, which is inevitable given how much emotion it arouses. The Québécois follow Francophone players with a particular pride, preferring Mario Lemieux to Wayne Gretzky. That's fair enough, but it can also make matters tense. Serious historians have traced the origin of the rise in Québec nationalism to the suspension of Maurice Richard in 1955. This suspension robbed Richard of the title of champion goal-scorer, the only title he was eligible for. For this, the NHL president at the time, Clarence Campbell, was booed and hissed at and stigmatized as an enemy of the French-Canadian people. Images from television—a recent invention at the time—immortalized the riot that followed, with tear gas explosions and everything. The ironic thing (and, perhaps for Richard, the lucky thing) is that there are no surviving images of the actions that led to the suspension. According to witnesses, he either hit the referee with his stick or threatened to do so; reports differ. Today, the act would have been recorded and shared around the world (the hockey world, that is), and we might determine that the suspension was in fact deserved. Regardless, in the heat of the moment, what mattered most was the feeling of outrage it triggered: a "*maudit Anglais*" (*maudit* being an adjective otherwise reserved for the French) had deprived a proud French-Canadian of his rightful honour. History forgets, however, that the player who did receive the honour was Richard's teammate, a Francophone no less, by the name of Bernard Geoffrion. But Geoffrion didn't personify the same sense of humiliation that stuck to Richard. The ensuing riot gave rise to the nationalist movement of the 1960s and 1970s. What could be more telling of hockey's metaphysical importance? Maurice Richard got his revenge in one sense: after his suspension in March 1955, the Montréal Canadiens won the Stanley Cup for five consecutive years, which helped make it one of the most dominant dynasties in hockey's short history. This points to another impressive quality of the metaphysics of hockey: there's no shortage of talk (call-in shows, blogs, etc.), but it's the action—the wins—that count in the end. Or, as a philosopher might say, there is a priority of being, and in this case action, over language.

English-speaking Canada has its share of controversial personalities too. The most well-known today would have to be Don Cherry, a man the Québécois love to hate. Granted, he has made some pretty derogatory comments about Francophones (surely because the Canadiens so often beat his Boston Bruins, who had more talent but whose results were less impressive). Francophones are supposedly less "macho" than Anglophones; like "Europeans," they wear visors. Comments like these offend the Québécois macho instinct. As a hockey fan, Cherry is as loud and proud as they come, and his main fault seems to be that he says what he really thinks (a practice that's becoming rarer, even in philosophy). Here is a man whose commentary is broadcast by the CBC with a 10-second delay so that he can be censored if needed. To look at him, he often gives the impression restraining himself, but no censor can bleep the unbleepable: those daggers in his eyes. Somehow, he still has a large audience in Québec. One careless comment that goes too far would do wonders for the nationalist movement.

Cherry is at his best when he sticks to hockey, a topic he speaks about with passion. He does so with the same ardour as one does when evoking the memory of fallen soldiers in missions abroad. One can only admire the heart and soul behind his words. No public figure—and certainly no politician or fellow commentator—does so with as much gusto and with as little political decorum. It would seem as though the metaphysics of hockey, in calling us to do better than our best, had something vaguely militaristic about it.

A decidedly physical metaphysics: War

Hockey fans are reluctant to admit this, but the vast majority of people in the world who have no interest in hockey, for what little they've heard of it, see it as a brutal, violent sport. Die-hard fans of the sport wouldn't disagree, even if they themselves see it as a rather graceful sport, with such finesse (oh yes) that it might even be compared to ballet—that is, if they were into ballet. The fans grant that brutality is part of the game, but hasten to point to other sports that are even more violent, like football and rugby. Either way, the same logic is at play: in a world where war and its "virtues" are incompatible with modern values, hockey is a stand-in for war. Obviously, the sport is full of attack, defence, and strategy, but what counts the most is courage and something euphemistically referred to as "physical play." Today's hockey journalists begin to resemble yesterday's war correspondents.

And hockey players, for their part, start to look like gladiators. No sport has equipment that is heavier, more complicated, or more expensive (as hockey moms and dads well know). But we just "deal with it." We also accept the violence involved. It's a sport with many injuries, and it's not hard to see why. There are a million wonderful ways to get hurt: the puck is a projectile that can literally kill (kill players, yes, but also spectators, as has recently occurred). Hockey sticks can also be lethal when used as clubs, javelins, bayonets, or tridents. The same is true of the boards and windows as well as the clothing itself, starting with skates, whose blades are sharper than swords. Some participants have had their throats slit (including Richard Zednik, in February 2008, who miraculously survived), and players at all levels have died. This is one of the great taboos of hockey. Actually, it's a wonder there have been so few deaths considering the number of weapon-wielding players who are blinded by their ferocious determination to win.

Hockey it is an incredibly virile sport. In a society that's been feminized and softened within an inch of its life, hockey remains one of the last bastions of pure, unbridled machismo. Women of course follow hockey, and more and more of them are playing it, and that's a good thing. But the fact is that hockey is infinitely more exciting to men than women. This claim I am basing on a small homespun survey I conducted (nothing scientific about it, unlike everything else I have stated here). I found that the vast majority of women I have had the pleasure of knowing don't follow hockey much, while the vast majority of men are incurable hockey addicts. What's the proportion of women who attend hockey games? Maybe 20 percent. That's not nothing, although they might be attracted by the sport's unabashed virility, which has become so rare in other areas of life. I know I should probably strike this paragraph from the text, as I am on thin ice, "genderly speaking." But then again hockey, with its metaphysics, isn't very politically correct to begin with. It's also profoundly meritocratic.

Meritocracy in an egalitarian society: The best man (usually) wins

We live in a society that's proud to call itself egalitarian, and rightly so. Yeah, hockey is in no way egalitarian. It's the best players who win, and it's the best players who play (at least in the upper echelons). Meritocracy operates at many strata. First you have to make the team, and that means outclassing many other high-calibre athletes, who (poor souls) will be relegated to the lower leagues, which are less glamorous and often even more brutal. Even if you do make the team, the pressure to perform is intense. "Lethargies" (which hockey nerds obsessively keep statistics on, and which fans pounce upon, crying "only one goal in the last eight games") aren't forgiven: you'll be moved to a different line or demoted to the minor leagues. Even a first-rate athlete may be sidelined or given less ice time if he doesn't perform consistently. A goalie who chances to let one or two "easy ones" through will be replaced immediately. And the coach's life is more precarious still.

Justice in hockey isn't egalitarian; it's meritocratic. Justice is accompanied by punishment: "bad boys" receive penalties or suspensions. It's the job of the referees (much maligned but critically important) to ensure that the game proceeds in an orderly fashion. They deal out "penalties" for infractions with extraordinary names, names whose poetic value we often underestimate: you can be penalized for "cross-checking" (which only die-hard fans will understand), but "checking" is generally seen as a good thing. You can, however, be penalized for "high-sticking," "elbowing," or "boarding."

For philosophers, there is something strangely fascinating about this meritocratic metaphysics: there are clear winners and a certain justice. This is almost unheard of in their world. Philosophers are accustomed to having endless debates on all kinds of questions, but when do they ever reach a final conclusion or decision? Quite rarely indeed, and when philosophical "research" leads to a publication, the discussion's still not over. It's just getting started. Virtually everything is up for debate, and ideology is a constant: there are rationalists and Nietzscheans, theists and atheists, liberals and communitarians, analytic philosophers and continental philosophers, leftists and rightists. Even the safest authors and the most traditional topics can be questioned. Descartes and Plato are two of our most eminent classics, but there will always be cranks claiming these men are responsible for all of philosophy's ills. While certain people will devote their whole lives to studying the philosophy of Hegel, others will forever dismiss Hegel as a fraud.

Hockey has its share of endless debates too, but its metaphysics requires that there be final scores and winners. There is a clearcut finality to it: whether you're on the left or the right politically, whether you follow the teachings of Kant or Hegel, the Canadiens *did* beat the Maple Leafs 3 to 2, the Red Wings *did* win the Stanley Cup, and there *was* one and only one top scorer, period.

Philosophers have nothing remotely similar to hang their hat on. Yes, we get good ideas from time to time; our manuscripts are accepted or rejected; and we do (rarely) get teaching positions, grants, or accolades. But such honours are always surrounded by an ephemeral cloud of uncertainty, as they may be called into question at any time. "Finality" is almost alien to philosophy, though it is the alpha and the omega of hockey and other sports. Each person is judged according to his merits and performance. In philosophy, doubt can be cast over any merit and any performance. One of the most iconic thinkers of our profession is Socrates, and he is regarded as such because he acknowledged that he knew nothing. Socrates wouldn't get very far in the world of hockey.

Group excellence, individual excellence

Hockey is often called a team sport. But this isn't completely true. Of course, the primary object of the game is for a team to win, and in order to do so, there must be cohesion among the players. The metaphysics of team spirit is very important; nobody doubts that. But by the same token, all hockey fans follow the individual achievements of their heroes and saints. No professional sport bestows more individual honours than hockey. Most other sports have a most valuable player (MVP, Ballon d'Or), and many have a Rookie of the Year, but that's about it. Hockey has all of these, but there's also a trophy for the "most gentlemanly player" (no laughing, non-hockey-fans!), another for the "best defensive forward," the King Clancy trophy for "the player who best exemplifies leadership qualities on and off the ice and has made a noteworthy humanitarian contribution in his community," not to mention trophies for the best coach, the best defenceman, and even the player with the best "plus-minus" statistic (that one's a little hard to explain, and it didn't exist until a few decades ago). The "Bill Masterton" trophy, named after a player who lost his life in a game on January 15, 1968, is awarded to a player who shows perseverance, sportsmanship, and devotion to hockey.

Every game begins with an anthem and ends with the metaphysics of hockey choosing its three "stars." This metaphysics also honours the careers of the hockey greats: heroes are deified and "elected" to the "Hall of Fame," a sort of pantheon of hockey's immortals and saints. Their jersey numbers are "retired" in a solemn ceremony, in which each jersey is literally raised heavenward to stay there for all eternity. Finally, there are also "records," not just for teams but also for individuals. All hockey fans know the main metaphysicians as well as the greatest ones, but there are so many of them that they fill a book many hundreds of pages long, which the hockey-minded read like a sacred tome.

The transformation of modern hockey in metaphysics and the media

In the almost total absence of a unifying religion (or at least its burial deep within us), hockey takes the place of metaphysics in the regions where it is appreciated. Today, this unifying religion is increasingly present in the media. As Henri Richard aptly observed in a recent interview, "It was big in my day, but it's even bigger today." So we should beware of idealizing old-time hockey and its glory. Formerly, hockey was played on ponds and outdoor rinks, far from the watch of the media, which didn't really exist at the time. Back then professional players were a little like the Greek gods: much talked about but little seen.

The flood of media attention has deified hockey and its idols. In bygone eras, few people actually witnessed "professional" hockey being played; they just heard about in short newspaper articles. These pages were perhaps the most widely read, but back then there were no dailies such as *Le Journal de Montréal* (the highest-circulating French daily in the Americas) that systematically devoted their front page to hockey (even in summer!). Later it became a sport you could follow on the radio, where the lack of visuals engaged the imagination. With the advent of television, hockey began to carve out a place for itself, but still a rather limited one: games only happened on Saturday and Wednesday nights, and it wasn't always the Canadiens who played. Curiously, the puck dropped at 8:00, but the coverage didn't start until 8:30. Apparently average spectator wasn't interested in seeing the first part of the game. I can remember sometimes the first period would already be over when the broadcast began—and there were almost no commercial breaks in those blessed days. There were also no replays of goals or important plays. Today it would be inconceivable not to show a goal again seconds after it happened, from every angle. (This is true even in professional hockey arenas, which bounce like dance clubs. This ambiance may sap the metaphysics of hockey of its aura only to replace it with another: the aura of spectacle, in whatever form this may take—most often dictated by the scoreboard.) There were also no TV channels dedicated exclusively to sports. The sports news were never the top story, as they have become for many fans today.

The deification of hockey and its stars plays a part in the culture of image that affects all other aspects of the contemporary world, not least in politics, where image is king (to think that US president Franklin D. Roosevelt was stricken by polio and unable to walk but that most Americans didn't learn this until after he died!). As we noted earlier, there are no recorded images of the incidents that led to Maurice Richard's "historic" suspension. Hockey is more of a spectacle today than it used to be: it's less about being played and more about being seen and especially sold. It participates in the metaphysics of stardom, of instant celebrity and victory. The spectacle of hockey, like the game itself, gained ground over the course of the twentieth century. Who could name, off the top of their head, even one or two athletes of the eighteenth or nineteenth centuries? (Okay, there's Spyridon Louis, but even he won the marathon in 1896, which suggests that the metaphysics of sport is relatively new.) This may also indicate that athletic achievements don't age as well as cultural and intellectual ones.

The end of the nineteenth century surely marked a metaphysical turning point with the revival of the Olympic Games in 1896, which sparked only mild interest from the public at the time. Back then the most well-known sports were mostly invented by the British or followed British rules: golf, football, cricket, rugby, and the most popular of all, polo. For the people of that era, at least initially, sport was more of a pastime and had nothing to do with money. (Athletes' salaries and contracts were never debated, whereas today these issues are sports of their own and spoken about as such. The Olympics were for amateurs, and the idea that an athlete could make a living from competition was scandalous for a long time.) In calling for a sense of fair play, it offered positive life lessons, and even ethical ones: we can always redeem ourselves, we can always make a comeback, we learn the most from our defeats, effort brings reward, etc. British colleges and universities distinguished themselves—and still do—by their sports teams (who's ever heard of the teams of the Sorbonne or the University of Bologna?). And sport, still regarded and practiced as a simple game, was a training ground for self-improvement. Gymnastics wasn't just a mental pursuit (*mens sana in corpore sano*—now there's a bit of metaphysics for you), it was primarily a mental pursuit. The *mens sana*, the healthy mind, was the main focus; the healthy body was seen in service of this. This priority of the mind over the body has taken something of a backseat in the cacophonous world of modern hockey: sport, and for us hockey, is now the only metaphysics, an ersatz religion. Bound up within it are hopes and dreams it cannot hope to satisfy. If, at least in our part of the world, there is no more compelling metaphysics than hockey, certainly there are better alternatives to be had.

3rd period

Ethical and aesthetic issues

Eulogy for the Tie Game

Daniel M. Weinstock

There are no more tie games in the NHL. Not since 2005. The last tie game *in regulation time* dates back even further, to the 1982–1983 season. Within a few years, the tie game will have been relegated to the dustbin of our national sport's history. I've searched far and wide but have found no one who has mourned its disappearance. It's as though every last fan of the game implicitly agrees with the late US Naval Academy football coach Eddie Erdelatz, who, upon seeing that his team had tied with Duke University, famously expressed his frustration by saying "a tie is like kissing your sister."

Despite the general lack of enthusiasm for tie games among the fans, and also despite the huge popularity of this crime against nature we call the "shootout," I will defend the position that the loss of the tie game represents a major loss for hockey. I will do so in three stages. First, I will develop a normative framework that will allow us to evaluate the many rule changes made every year to NHL hockey. I will defend a position that sits between *nostalgic purism*, which condemns any change to the rules as an affront to the original purity of hockey as practiced since its beginnings, and *revolutionary enthusiasm*, which automatically praises any and all changes as inherently good. The position I will defend is called *moderate progressivism*. To put it briefly, I think that hockey, like all sports, has room for improvement, but that rule changes are improvements only if they bring the practice of the sport closer to its *spirit*.

Second, building on the normative framework I mentioned above, I will demonstrate how the mechanism used since 2005 to declare a winner after 65 minutes of play violates the spirit of hockey. This conclusion will be insufficient as a positive defence of the tie game; it will simply allow us to reject one specific method of tiebreaking. This section will leave open the possibility that other methods of declaring a winner may be preferable to keeping the tie. Finally, in the third section I will develop a positive argument *in favour of* the tie game. This requires me to outline what I see as the *educational function* of hockey. For better or for worse, hockey plays a part in the moral development of our young people (and their elders too). I will argue that the sport fulfils this function better with the inclusion of the tie game than without it.

I

Every year, NHL officials make changes to the rules of hockey. At the risk of oversimplifying, we can distinguish among three categories of rule changes.

1) *Essential changes:* Changes to observable practices in the game that, while they comply with the rules, push the game further away from its spirit or essence.

2) *Protective changes:* Changes intended to protect players from injuries that could imperil their careers.

3) *Populist changes:* Changes intended to increase the appeal of hockey in a market where it is bound to compete with other sports in attracting spectators and sponsors.

Hockey fans will instantly recognize these three categories and will not have much difficulty using them to classify many of the rule changes made in recent years. Having said this, I don't think the boundaries of these categories are perfectly clear in all cases. Grey areas definitely exist, and any attempt to define these categories neatly in terms of necessary and sufficient conditions is destined to fail. I will attempt to provide a preliminary description of each category using clear examples. Next I'll show how they can sometimes come into conflict with one another (in other words, how a change that is justified for one end can come at the expense of a different end). Finally, I'll propose a method for establishing priorities among the three categories when such conflicts arise.

Recent hockey history provides us with a good example of an essential change. During a playoff game between the New Jersey Devils and the New York Rangers, the forward Sean Avery of the Rangers turned his back on the play during a 5-on-3 power play for his team and began waving his arms and stick in the air to break the concentration of the Devils' star goalie, Martin Brodeur. The Rangers scored, and Avery received no penalty. Apparently there was no rule in place to stop him from doing this, although everyone agreed that he acted in a manner that went against an "unwritten rule" of hockey. The following day, the NHL responded by creating what is now called the "Avery rule," which dictated that this type of behaviour would thenceforth be considered unsportsmanlike conduct.

Why does this count as an essential change? Because anybody who watches a lot of hockey, either as a participant or as a spectator, can see right away that "you don't do that." It's part of the implicit ethics governing players' behaviour on the ice: there are some things you can do with your stick and other things you can't. Most of the time these rules don't need to be codified, as they form part of the *ethos* of the sport.

Let's formalize this a bit by turning to one of the classic distinctions from the history of philosophy. The philosopher Georg Wilhelm Friedrich Hegel made a key distinction between what in individual and group morality are termed *Sittlichkeit* and *Moralität*. (Philosophers are fond of saying that these terms are "untranslatable" because doing so increases their social capital. But they are perfectly translatable. The first term refers to a community's customs, traditions, and mores, which are most often implicit and unwritten; the second refers to the explicitly formulated ethical rules.)

It's well known that Hegel was one of philosophy's great plunderers of ideas: specifically, he lifted the idea of *Sittlichkeit* from Montesquieu, who had formulated the idea of the *spirit* of the laws six decades earlier. Therefore, in homage to Montesquieu (who never got the chance to apply his ideas to hockey, a sport that wasn't played in Bordeaux in the eighteenth century), I will refer to the implicit customs, traditions, and mores of the sport as the spirit of hockey.

Sean Avery's action undermined the spirit of hockey. Because the incident went unpunished and his team scored as a result, there was a risk of setting a precedent that would be liable to further erode the spirit of hockey unless an explicit rule (a piece of *Moralität*) was established.

Let's agree that a rule change fits into the category of *essential changes* if it seeks to protect hockey from practices and behaviours that could undermine its spirit.

Protective changes and *populist changes* are much more straightforward. The purpose of a protective change is simply to protect players against injuries, which, because the game is so fast and contact is allowed, could prematurely end a player's career. The clearest cases have to do with the equipment players are required to wear. But other changes and proposed changes are intended to protect players too. For example, if the NHL were to adopt the automatic icing rule (i.e., not requiring that a player from the defending team get in front of a player from the attacking team), this would be to avoid the kinds of injuries caused by the epic races allowed under the current rules, with the attendant risks of terrible falls and vicious slams against the boards.

A populist rule is intended to make the game more exciting. While everybody knows hockey is objectively the best game you can name, it's not always the most popular game you can name, especially in the United States, where it vies with other sports for the fans' and sponsors' money. Many rules are adopted with the *sole function* of making hockey more "saleable." Some are specific-ally intended to increase the number of goals scored during games. I will argue that the shootout rule constitutes one example of this logic. Examples of rule changes made mostly or exclusively for populism's sake include restrictions on goalie leg pad sizes and the rule prohibiting goalies from touching the puck anywhere behind the goal line outside of a very restrictive trapezoidal area.

I mentioned above that these categories don't have clear boundaries. For every case that fits into a given category, there will be others that fall into a grey area of debatability. Is the elimination of the red line used to determine offsides an essential or a populist change? The much-hated "trap" strategy helped propel the soporific New Jersey Devils to victory in 1995, and this rule change was meant to thwart this strategy. Does trapping undermine the spirit of hockey, or merely the spectacle thereof? The issue is debatable. Personally, I feel that there is overlap between essential and populist changes, given that spectacle is a part of hockey's essence.

If my proposed categories for classifying rule changes in NHL hockey have fuzzy boundaries, it's because the ends that motivate them (the spirit of hockey, player safety, the popularity of the sport) sometimes come into conflict. For example, the speed of the game and the allowance of intentional contact both contribute greatly to the spectacle of hockey, but these are also factors at play in most serious injuries. Both should be constrained in various ways for the sake of player safety, even if this means the spectacle isn't as rousing as it could be.

Similarly, populism can also clash with the spirit of hockey. I will argue in the following section that the shootout constitutes a prime example of this. But other conflicts can also arise.

We can imagine various ways in which these competing ends could be prioritized (or opt not to prioritize them). For example, an end might receive priority if it somehow served as one of the organizing principles of the different categories of rule changes. We could also be opposed to any change, regardless of its end. Conversely, we could see any and all changes as desirable, so long as they are justified in terms of one of these principles.

There are doubtless some nostalgic purists out there for whom the changes made to hockey since March 3, 1875 (the date on which the first hockey game was played according to codified rules—all seven of them!) have been a steady path of degeneration and decline. These people commit what one might term *original sophism*. This sophism consists of thinking that the essence or spirit of a phenomenon is fully and completely revealed in its first manifestation and that any departure from this historical origin therefore constitutes a loss. There is no shortage of cases exposing this as a sophistry. For example, democracy was still in its infancy when it first appeared in Greece about 2,500 years ago. It was a long way from achieving the ideals that lay dormant within it: notably, women and slaves were deliberately excluded from the political community. Many centuries would pass before democratic practices began to approximate the ideas embedded within the concept of democracy. Perhaps what is true of democracy is also true of hockey: loyalty to its historical origins is not the best way to be loyal to the *spirit* of the practice in question.

It would seem that nostalgic purism isn't a viable attitude to adopt with respect to rule change processes. But if that is the case, then revolutionary enthusiasm cannot be the alternative either, as it fails to establish any priority among the three ends we've identified. Endorsing all ends at once can lead to contradictions. For example, if we choose safety as the priority, we may favour the protection of players by adopting the automatic icing rule. If on the other hand we prioritize populism, we may, in the name of spectacle, choose to defend the rule prohibiting goalies from leaving their zones and going after the puck in the corners, which puts skaters in the position of having to do faster defensive withdrawals and poses the very dangers that the automatic icing rule seeks to prevent (i.e., falls and violent boarding).

Only moderate progressivism, in which priority is assigned to one of the three motivations behind rule changes, can be justified. Why should moderate progressivism be required to prioritize essential changes as opposed to protective or populist ones? Because this is the only ordering that preserves the sport's *conditions of identity*. Allow me to explain.

Suppose we gave progressive populism absolute priority. Someone motivated only by the desire to make the sport attract as many spectators and sponsors as possible, seeing that a profusion of hockey fights has a tendency to increase sales, might end up supporting changes that greatly increased the allowable time for fisticuffs during games. Or this person could decide that what the public wants to see more than anything else is *lots of goals*, and make changes that would allow players to score almost as frequently as they do in basketball. At some point a line would be crossed, and the sport in which two opposing groups of people wearing skates and fighting over a chunk of rubber on a rink *would no longer be hockey*. If populism went completely unrestrained by the essentialist approach, there would be nothing to prevent rule changes from creating a situation in which we would no longer be dealing with the same sport.

The same thing could be said in a case where changes made for safety's sake were given absolute priority. Effectively, if populism unconstrained by essentialism could distort the sport beyond recognition, putting safety at the top of the list could ultimately suffocate the sport out of existence, as the surest way not to get injured in the sport is simply not to play in the first place! Because of the speed and rough contact involved in hockey, injuries will never be completely eliminated. The desire to protect players from all risk of serious injury could, just like the desire to maximize the spectacle of hockey, fundamentally unmake the game.

Moderate progressivism places the emphasis on essential changes, and limits changes made for the sake of safety and populism by stipulating that they not alter the spirit of the sport. This makes it the most defensible attitude to adopt in managing rule changes in hockey. In the following section, I will attempt to demonstrate that the shootout, the method the NHL currently uses to declare a winning team if the game is tied after 65 minutes of play, does not fall within these constraints and therefore goes against the moderate progressivism we defend here.

II

The lengthy preliminary considerations above allow me to state rather succinctly why I think shootouts are regrettable as a rule change. In my opinion, the change was made for exclusively populist reasons and pushes hockey away from its spirit. Allow me to explain.

It's hard to express exactly what we mean by the spirit of a sport; its implicit norms, traditions, and mores are hard to pin down. These form the unspoken code of the sport, the aspects of the game that are so central and so essential that they pass right under our noses—at least until some action brings them to our attention, like when Sean Avery waved his arms in front of Martin Brodeur with the sole aim of breaking his concentration.

This is murky territory, and there's no consensus on exactly what this set of implicit norms includes. But if we can all agree on one thing, it's that *hockey is a team sport*. Individual talent certainly plays a role, but it's of secondary importance to group cohesion—the ability to combine the efforts of many individuals.

Except in very rare cases, a goal is the product of multiple players working together. At the end of this group effort, the person who scores the goal is frequently not the one who contributed the most: the scorer often takes advantage of a play that allows him to shoot into a net that's been left almost deserted. This is why both assists and goals count towards a player's total point count. The top scorer in the NHL is rarely the person who scored the most goals. And while for the last few years a trophy has been awarded for scoring the most goals (the Maurice "Rocket" Richard Trophy), it is clear that the top honour for an offensive player is the Art Ross Trophy, which recognizes the player with the most points overall (goals and assists combined).

The shootout between the skater and the goalie, baldly positioned opposite each other, has no equivalent in game play. Breakaways are rare in hockey; they are situations to be avoided and are symptomatic of a defensive failure. "Pure" breakaways are rarer still: lone players facing a goalie almost always have an opponent hot on their heels or get hounded in a defensive withdrawal.

Some readers will retort that shootouts are subject to the same rules as penalty shots and therefore not as alien to the spirit of hockey as I suggest.

My reply is twofold. First, penalty shots are rare. The profusion of this kind of situation created by the shootout rule might well end up trivializing "real" penalty shots that are filled with dramatic tension precisely because of their rarity.

Second, penalty shots don't just come out of thin air. Most often they result from a play that was so well set up that it left the opposing team with no choice but to act in desperation. As in soccer, the penalty shot is the result of a group effort that has been short-circuited by an illegal action. The spirit of the penalty shot can be interpreted as giving the team that might have scored the position it would have had were it not for the illegal action.

Unlike penalty shots, shootouts have no function other than to artificially create, by imposing a sort of *deus ex machina*, a winner in a situation where none could be determined from within the game itself.

In other words, shootouts determine a winner by using a type of competition that bears no resemblance to the intrinsically team-oriented sport of hockey. We could just as easily declare a winner based on a series of fights between various players, speed skating races, or a precision shooting contest. Readers of my vintage will remember that in the 1970s, during intermission, Radio-Canada presented a skills competition called *"Confrontation dans la LNH,"* which pitted players against each other in precision shooting exercises, obstacle courses, etc. The goal was simply to entertain the fans. People back then understood something we seem to have forgotten today. Individual skill is one thing; hockey is another. And the spirit of the game suffers when we leave the outcome of a game entirely up to the former.

III

By this point, you may be persuaded that shootouts are not the way to break a tie. But nothing stated so far makes the case that tie games are a good thing. If, like Eddie Erdelatz, you feel that a tie game is about as appealing as kissing your sister, you might assume that a *different* way of determining winners in hockey is what's needed here. In other words, you might see the shootout as the *lesser of the two evils*, even if it does disfigure the spirit of the game. The other option would be to apply the playoff rules in the regular season and just keep playing until a goal is scored. Obviously, this is not a feasible option. The regular season is 82 games long (not counting the playoffs and exhibition games), and players often play two games in as many nights. The playoff system simply doesn't work in the regular season.

In the following pages, I would like to submit to the reader that despite our natural tendency to desire a clear winner and a clear loser in every game, perhaps we ought to overcome this desire and recognize that there is something morally noble about a tie game. Given the educational role that sport plays in the lives of our young people, we should be rooting for a revival of the tie game in professional hockey rather than seeking alternatives to shootouts.

It is clear that sport serves an important moral function in modern society. First of all (and this is probably the most basic moral dimension of team sports), it sublimates aggression and the natural human tendency to identify with certain groups in opposition to other groups in a socially acceptable manner. To put it a different way, the passion and fanaticism we feel towards the Montréal Canadiens (to cite an example that applies to me personally), can be traced back to the same source in our psychic and affective economy as the aggressive and potentially destructive emotions that underpin war. As Freud said, human civilization could not exist without sublimation. Insofar as sport is involved in this process of sublimation, it follows that there could be no civilization without sport.

Second of all, our conception of sport, and more specifically of ethical sport, is a unique setting in which to affirm and illustrate the belief—a belief that is so important for the cohesion of society as a whole—that morality and personal advantage need not be in conflict but rather complement one another. For example, egoism is seen as the cardinal sin in team sports, not only because it is morally reprehensible in and of itself, but also because it is harmful to the interests of the team, and therefore ultimately to the interests of the individual himself, who cannot win without the help of his team no matter how skilled he is. Sports interest properly understood (to speak like Tocqueville), requires a moral attitude of cooperation and sometimes even sacrifice.

We are aware, if only vaguely so, that sport functions as a school of morality by virtue of its ability to sublimate our destructive emotions and affirm the belief on which social cohesion rests, namely that morality and personal advantage are not in conflict. This vague awareness is doubtless what impels us to enrol our children in sports. Surely some parents do so because they fancy Junior the next Sidney Crosby (as I do my son, for example), but most of us do it because, in addition to encouraging them to stay physically active, we want to teach our children "important life lessons" through their participation in sports, especially team sports.

In order for sport to fulfil its educational and civilizing func-tion, it has to teach children the right lessons, lessons that will help them to be and to live in the world around them. Breaking a tie in a sporting match, by shootout or by any other method, encourages the belief that there are always winners and losers in life. *And that is a terrible life lesson to be teaching people.*

Even the dimmest of adults knows how often life hands us out-comes that are plumb *inconclusive.* We invest all kinds of effort into reaching an objective, dreaming of "our big night" that will some-how see our effort rewarded with either a gleaming success or an abject failure. But the fruits of our labour are seldom as clear-cut as that. We may achieve some but not all of our objectives, or achieve different objectives from the ones we had in mind. In competitive contexts, for example in the business world, we frequently have to share a small victory with someone we formerly viewed as a bitter enemy. Love, politics, business, art—all of these have their share of triumphs and failures. *But they also all have their share of tie games.* In excising this unavoidable truth from our young (and not-so-young) people's conception of reality as constructed through sport, we cause sport to fail in its educational duty. A life well lived is one in which we are properly prepared to handle successes and failures as well as the more indeterminate results of our various undertak-ings. By eliminating the tie game from our young people's moral ontology, we diminish their ability to face up to this elementary dimension of human life.

It is worth noting that the world's most ethical sport, cricket, has successfully resisted the tide that has wiped out the tie game from so many other sports. In fact, cricket has not one but two forms of tie games. A match can be tied when both teams score the same number of points. (This happens very rarely indeed, given the large number of points that can be scored in a game.) *But it can also happen when the time allotted for the match runs out without both teams having the turn at bat to which they are each entitled.* The first case is called a tie (stricto sensu), and the second is called a draw. What a beautiful life lesson to teach our children: that there can be situations of equality, but also situations where the results are inconclusive.

We shouldn't hold our breath for hockey to display moral subtlety and refinement of cricket. But at the very least we should hope that it recovers the moral nuance it had until 2005 by reinstating the tie game.

The greatest tie of all

From a very young age, I had a special place in my heart for the masters of the puck. As I grew up, hockey cards, jerseys, and sticks autographed by Orr, Esposito, Mahovlich, and Lafleur piled up in the basement of our apartment, much to my mother's displeasure. Then one night, on New Year's Eve, 1975, a new group of players from a strange, faraway, and despised land would also win my heart. I had had a chance to admire them—briefly before bedtime—in 1972, during the Summit Series, during which they clobbered our team with their zone entries, their never-before-seen fakes, and their criss-cross plays. People had been talking about this "historic" game between the two hockey dynasties (the Montréal Canadiens and the Red Army), and while I didn't fully grasp the issues at play, I sensed that something important was happening that day. The two team's systems of play, their traditions, their mentalities, their countries, and their ideologies—all of these were going head to head on the ice. I remember marvelling at the artistry of Mikhailov, Petrov, and Kharlamov, who were just as deft as my favourite players, if not more so. After three periods and a smattering of goals here and there—in what is now considered one of the greatest games in history—I was disappointed by the final score of 3 to 3. I would have preferred it had the "enemies" won!

Not long afterward, I came to appreciate what a blessing this balance of powers had been for hockey. The Communist bloc would soon begin to crumble on all sides, but the metaphor of a sport that crosses all borders and blends together differences was born. And we all know how that turned out. Every New Year's Eve since then, I've thought back with a hint of nostalgia to that little boy who had just received an extraordinary life lesson without even realizing it. (C.B.)

Fisticuffs: When do We Say Enough's Enough?

Christian Boissinot

> I went to a fight the other night and a hockey game broke out.
>
> Rodney Dangerfield

> The police had to hold back about 20 spectators who were attempting to attack one of the Lavals. Argall, the Laviolettes' goalie, attacked the referee several times; the players kicked each other, punched each other, and hit each other with their sticks.[1]

Don't bother searching online for further details on this sorry scene. Contrary to what you might be thinking, these events didn't transpire recently—they happened in 1899! Ice hockey has been dealing with the problem of violence since it first began. Violence continues to be a thorn in the side of the NHL (founded in 1917), where unsavoury behaviour has unfortunately become par for the course and frequently makes the headlines.

Hockey is by no means the only sport that's known for violent outbursts—far from it. However, there is one unique aspect of our

---

1. Donald Guay, *L'Histoire du hockey au Québec* (Montmagny: JCL, 1990), p. 206. The first description of a game in a newspaper article, dated March 3, 1875, mentions that it ended in a fight!

national sport that has long provided fodder for discussion: fisti-cuffs, otherwise known as fighting. A few years ago, a series of events reopened the debate on violence and whether fighting ought to be banned. A monster of a player, Todd Fedoruk (a sort of bionic man whose face is adorned with nine titanium plates from past fractures), was knocked out by a friendly hit from another monster of a player, Colton Orr. Goaltender Jonathan Roy crossed the ice to beat up his counterpart Bobby Nadeau, who chose not to respond in kind.[2] In something of a Groundhog Day revival, George Parros (457 games, 18 goals, 164 fights) got a concussion from fall-ing face-first on the ice following a fight with the aforementioned Colton Orr (444 games, 12 goals, 118 fights). Goaltender Ray Emery viciously attacked his fellow goalie Braden Holtby, who didn't want to fight. All of these incidents have brought the debate to the fore. I am writing this now—and I'm not the first to do so—at the risk of being labelled a wuss: for the good of hockey, it's high time we banned fighting. I would like to contribute the debate by asking a simple question: when do we say enough's enough?

The pro-fighting camp

When you start teasing them apart, the arguments currently used to justify fighting don't have much substance. First of all, let's consider the particular nature of this ultra-high-speed sport, with its many bangs and bumps involving athletes who are armed to the teeth (if they have any left) and flying down the ice at 30 kilometres an hour. Getting clocked or slashed by a fellow player is enough to make any-one's blood boil, especially if the aggressor goes unpunished: this is only natural. Referees are only human, and they can't catch every-thing. So rather than retaliating against somebody who's just elbowed you by checking them, you drop your gloves, settle the matter in a fist fight, and calmly get back to the game. Fighting

---

2. Shocked by this act of aggression, the Québec Minister of Education, Recreation, and Sport, Michelle Courchesne, said she wanted to see fights dis-appear from Canadian junior hockey. Hockey Québec produced a report that, among other things, made changes to penalties for participating in fights—without banning them, of course. Roy, who was charged with simple assault (no injury), avoided a trial by pleading guilty and received an absolute discharge.

allows us to channel frustration that would otherwise have built up if not for this therapeutic release. Second of all, the talented players, with some exceptions, are too busy playing hockey: they prefer to spend as much time on the ice as possible and leave others the hassle of throwing down the gauntlet. But who's there to protect them? That job goes to the recognized enforcers (the fighters, the heavies, the goons), whose given mission since the birth of hockey has been to police the game, to "make space," or to change the course of a game with a little scrap here and there, effectively sacrificing themselves for the team. Even if we prefer not to admit it, the longer we keep fighting in hockey, the longer we maintain a highly lucrative industry. Fighting is part of the "spectacle" of hockey; it taps into the fans' primal instincts. As the main actors in the industry will tell you, "The fact of the matter is that violence sells. It always has."[3] A ban on fighting would be a death sentence for hockey.

These arguments, which invoke anthropology, tradition, and economics, have always seemed to me as bizarre as attendance at Florida Panthers games. Here's why.

From the nature of hockey to the nature of humanity

"That constant threat of pain and suffering is what separates hockey players from other athletes."[4] Some people would have us believe that hockey is unique among all sports and requires an extraordinarily tough mind and body. The "martyrdom" endured by hockey players, worthy of Golgotha, explains the otherwise inexplicable, namely that bottled-up pain and frustration must *necessarily* be released through fighting and other means in order to prevent an overload of violence. This is why fisticuffs are tolerated in the NHL and a few other North American leagues, making hockey the only professional sport that states explicitly, *in its rules*, that two individuals are allowed to punch each other in the face, ladies and gentlemen, with their *bare fists*, before taking a short "union break" on the penalty bench. This argument is so daft it almost merits a penalty of its own.

3.   Ross Bernstein, *The Code: The Unwritten Rules of Fighting and Retaliation in the NHL* (Chicago: Triumph Books, 2006), p. 187.
4.   Ibid, p. 32.

First, let's be clear: *North American hockey does not have a monopoly on rough play.* Anybody who's ever played rugby or football will tell you that. Having your rib cage compressed by a defensive back's helmet is far cry from a friendly squeeze. And imagine what it's like in the pro leagues! Are the other contact sports less underhanded, less aggravating, or less violent than hockey? The answer is obvious. It would seem that football has the most barefisted fights. However, these fights are against the rules, even if your opponent has gone after your ribs 15 times in the first two quarters and you're getting peeved. Hockey is no less rough in the 63 other countries where it is played, and in many North American leagues too. No. If fighting exists in professional hockey, it's because we tolerate it. Period.

Second, the point of hockey, to the best of my knowledge, is to shoot a puck into the other team's goal using a stick with a blade at the end. This is a truism: without these basic features, plus a few specific rules (line changes, etc.) and allowances for legal contact, hockey can't be said to exist. Only Canada and the United States allow fighting as an indirect means to score a goal, and they consider it an extra feature, a distinctive trait. Unlike, say, the goalposts (which Réjean Houle could tell you a thing or two about), fights are in no way consubstantial with hockey. Like Gretzky behind the net, I've looked at it from every angle, but I can't for the life of me see any link, not one, between fighting and the essence of the sport. Pardon my intellectual myopia! When the players decide to ditch their sticks, their gloves, or even their jerseys (ahem, Rob Ray) to fight, can you really tell me *with a straight face* what this striptease has to do with hockey? Why not just go the full Monty like in the movie *Slap Shot*? If you've got an answer for me, bring it on. When I'm watching a football game, I don't expect the game to be interrupted by strapping 300-pound lads in tutus doing ballet or figure skating. But in hockey we sometimes stop the clock so some people can satisfy their itch to peel it off. Can we get a pole and some mood lighting please?

Third, and this is the most pernicious point of all, the anthropological view that underlies this argument suggests that the aggression we associate with hockey is an innate need, and essentially can't be controlled on the ice. Apparently the philosophers

Thomas Hobbes (1588–1679) and Sigmund Freud (1856–1939) had it right, then. Hobbes wrote that men in a state of nature were beings of violent passion, wolves of men who used all possible means (force, war, trickery, violence, etc.) to protect themselves from their enemies. Freud thought that the kindness often associated with human nature was an illusion. In this view, violence and war are an intrinsic part of us. They are the manifestation of this urge to kill, from Thanatos, an urge that pushes us towards self-destruction and, when turned outward, manifests as aggression against others. The hockey rink embodies this state of war: at any moment Thanatos may suddenly appear, usually when a good shoulder check isn't enough and we encourage and applaud interference, hip checking, and so on—basically any form of violence short of causing serious injury. The rebelliousness of human nature makes rules almost inapplicable, so we might as well give in to this epiphenomenon of fighting, which is "impossible to ban,"[5] in order to avoid an even greater escalation of violence.

The thing is, there's no serious scientific, philosophical, or sociological position that supports such a view of humans. The latest genetic research reveals that apart from belonging to a certain blood type, for example, there is no direct causal link between our biology and sexual orientation, alcoholism, or violent behaviour. We are certainly influenced by our biological makeup, our education, socio-economic factors, and so on, but this does not make us slaves to nature or history. This determinism or primary materialism, which depicts humans as automatons held hostage by forces beyond their control and bereft of freedom or choice, is supported by only a handful of enlightened "academics."[6] Furthermore, if the urge to kill is irrepressible, why then are humans not in a constant state of violence or war? Why are wars declared at certain times and not others? Furthermore, if humans share the same fundamental biological makeup, why is it

---

5.   Bertrand Raymond, "Le commissaire Courteau s'explique," *Le Journal de Montréal*, August 30, 2008. This comment is from the president of the Québec Major Junior Hockey League, Gilles Courteau.
6.   The following is heavily inspired by Jean-Claude St-Onge, *La condition humaine*, 2nd ed. (Montréal: Gaëtan Morin, 2000), especially chapters 1, 7, and 10.

that certain peoples are more peaceful than others? Archaeological digs have conclusively shown that humans have existed peacefully for millennia at a time. Indeed, while our species has been burying its dead for the last 100,000 years, evidence from human gravesites indicates that war first appeared only 6,500 years ago. In this view, then, violence and war are the result of economic and social motives (competition, social differentiation, seeking markets and resources, etc.) that are linked to traditions, customs, and institutions. So, if socioeconomic conditions push our instincts towards violence, it would appear that other conditions pull them away from it. Therefore, there's no point in citing history to justify human cruelty, since there are just as many examples of human kindness (love, mutual assistance, etc.). Neither science nor history corroborates the hypothesis that human nature is fundamentally violent.

The vast majority of philosophers (Rousseau, Kant, Sartre, etc.) have also supported the thesis of the relative indeterminacy of human nature, namely that it is possible to divorce ourselves from nature and history. This form of liberty, not found in other animals, makes it possible to invent ourselves; the whole ideal of human rights is predicated on this notion. Hobbes thought that entry into civilization ended the insecurity that came with the state of nature and brought citizens peace. Finally, as proof positive of human liberty and perfectibility, to use Jean-Jacques Rousseau's term, sociologists have shown that the rise of the parliamentary political system and the capitalist economy helped make social life more peaceful over time. One of its effects was to reduce sanctioned violence in sports: we see a *total rupture* from the Greco-Roman games and medieval jousts, in which competitors' lives were on the line and which may have resembled something of a "state of nature." Modern sports are confrontations that have become regulated (length, technical conditions, enforcement of physical safety standards, secularization, etc.) and also less violent by virtue of their transformation into mimetic or proxy activities that generally don't endanger participants' lives.[7]

---

7. See the classic book by Norbert Elias and Eric Dunning, *Sport et civilisation: La violence maîtrisée* (Paris: Fayard, 1994). The effect of this transformation has been to profoundly alter "the sensibility of players and spectators, who no

Whew! Now there's something reassuring for you: hockey players are no different from their fellow athletes and or other mortals. It'll be a long time before scientists discover an impulse, a special gene or a new form of testosterone that triggers an irrepressible need to pick fights. Nor will we hear on the news anytime soon that goons, who manage to comport themselves like gentlemen off the ice, are an intermediate species between Cro-Magnon humans and Homo sapiens, or that they drink a secret potion before the game that transforms them into Mr. Hyde. If this argument had even an ounce of truth, the best players would seek catharsis by putting up their dukes rather than racking up points, since they are the most addicted, the most crazed, the most charged up. Oh, and this is to say nothing of the 90 percent of NHL players who never fight, a figure that's close to 100 percent elsewhere in the world and in the minor North American leagues.

When you look at the data, it's legitimate to ask what makes North American hockey so resistant to this civilized progression that other dangerous sports, *without exception*, have espoused for about two centuries. Why did the NHL wait 29 years after Bill Masterton's death in 1968 from a skull fracture to make helmets mandatory for all players, both the old guard and the new guard? Why is the organization so reluctant to protect its athletes from certain risks, specifically through the use of visors, which only 38 percent of players wore in 2005? Why are the consequences of

---

longer tolerate the sight of killing or bloodshed" (Jacques Defrance, *Sociologie du sport*, 3 ed. (Paris: La Découverte, 2000), p. 18). This view is shared by sociologist Eliane Perrin: "Our era is hungry for violence but refuses blood and hates death," (Sophie Davaris, "Sport et université: des intérêts communs," *Campus magazine* vol. 53, no. 1 (Université de Genève), pp. 12–19. www. unige.ch/presse/campus/pdf/c53/eclairages.pdf.) Of course, there are still those executioners, vampires, and hockey fans who refute this view, saying, for example, that nobody's looking the other way when a fight breaks out. Freud would call this a vestige of Thanatos, who reminds us of people's fascination with public executions (burning at the stake, stoning, quartering, etc.), which have by and large disappeared today. When the public is informed about the serious physical and psychological repercussions of this gratuitous violence for athletes, their perception of it changes completely. This rejection of violence is confirmed in survey after survey: "Which puts the safety and dignity of people at risk disgusts our consciences, the public likes to consume violence in the media but condemns it with extreme severity in real life." (Gilles Lipovetsky, *Le crépuscule du devoir* [Paris: Gallimard, 1992], p. 151).

> ### Hockey? Dangerous?
>
> According to studies cited by Lawrence Scanlan in his book *Grace Under Fire* (Penguin Canada, 2003), hockey is still the most dangerous sport, with 37,000 injuries per million participants, at all levels combined—far ahead of football (18,000) and snowboarding/skiing (11,000). Most of these injuries occur as a result of checking from behind against the board. Even though they know the hazards this kind of checking poses for their enemies, 26 percent of young hockey players said they would still do it if they were angry, and also to emulate their heroes in the professional leagues. Since 1972, there have been 1,906 recorded eye injuries in Canadian hockey, 309 of which have resulted in total loss of vision, and 40 NHL players have been forced to retire as a result of such injuries.

and punishments for gratuitous violence (boarding, spearing, knocks to the head, etc.) and for fighting so laughably toothless when we know that North American hockey is by far the most dangerous sport out there?

Why do the NHL and the leagues that model themselves after it overlook the fact that millions of young people all over the world have been taught to play in a civilized manner, developing different virtues that should be encouraged by any athletic activity, such as sportsmanship, self-improvement, courage, effort, and self-control? Yes, that includes those who currently fight in the NHL and in other leagues, and the millions who continue to play in this fashion. Why does the league turn a blind (or black) eye to the huge amount of educational work being done in other leagues and other sports, where young people are taught that if they cross the line they'll be punished and that they must control themselves no matter how frustrated they feel? Why does it so mulishly uphold the law of retaliation, while we teach children almost from the cradle that the self-control required in modern society must be "generalized to all areas of experience (work, play, affection, intimacy, etc.)"?[8] In other words, why does this sport reflect the extremes of society (violence, trickery, etc.) to the point of legitimizing them as a distinctive feature in its rules and in its "essence"? The theologians of hockey point to pseudo-historical and financial motives, which I will examine presently.

The sacred tradition

People's justifications for the obscene insensitivity that North American hockey has towards the issues I have just raised are rooted in sacrosanct "tradition." Defenders of the sport that glorifies the perfect fight as much as it does the perfect goal hide behind this all the time. These people will argue tradition till the cows come home. Fighting has been part of the game from day one; it lets players settle their own scores and allows enforcers to "serve and protect" their teammates, sacrificing their teeth, their noses (just ask Tim Hunter), and joints in the process.[9] But the enforcers' role is actually much more far-reaching and complex: they are there to punish, to make space, to dissuade, to change the feel of the game, to intimidate, to send a message, and to give the other team a penalty. The appeal to tradition also bolsters the defence of a form of machismo that has vanished from other contact sports. This makes hockey the last bastion of masculine hegemony and brute virility, the last rampart against civilization, where real men settle their disputes "like men."[10]

But what exactly do we mean by "tradition" anyway? *Tradition* comes from the Latin *tradere* (meaning to pass on, to hand over). It refers to the passing on of doctrines and ways of acting and thinking. It's not hard to see that tradition in hockey is not a monolith. Significant changes have come about since the days when each team had nine players on the ice at once—and zero helmets. These

---

8. Jacques Defrance, *Sociologie du sport*, pp. 18–19.
9. This sacrifice is wonderfully expressed by Basil McRae: "Fighting wasn't about me; that is selfish. It was always about being there for and protecting my guys." (Ross Bernstein, *The Code*, p. 94).
10. As Bernstein writes countless times (pp. 54, 146, 232, and others), which echoes a certain discourse.

The fighting tradition

The year 1922 saw everything turned on its head, so to speak: "At the time, in university hockey games and even into the amateur leagues, both opponents were kicked out of the game; the NHL introduced the notion of acceptability by giving the aggressors a five-minute penalty" ("*Combat au hockey sur glace*," Wikipedia. http://fr.wikipedia.org/wiki/.). The famous Rule 56, entitled "fisticuffs," would eventually trickle down into the minor leagues. As a result of the many brawls and (coincidence?) the success of the movie *Slap Shot*—a parody of the minor hockey leagues in which the spectacle becomes overshadowed by violence—the authorities established the "third man in" rule in 1977. Under this rule, any player who gets involved in a fight that is in progress (for the record, the last general fight took place in 1987) is to be expelled from the game. This was followed 15 years later with the addition of an additional minor penalty and a match penalty (reduced to 10 minutes in 1996) for instigating a fight. This "instigator" rule was made more stringent in 2005: any player who started a fight in the last 5 minutes of the game would now receive a match penalty and be automatically suspended from the game, with the duration of the suspension being doubled with each additional offence, and the coach of the player at fault having to pay a fine of $10,000 US. Finally, in 2007, the NHL decided to increase the number of penalties for instigating fights before suspending the instigator from three to five.

Fights were relatively rare between the 1920s and 1960s (we're talking an average of 0.20 fights per game in 1957–1958 and 0.18 in 1967–1968). They became more frequent with the introduction of franchises—which involved a clear dilution of the "product"—and reached record high levels in the 1980s. While it has fluctuated, the overall number of fights has been falling for a few years to about one fight for every two games (0.44 in 2011–2012 and 0.48 in 2012–2013). The new rules and speed-oriented plays are even leading some hockey buffs to predict, with heavy hearts, the inevitable demise of fisticuffs.

changes show how futile it is to draw comparisons, for example, between the era of the Original Six and the present day, between straight sticks made of wood and curved ones made of composite, between the lukewarm Molson brew (and cigarette) between periods and the rigorous health regimes that today's athletes follow. The same goes for the short history of fighting, which has gone back and forth so many times, from its formal prohibition in the NHL from 1917 to 1922 (ahem!) to its decline in recent years. So what exactly is the tradition that defenders of slapstick hockey are arguing for? Before or after 1922? The golden age of the 1980s or today?

That's a load of bull, I can hear the brain-stricken traditionalists, who aren't usually noted for their subtlety, retorting: we allow fighting to continue because it has (almost) always been thus. Enough with the twisting of the words, already. What's important is the crucial role fighting and fighters play during the game. Forgive my insistence, reader, but I really do need to get this straight.

First of all, how is the mission of dissuading, intimidating, making space, and so on, specific to fighters? Those jobs apply *mutatis mutandis*, not just in hockey but in all contact sports. It's the determination, speed, talent, intelligence, tactical ability, and combativeness of a Brendan Gallgher or the violent checking of a Niklas Kronwall that changes the feel of the game. No need for cockfighting! Second of all, if these nonsensical duties we retroactively attribute to fighters were really necessary, why is it they're almost never seen (like fighting, by the way) in the playoffs, when the stakes are the highest? Why are goons not welcome at important competitions like the Olympics or the Canada Cup?

Obviously, this use of the fighting tradition as a defence is an example of what Nietzsche described, better than anyone else, as the "herd instinct": a comforting mentality but also one that suffocates individual freedom of thought and critical reflection. Examples of calcified traditions are legion. And none of them avoids the trap of intolerance. Philosophers would call such a blind and simplistic appeal to tradition a "sophism," which is defined as an argument that seems acceptable without actually being so. Simply invoking the oldness of something to support one's claims is a truly cheap shot. Certain values and behaviours stand the test of time, while others do not. It wasn't so long ago that indulging in a wee beer while driving a car was considered pretty cool. But today, impaired driving is considered a criminal act and isn't cool at all. Different times, different values.

There are many different ways to interface with a tradition: you can just go along with it, of course. But you can also refuse it, adapt it, or enrich it. Once again, humans are not prisoners of some natural code or a deterministic history. Cases in point: the CBC changed the theme song to *Hockey Night in Canada*, and the tradition of hockey has been enriched over time, such that young players aren't allowed to play without a mask anymore. The machismo associated with hockey, which is in relative but inevitable decline, is ripe for just this kind of enrichment. This is 2014. It's time to face the music, lads: the patriarchal system received the kiss of death decades ago, and our image of manhood has changed.[11] No one denies that such a decline in so-called masculine values can cause some men to question their identity. For those who subscribe to a classic model of masculinity in which force, power, domination, aggression, vigour, bravery, etc., are prized, it can mean full-on crisis. Masculinity has many faces: macho, metrosexual, übersexual, the sensitive type, and others. Are Tiger Woods, Michael Phelps, David Beckham, or Roger Federer any less "male" because they don't fight? Ask anybody who's been checked by Alexander Ovechkin or Alexei Emelin how tough those guys are! While we're on the topic, would you call any player who throws himself onto

---

11.   Élisabeth Badinter, *L'un est l'autre* (Paris: Odile Jacob, 1986), p. 214.

the ice to block a puck of frozen vulcanized rubber speeding towards him at 160 kilometres an hour a sissy? How about some-one who plays on an injury? Manliness isn't necessarily synonym-ous with war, muscles, or fists.

The time has come to shed this shameful vestige of athletic his-tory, this anachronism we call fighting. Canada, a peaceful country, has no need to associate herself with the image of a Neanderthal brute and to rejoice that other primates cheer her on. Fights and goons will disappear automatically when we decondition ourselves and get it through our skulls that enforcing the rules down to the letter is the best way to *serve* and *protect* athletes, just like in any other legitimate sport. Building a tradition without fighting is indeed behaving "like men" and then some.

The economic argument

Trailing 2 to 0 with just a few minutes to go, the pro-fighting camp usually decide to call in the big guns. Their secret weapon? The argument that hockey is first and foremost a big business, that fighting is an essential marketing tool. . . and that if it disappeared, the sport might disappear with it. According to a recent survey, 76 percent of "avid fans" would actually like to see fighting kept.[12] This makes using the economic logic a straightforward affair.[13] The

---

12. "Hockey Fans Don't Want to See Fighting KO'd: Poll," *Canadian Press*, April 4, 2007. Among the 1,000 people interviewed, only 22 percent described themselves as "avid fans." As for the rest, 43 percent of those who follow hockey occasionally want a ban, while 52 percent of those who don't follow hockey at all do. Another interesting piece of data: 8 percent more Franco-phones than Anglophones want fighting out of hockey.

13. Consider the many fan clubs and websites devoted to fighting (www.hockey-fights.com, www.hockeyfightsdump.com, www.dropyourgloves.com, etc.), the astronomical sales figures of the ever-subtle Don Cherry's DVDs, the popularity of guaranteed fight nights as in the Québec Senior Hockey League, in which braggarts only leave their benches to get beaten up, the pre-game shows dedicated to various fights in many NHL arenas, and so on. Did you know that Tie Domi, at the peak of his "art," sold as many jerseys as the great Mats Sundin? That after the Nashville Predators entered the league in 1998, it was the sale of fighter Patrick Côté's stick (!) that raised the most money for a charity fundraiser? The text accompanying the DVD *Honor and Courage: Tough Guys of the NHL* even very nearly made me misty-eyed: "Only in pro-fessional hockey is a man's role to use his fists on behalf of his teammates. Physical intimidation is a large part of determining a team's success. This DVD takes an in-depth look at the on-ice/off-ice life of the NHL 'Enforcer'

strategies have changed a bit since the 1920s, but the end goal is the same: to capture the attention of the reptilian brain of those "blood-thirsty folks."[14] Take me out to the brawl game!

Let's contextualize the popularity of fighting using a basic truth we expressed earlier: the higher the stakes of game, the less fighting we see. Why? Those in the pro-fighting camp (and there are many) lay it bare: "The NHL season is 82 games long and fighting helps make the games more entertaining and interesting during the long season."[15] Like magic, we see tradition, protection, and all that other stuff vanish, leaving behind only spectacle and cold, hard cash! This argument shines in all its glory in "natural" hockey markets like Miami (whose average annual temperature is 26°C) and Phoenix (which has received more than 0.25 centimetres of snow only seven times since 1896), where officials have to attract spectators any way they can. "They may not understand hockey, but they understand fighting."[16] Let's be real for a second. Is it because there aren't enough fights that many hockey arenas sit empty and televised games rank behind women's basketball, poker, and demolition derbies in the United States (causing ESPN not to renew its contract with the NHL, which had to settle for the Outdoor Life Network for a time before eventually signing a contract with NBC in 2011)? And is it due to a lack of fighting that the NHL has its eye on Europe and basically has to rely on northern markets to make money, with the seven Canadian teams generating over 50 percent of the revenue of the 30 teams in good years and in bad?[17] What if

and the importance this man has to his team." (http://shop.nhl.com/sm-warner-brothers-honor-and-courage-tough-guys-of-the-nhl--pi-2989677.html).

14. Tex Rickard is without a doubt the pioneer in this regard. He rebuilt Madison Square Garden in 1925, and he was a boxing and wrestling promoter. He quickly saw that hockey fans were the same as the people who attended his events. That was all it took for him to send publicity ambulances driving around the streets of Manhattan displaying posters and putting up posters that said "Wanted: Dead or Alive" nearly everywhere in sight.

15. Christy Hammond, "Keep Fighting in the NHL," *Kukla's Korner*. http://www.kuklaskorner.com/index.php/hockey/comments/keep_fighting_in_the_nhl/.

16. Cf. R. Bernstein, *The Code*, op. cit., p. 186.

17. Every year, the business magazine *Forbes* releases a report on the NHL's financial health. In 2012, the profits of Canadian teams were as high as $218.9 million, or 57 percent of the $380.5 million accumulated by the 30 teams. By the way, 13 American teams are in deficit.

it were in fact because of economics that fighting ought to be banned? Commissioner Gary Bettman and his associates understand the truth: hockey will never be remotely as profitable as other North American professional sports.[18] However, by focusing on rivalries and natural markets, and by abandoning gratuitous violence and fighting in favour of the natural beauty of the game—in other words, returning to the essence of the game—hockey may see unprecedented success.

Fight-free hockey pulls in profits that speak for themselves. You don't need a Ph.D. in economics to see that the Canada Cup, the World Cup, and the Olympics generate astronomical ratings (and revenues). Hold on to your helmet: 38 million Americans watched the gold medal game between the United States and Russia in 2002, which is three times the audience for any Stanley Cup final in history! And besides these occasional competitions, even a cursory glance at European professional hockey shows that millions of fans tune in to the game. Even though many countries have seen an exodus of their best players, arenas are still packed, television and radio contracts are lucrative, and sponsorships abound.[19] And of

18. *The Sporting News* (http://www.sportingnews.com/blog/aajoe7/135024) reports that in 2007, sales figures for the National Football League (NFL) were $6.7 billion, compared to $6.07 billion for Major League Baseball (MLB), $3.384 billion for the National Bastketball Association (NBA), and $2.25 billion for the NHL—and again, 40 percent of this was generated by the Canadian teams. Attendance at junior hockey games in the United States, to cite just this one example, doesn't lie. While the United States Hockey League attracted 1,051,897 spectators in 2006, there were 27,008,920 and 36,814,468 spectators who attended the NCAA Men's Division I Basketball Championship and the NCAA Division I Football Bowl Subdivision! Would someone lend the high priests of hockey a copy of La Fontaine's fable "The frog that wished to be as big as the ox"?
19. For example, the Swedish Hockey League (the first incarnation of which was founded in 1921), brings together the top 12 teams in Sweden, which play a season of 55 games. The largest arena fits up to 12,000 people and, while my Swedish is a little rusty, the game summary indicates that games are always sold out. Svenska Spel, the equivalent of Loto-Québec, is the main sponsor of this league. A number of games are broadcast throughout Scandinavia by Canal+, while all 330 games of the regular season are available by cable or on the radio. Unfortunately, I was unable to track down the salaries of the players in this league. However, in 2008, Jaromír Jágr received $5 million from the Russian team Avangard Omsk, at a fixed income tax rate of 13 percent, reasonably better overall than he would have in the NHL. It's no surprise that many players (Yashin, Radulov, Kovalchuk, etc.) decided to play for one of the 28 teams

course, this is to say nothing of the NHL playoffs themselves, which are generally free of fights: here the shot at winning the cup is what galvanizes fans.

Here's a thought: what if, like European hockey or football, North American hockey were to take on the atmosphere of a celebration rather than vaudeville? What if it became a genuinely family-friendly spectacle, in which young people could admire and identify with athletes who play to outdo themselves while still respecting both their opponents and the public? The "adults" would stop awkwardly squirming when the "children" ask them why some players get to fight while they themselves are told ad nauseam that physical violence solves nothing. The celebratory approach might encourage more young people, including those from Québec, to rediscover the joy of *playing* hockey, disheartened as they currently are by the culture of violence that's become so prevalent.[20] Clearly, the joy of playing hockey isn't something they would learn at those repugnant children's hockey fighting camps, which for a few years were led by the skilful enforcer Derek Boogaard (who died tragically in 2011) and whose objective was to teach them how to defend themselves (!) by forcing them to wear jerseys stained with blood.

I'm convinced that, given a certain adjustment period and a brilliant marketing strategy, this approach would translate into a spectacular increase in hockey's popularity, which certainly can't get any lower. The public that has thus far been reluctant to embrace the sport would definitely welcome such a change in image and mentality, not to mention the many sponsors that would finally feel comfortable associating themselves with a game that's "tough but clean."[21] "Molson and Mattel salute the greats." How

---

in the Kontinental Hockey League, which already has a few teams in countries that border Russia, and whose stated ambition is to have franchises all over Europe, including in London, Paris, and Milan.

20. The figures are dizzying: in 2000–2001, Québec had 3,332 teams in the Atom to Midget leagues, compared to 7,170 in 1974–1975. Five studies conducted since 1979 have given reasons for this drop in popularity: too much competitiveness, too much violence, the behaviour of coaches and parents, interest in other activities, and excessive cost.

21. This view is shared by Dan Doyle, chair of the Institute for International Sport. See Michael Morrison's article entitled "To Protect and Serve: Is

Loss of jobs

Did you consider the loss of jobs? Of course you did. Statistics show that the same 30 to 45 players account for 90 percent of fights. Like so many other workers in their prime, crushed by the pitiless invisible hand of the market, these gents will just have to find a more suitable line of work. If they're still hell-bent on lacing up their skates, I would strongly recommend they tap into the market of the *Battle of the Hockey Enforcers* event, which took place in 2005. It was an amazing round-robin tournament of on-ice fights involving 14 Neanderthal men—with no actual hockey game. The star attraction was Link Gaetz, nicknamed the "missing link" for obvious reasons.

does that sound? Once deprogrammed, the fans would remember that a shoulder check is nobler than a punch in the teeth. And for the truly constipated, the ones who use hockey players to vicariously release unacknowledged or unexpressed aggression, well, they can always turn to boxing or paintball. (Having such a choice available is one of the advantages of living in a liberal society!) As a last resort, some figure-skating cheerleaders might draw them back to the arena—everyone knows a little sensual titillation is an easier sell than violence.

Owners who persist in thinking their business needs a few rousing skirmishes to stay afloat financially should bear in mind that the rules and discipline committees of organized sport do not make athletes or managers a separate class of citizens who are somehow immune to courts of justice and the Criminal Code. In adhering to the notion of "implied consent," hockey players know well that they are participating in a risky business, but they also know they are on thin ice in terms of acceptability. How can we know when the line of what is acceptable and tacitly consented to

vigilante justice necessary in hockey?" *infoplease*. http://www.infoplease.com/spot/hockeyfighting1.html.

has been crossed? This is where the quest for accountability and profit transforms into a vicious game for two. The brotherhood of players would appear powerless against the individualist economic logic. Since 1968, the NHL has seen a good number of its clubs come under fire from the Canadian and American justice systems for actions that occurred on the ice that were deemed unacceptable.[22] The famous Todd Bertuzzi case, for its part, was still pending at the time of writing. Steve Moore, its victim,[23] claimed a jaw-dropping $38 million in damages, while his parents also filed a lawsuit for "shock and distress." On top of all this, Bertuzzi maintains, along with the former general manager of the Canucks, Dave Nonis, that his erstwhile coach, Marc Crawford, was the one who encouraged him to avenge his captain. It's been quite the imbroglio, and it's far from being resolved. It shows how players, coaches, teams, and the league are all at risk of being tarred with the same brush when their sport refuses to deal seriously with the problem of gratuitous violence and even makes it its *primum movens*.

It's clear that the complicity of the owners, the players' association, and the public in this grim spectacle poses enormous risks to the athletes' well-being—and to their lives. Even if they are lavishly paid, even if there is an unwritten "code" surrounding fist fighting, how many bone fractures, scars, concussions, shortened careers, and lifelong pains result? Nobody doubts the players' bravery (or their stupidity or their desire to further their careers at any price). Taking a smack in the face from a 220-pound brute? That's got to hurt. But taking pleasure in getting hit like that? Come on. Just read the confessions of the pugilists. That should knock some sense into you.

Straight up, I believe these athletes are being sacrificed on the altar of money and spectacle, just like the gladiators of Ancient Rome.[24] Here's a sobering question: for every McSorley and

---

22. The list is very long: Wayne Maki, Dan Maloney, Dave Forbes, Mel Bridgman, Don Saleski, Bob Kelly, Joe Watson, Wilf Paiement, etc.
23. Remember that Moore, a marginal player, had purposely struck Markus Näslund, former captain and leading scorer of the Vancouver Canucks, without receiving a penalty. Näslund was never the same player again, and Moore never played again.
24. If I dare, I would even amend what I said above about the adulation fighters receive and this stubborn desire to keep fighting in the game at all costs. This

Confessions of the pugilists

Enrico Ciccone: "Pat Burns said that players like me enjoyed doing this kind of work, but I'd just like to tell him no, I didn't like it. I couldn't sleep at night, and it gave me stomach pains. I did it because I realized I had to do it to go as far as I could. But I didn't like it." (Jeremy Filosa and Frédéric Bhérer, "*J'en faisais des cauchemars*," Corus Sports, September 4, 2008).

Dave Morissette: "When you're 16 years old, when there are 2,000 people in the stands including your buddies and your girlfriend, you don't want to disappoint anybody. And every game, you have to push yourself to fight. Sometimes I wouldn't sleep. I would try to motivate myself by cultivating hate for my opponent the next day; I developed the desire to kill the other team's fighter. I felt stuck in a dead end. I had no desire to fight on command, but I felt that if I didn't follow orders, my dream of playing in the NHL would slip away... There's no such thing as a guy who's never afraid before a fight... That doesn't exist. A tough guy who tells you he's never afraid is a liar. You can't not be afraid with all that pressure from millions of spectators, 20 players, your coach, not to mention the feeling that your career depends on it. It's horrible." (Jean-François Bégin, "La peur au ventre" *La Presse*, March 13, 2004, p. S3).

Dave Schultz: "I didn't like fighting. Off the ice, I've never fought in my life." (Kevin Allen, *Crunch Chicago*: Triumph Books, 1999, p. 98).

Georges Laraque: "I do it because it's my job, not because I enjoy it. It's not something that excites me, really. It

can be seen as a mechanism of managing violence that is specific to human societies, as described by René Girard, *La violence et le sacré* (Paris: Grasset, 1972), p. 122: expulsion, the stigmatization or sacrifice of a victim, the scapegoat, the sin eater, which makes it possible to regain the threatened coherence and the purification of the person who sullied it. But I don't dare.

allows me to stay in the NHL, and I'm here because of it."
(Renaud Lavoie, "*En donner davantage*," *RDS*, November
3, 2008).

Laraque who rises to the top, how many more out there didn't
make it? How many guys are there like Dave Morissette, who
played only 11 games in the "big" league? What if the monster that
the managers have created turned on them and the players decided
to sue the "big" league to compensate for a career shortened by a
blow to the head, a punch, or related complications?

The notion of implied consent, which the NHL guards so pre-
ciously, melted like ice in the sun when the Supreme Court of
Canada ruled that two individuals may consent to fighting but,
"from the fact that one or the other was assaulted, it is not possible
to consent to assault causing bodily harm or assault with a weapon.
Such an action could constitute criminal assault independently of
consent."[25] I shudder to imagine the potential spin-off cases, especially when you add in the junior leagues, where minors aged 16 or
17 engage in fights with adults. Need I remind you that bare-fisted
fighting (à la *Fight Club*) goes against all kinds of laws? Or that
combat sports have their own federations and governing bodies?
Or that "extreme" forms of combat, which were originally brutally
violent, began evolving ages ago into rigorous and acclaimed sports
in which the protection of fighters is a central concern? Finally,
even if few people care to admit it, the way players are built these
days is reason to fear the worst: crashing down onto the ice from
six feet high during a manly brawl, shattering your skull, and wind-
ing up six feet underground. One hockey player from a senior
Ontario league, Don Sanderson, died in 2008 after cracking his
skull on the ice following a fight in which his helmet came off. Must
we wait for another tragic event like this to happen in the big
leagues before we get this sport under control?

---

25.   Steven G. Slimovitch, "Les sports et la violence. . . La justice se rend à la
patinoire," *Réseau juridique du Québec*, March 2000. http://www.avocat.
qc.ca/public/iihockey-violence.htm. The author is a lawyer.

Lawsuit brought against the NHL

The NFL and over 4,500 former players recently reached an out-of-court settlement of $765 million as part of a lawsuit pertaining to concussions. With scientific studies in hand, the players alleged that the league was aware of the risks associated with concussions. It is now proven that they suffer long-term physical, physiological, and psychological consequences: chronic encephalopathy (a degenerative brain disorder), Alzheimer's disease, depression, etc. (See Dave Ellemberg's excellent book on this topic, *Les commotions cérébrales dans le sport*, Québec-Livres, 2013.)

In the hockey world, the NHL has always claimed to take the health and safety of its players to heart. Rule 48, which was established in 2011, prohibits blows to the head. Yet in a conceit worthy of absurdist theatre, it continues to allow fights that necessarily involve this type of hit! In November 2013, over 200 ex-NHLers filed a lawsuit similar to the one brought against the NFL. This was the first in what many observers expect will be a long series of such cases. Given that three former fighters (Derek Boogaard, Rick Rypien, and Wade Belak) were found dead in their homes in 2011, all having suffered from serious health problems for years, it's only a matter of time before the issue of blows to the head hits the league managers' heads too.

Open-mindedness: The real fight we should be having

The about-face taken by Minister Courchesne on fighting in junior Québec hockey shows just how wide the gulf between theory and practice can be.[26] I dare say we are witnessing the dawn of a major

---

26. The report she commissioned from a consultation committee, 12 (!) of the 14 members of which were from the Québec Major Junior Hockey League, was tabled in September 2008. Certain measures have fortunately been implemented, but fighting is still a reality.

shift in this sickening culture. After all, if Spain, the home of bull-fighting, passed a resolution a few years ago to confer fundamental rights upon gorillas, chimpanzees, and orangutans in order to better protect them, then indeed "the best is yet to come" in this country, to borrow the old slogan of the Québec Nordiques!

That said, as long as certain members of the "old guard" noted for their "man's man" vision of the game continue to be involved in the sport as managers, coaches, and commentators (Don Cherry, Brian Burke, Mike Milbury, Pat Quinn, Paul Holmgren, and the list goes on), the higher-ups will continue to suffer from myopia and hockey arenas will continue to be treated like gladiators' arenas.[27] Nothing will be achieved without a firm desire to profoundly change the spirit of violence that currently pollutes hockey. There is no shortage of examples of radical "spring cleaning" being done in other sports to maintain their integrity and increase their popularity.[28] For its part, the NHL continues to drag its skates in quite a few areas.

The spirit of the times. Public outcry. Pressure from all sides: the public, the political sphere, the legal system, the scientific community, the insurance companies, the players themselves. Even the sight of a gory death. Could any of these finally set North American hockey free from this caricature of an image that sticks to it like hockey tape? Could we dream of a new day in the history of this magnificent sport in which all parties would take their fair share of responsibility for this senseless cult of gratuitous violence, a day when the only fight worth fighting would be to return to "the elegant movements and the courteous etiquette of the culture of gentlemen"[29] that characterized the sport in the nineteenth century? Oh, to see the words "Fair Play and Respect" emblazoned on every

---

27. This opinion is shared by former player and general manager Lou Nanne (R. Bernstein, *The Code*, p. 203).
28. A few examples: in 2006, NBA commissioner David Stern suspended the star player Carmelo Anthony for 15 games for punching a fellow player. The revelations of Jose Canseco incited MLB to give itself a dose of credibility (commissions, investigation, etc.) to counter the growing problem of doping. The NFL tightened its rules in order to better protect its star players *par excellence*, the quarterbacks, who are too often victims of excessively rough play.
29. Donald Guay, *L'histoire du hockey au Québec*, p. 203.

Breaking the code of silence

Serious consideration regarding fighting dates back at least as far as 1975, when the players' association recommended that the league bar violators from the current game as well as the following one. The owners categorically refused. Later, in a 1992 NHL Board of Governors meeting, only seven of the then 24 teams voted to ban fisticuffs; 13 votes were required for the rule to be overturned. What resulted instead was the instigator rule. There have been many such missed opportunities. For example, Gil Stein was elected president of the NHL and campaigned against fighting but was eventually beat by Gary Bettman. In recent years, a number of dissenting voices have dared to break the code of silence. And these aren't voices in the wilderness either: we're talking Ken Dryden, Scotty Bowman, Pierre McGuire, Bruce Hood, Jean Perron, Réjean Tremblay, all of whom are vehemently opposed to the concerto for four fists. After the Todoruk incident, even the NHL's Dean of Discipline, Colin Campbell, a former fan of the two-man tango, questioned the relevance of fighting. This serves as proof that some people in the league are now, for the first (or second) time, starting to see how rough play can spiral into violence, violence into brutality, and brutality into fatality.

Let's note that even before the NHL was born, the presidents of the National Hockey Association and the Pacific Coast Hockey Association, the wise Emmet Quinn and Frank Patrick, went to great lengths to reduce gratuitous violence: on their watch, any reprehensible action could be brought before the courts and would automatically lead to heavy fines and suspensions. These measures obviously calmed people's minds in the years that followed, gave referees some elbow room, and allowed the minor leagues to follow suit.

jersey in the International Ice Hockey Federation. To witness a player helping his opponent to his feet, as we do in football. To watch teams shake hands after every game, and have this be the only time the gloves are dropped. To behold a pure version of the sport in which it would no longer be the minor leagues, the "little guys" with their code of fair play and non-violence, that would set the example for the "big guys." Let's be clear: this is not a case of falling into pious moralism or conflating the roughness of a contact sport with violence. Rather, it is simply about remembering the hockey is an art of dodging, not a boxing match—where to refrain from fighting is to act like a man and then some.

Further reading

ALLEN, Kevin. *Crunch. Chicago*: Triumph Books, 1999.
> To get inside the special world of fighters.

BERNSTEIN, Ross. *The Code: The Unwritten Rules of Fighting and Retaliation in the NHL*. Chicago: Triumph Books, 2006.

ELIAS, Norbert and Eric DUNNING. *Sport et civilisation: la violence maîtrisée*. Paris: Fayard, 1994.
> To see the links between pacification of social life and the reduction in authorized violence in sport.

ELLEMBERG, Dave. *Les commotions cérébrales dans le sport*. Montréal, Québec: Les Éditions Québec-Livres, 2013.
> To learn about the troubling reality of head injuries in athletes.

NIETZSCHE, Friedrich. *The Gay Science: With a Prelude in Rhymes and an Appendix of Songs*. Translated by Walter Kaufmann. New York: Vintage Books, 1974.
> To delve deeper into what Nietzsche wrote about the herd mentality.

ST-ONGE, Jean-Claude. *La condition humaine*. Montréal: Gaëtan Morin Éditeur, 2000.

FERRY, Luc and Jean-Didier VINCENT. *Qu'est-ce que l'homme?* Paris: Odile Jacob, 2001.
> To learn more about what theologians, philosophers, and scientists think about human nature.

Twist vs. McFarlane

Tony Twist, affectionately known as The Twister, caused many of his enemies to tremble—and fight—during his decade-long career with the Québec Nordiques and the St. Louis Blues (1989–1999). At 230 pounds, the man was a fridge. He spent 1,121 minutes on the penalty bench and scored 10 goals in 445 games. His most important confrontation, however, took place before the courts, after his career as a fighter was over. The facts were as follows. In 1992, Todd McFarlane, the brilliant Canadian cartoonist, created a successful series called *Spawn*. The series follows the harrowing journey of a US Secret Service special agent who gets assassinated by his superiors. The agent strikes a deal with a demon in order to be able to see his wife again and avenge his death. McFarlane named one of the many characters in the series Antonio Twistelli, a cheery wink, or so he thought, to his passion for hockey. Meanwhile, he became co-owner of the Edmonton Oilers. Twist didn't want his name associated with a villain mobster and sued McFarlane for $15 million. The artist's many appeals and defences were unsuccessful. His publishing house was forced to declare bankruptcy after a $5 million settlement out of court.

Today, McFarlane has all but stopped drawing, preferring to focus on other artistic pursuits. *Spawn*, however, continues to be published. For his part, Twist owns the Twister's Iron Bar Saloon and makes regular radio and TV appearances. It's not known whether he gives a "cheery wink" when he does appear. (C.B.)

The Aesthetics of Hockey

Normand Baillargeon

Picture this.

You're at the Place des Arts in Montréal. It's a beautiful evening in May, and a prestigious event has just begun.

The master of ceremonies steps up to the podium and gives his opening remarks. Then he invites the person who will announce the first of many awards to be presented tonight.

Jean Béliveau comes up to the stage. He looks as dapper as ever in a sleek black suit and holds an envelope in one hand. He greets the audience, which applauds him at length, then begins to read, obviously from a teleprompter:

"This year's nominees for Most Beautiful Goal of the Year are:

"Rick Nash, for his goal scored against the Phoenix Coyotes. . ."

Video clips of the goal are shown on a large screen at the back of the stage. Oohs and aahs of admiration are heard from the crowd, even though everyone has already seen the goal before. Rick Nash is in the house; he stands and is vigorously applauded.

When the cheers subside, Béliveau continues:

". . . Pavel Datsyuk, for a goal scored in a penalty shot against the Nashville Predators. . ."

More footage is shown, depicting the goal etched into everyone's memories, and more oohs and aahs are heard.

After a time, Béliveau takes back the floor and reads the names of the remaining nominees in the same fashion. Then comes moment of truth: the room holds its breath as Béliveau breaks the seal of the envelope:

"And the winner is. . ."

Welcome to the inaugural Academy of Hockey Aesthetics awards ceremony.

Is this a plausible scenario? Can we imagine that hockey has such a significant aesthetic component that one day we'll look back on the days when it wasn't recognized and rewarded and shake our heads?

To answer these questions, I propose we begin by reminding ourselves exactly what this branch of philosophy we call aesthetics entails. After that, we'll try to determine see whether the idea of an "aesthetics of hockey" has any meaning. I'll end the text with a proposal that I hold very close to my heart. Hopefully, after reading the chapter, you'll agree with me. But let's start at the very beginning: what is aesthetics anyway?

Aesthetics in philosophy

Aesthetics is the branch of philosophy that deals with art and beauty. Questions and issues in the field of aesthetics have to do with defining concepts such as art, beauty, and creation; determining the exact nature of the aesthetic experience; examining the relationship between certain social, economic, or political conditions and works of art; determining whether objective norms and standards for evaluating works of art can exist; and much more.

These questions are highly complex and difficult to answer, and admittedly the answers that have been given remain hotly debated for the most part.

Consider, for example, the question of the nature of art. To appreciate how difficult this question is, consider what we commonly classify as works of art: films, novels, dance, plays, sculptures, drawings, paintings, installations, collages, photographs, music in its many forms, sound installations, and thousands of other things. What is it about all these things that makes them works of art?

To answer a question like this, philosophers have typically used a method of reasoning and research invented by Socrates

A little etymology
Like so many other philosophical disciplines (epistemology, metaphysics, political philosophy, and so on), aesthetics traces its roots back to the Ancient Greek thinkers, who were the first to deal with such matters; their ideas remain relevant even today.
The word "aesthetics" also comes to us from the Greeks, who used the word *aisthêtikos*, to mean "able to feel" and "sensitive perception." It was only in the eighteenth century that a German philosopher began using the word *aesthetica* to refer to philosophical reflection on art and beauty.

(469–399 BCE) called *elenchus*, which can be translated as "testing" or "refutation."

We begin by proposing a definition that lists the necessary and sufficient conditions for what we want to define and only what we want to define. Next, we test this definition against various examples. If we come across a counter-example (i.e., a specific instance of the thing we are trying to define that doesn't fall within our definition), we go back to the drawing board and start again.

For example, we might be tempted to define a work of art as any one of the human creations that tries—and sometimes succeeds—to produce something beautiful and pleasing. But quickly we realize that this definition isn't entirely adequate: many works of art are not beautiful and not intended to be pleasing. On the contrary, they may shock us, disgust us, or make us indignant.

Several famous definitions of art have been advanced over the course of history, and examining them all is beyond the scope of this chapter. We'll simply state that some, taking their cue from Plato, suggest that art is representation or *mimesis* (that's the Greek word used by Plato himself and by many contemporary thinkers). Others, such as Leo Tolstoy, have put forth the idea that art is the expression and communication of feelings. And still others have said that it is a meaningful organization of forms.

> **Duchamp's famous urinal**
> In 1917, Marcel Duchamp submitted this urinal signed R. Mutt (his alias) and entitled *Fountain* to the organizers of an art exposition. He called this type of object, which became art by virtue of the arbitrary choice of the artist, a "readymade." Duchamp's many famous readymades form an integral part of art history and are found in several different museums.

All these definitions have been attacked and defended, and none has succeeded in getting everyone on board. Perhaps because of this frustrating difficulty in defining what art is, certain authors have begun subscribing to a so-called institutional theory of art: art is simply that which is acknowledged as such by institutions; their recognition is what makes a thing art. "A work of art . . . is 1) an artifact 2) upon which some person or persons acting on behalf of a certain social institution (the artworld) has conferred the status of candidate for appreciation," wrote George Dickie, one of the defenders of this idea. In my view this theory resembles (how should I put this?) a vicious circle of a pirouette. I find it highly unsatisfactory because it says nothing about the reasons why we choose to elevate an object to the status of work of art, nor does it say anything about the value of these reasons. Nevertheless, those who subscribe to the institutional theory of art will find support for it in the work of many modern artists including Marcel Duchamp (1887–1968), one of the most influential and distinctive artists of the twentieth century.

Unless of course—and this perspective, inspired by an idea of Ludwig Wittgenstein's, has many supporters these days—the search for the essence of art is itself mistaken.

This inevitably raises another question: is the concept of sport itself one whose elements bear a "family resemblance" to each other but lack a single shared essence? What do you think?

Whatever the definition of art is, the fact remains that sport in general and hockey in particular are obviously not works of art. So

Wittgenstein and the definition of art

Many people consider Ludwig Wittgenstein (1889–1951) to be the greatest philosopher of the twentieth century, and those who don't agree still acknowledge that he definitely ranks among that century's most important and influential thinkers.

Wittgenstein's very strong and colourful personality made him a character like no other. He was by turns an engineering student who drew plans for airplane engines, a philosophy student, a logician, a war hero, a monastery gardener, an elementary school teacher, and an architect. Born into a fabulously wealthy Austrian family, he declined most of his inheritance and donated the rest, regarding money as incompatible with a life devoted to philosophy.

Another remarkable fact about Wittgenstein is that he authored two works of philosophical systems that are radically different from each other, yet equally respected and influential—a very rare feat.

When he was still a young man, he developed the ideas set out in the *Tractatus Logico-Philosophicus*. Then he up and left the field of philosophy altogether, having decided that he had solved all the problems he wanted to solve. It was mainly during this period that he practiced the different occupations mentioned above.

Many years later, Wittgenstein called into question the ideas in his book and went back to university to do philosophy again. The influential ideas he developed in this period were set out in *Philosophical Investigations*, which was published after his death.

One of these ideas might well be the key to solving the enigma of defining art: Wittgenstein suggests that the very search for an "essence" of art is erroneous and destined to fail. To clarify this perspective somewhat, let's join Wittgenstein in considering a concept that is very close to sport: the game.

We use the word "game" in everyday speech with no difficulty whatsoever. It seems that all games have something in common, an essence, and classic philosophy invites us to uncover what that essence is. Instead of using this approach, Wittgenstein invites us to examine how we use this word, what we use it to refer to, and what contexts we use it in. He suggests that such an examination will show us that the word takes on different meanings in different situations and that it does not refer to any single characteristic that is common to all games. Some games are competitive; others aren't. Some games are for one player, some for two, others for teams. Some games have one or more winners, others have none. You get the idea. Wittgenstein's advice is to take the time to observe how we use the word—and I invite you to give it a serious try. If you do, you may reach the same conclusion as Wittgenstein: there is no single criterion that characterizes all games. What we find instead is a complex network of overlapping similarities and differences, and the whole set of elements to which we apply the word game simply share a "family resemblance." Therefore such elements make up "families."

The concept of *work of art* would be one such concept; *work of art* has no essence in and of itself.

why should we examine our national sport from an aesthetic point of view?

The answer is simple: the emotions aroused by works of art are not generated exclusively by them, and we often experience such emotions (aesthetic ones) when we see many objects that are not works of art. Everyone has found beauty in and has been moved by nature (a beautiful sunset), by a person (a beautiful elderly person), by an animal (a beautiful cat) or by some technical achievement (a beautiful bridge, a beautiful building). What, then, is the nature of this aesthetic experience? And what would be the nature of our experience of a hockey game, which is obviously not a work of art, nor a natural phenomenon, nor a technical achievement?

It seems we need to unpack the type of aesthetic experience a hockey game can produce.

And unpack we shall.

Hockey and aesthetics

This reflection is all the more appropriate when, as you have surely noticed, the vocabulary we use to talk about hockey (and sport in general) regularly borrows from artspeak.

We say that such and such a player is graceful, that his skating is elegant, or that a particular game (and not just a goal) was beautiful—or ugly, as the case may be. We may praise a player for his creativity, declare another one imaginative, or congratulate another on playing a particularly inspired game. We could easily go on. This shows the degree to which the language we use to describe art overlaps with our conversations—and our writing—about sport.

But philosophers are a demanding breed. Never content with just an observation, they'll press for more details. What we want to understand, they'll say, is precisely what this use of the vocabulary of aesthetics means when applied to sport. What exactly are we referring to when we speak in these terms?

By way of a first stab at answering these questions, I'd like to draw inspiration from the writings of David Best (without claiming to be entirely faithful to them) and suggest what I think is a relevant and interesting distinction between what he calls the **artistic dimension** and the **aesthetic dimension** of sport. Let's take a closer look.

On the one hand, there are some sports in which references to elements of artistry and artistic appreciation are, so to speak, internal; they are an inherent part of these sports. Participants deliberately seek to achieve artistic effects and accept these as being an intrinsic part of the athletic activity in question, such that their performance is at least partly judged by such criteria. Best says that these sports have an **artistic dimension**. Diving, synchronized swimming, pommel horse, and figure skating (note that the French term is literally *patinage artistique*) are perfect examples of these.

The vocabulary of the aesthetics in hockey
"Rookie Thrasher linemates Ilya Kovalchuk and Dany Heatley are poetry on ice."
M. Farber, *Sports Illustrated*, No. 56, November 12, 2001.
". . . Jean-Michel Boisvert, the author of **some brilliant pieces of poetry** on the ice last night."
Richard Labbé, *La Presse*, December 15, 1999, p. S7
"Mikhail Grabovski helped the Canadiens force an overtime by completing a **beautiful play** by Sergei Kostitsyn."
Guillaume Bourgault-Côté, *Le Devoir*, March 19, 2008.
"We had lost hope in Charles Vouligny, but he seized his chance in October when he was recalled by default. His vision is sharp, and he is a **graceful skater**."
Dany Allard, *La Tribune*, December 18, 2007, p. 44
"**The elegant** and quick-footed Brassard tore up the ice and stunned his opponents with his precision."
Danny Allard, *La Tribune*, February 18, 2008, p. 36
"However, the period belonged to Price, the young goalie who fended off 20 shots by the Devils. Zach Parise took four shots and Jamie Langenbrunner took three without managing to thwart him. **A masterpiece!**"
Canadian Press, *Le Soleil*, March 12, 2008, p. 66
"Christopher Higgins was in a line with Belarusians Mikhail Grabovski and Sergei Kostitsyn, two players who are noted for **their creativity**."
François Lemenu, *Le Devoir*, March 15, 2008
". . . we saw all kinds of **beautiful plays**. . .: Markov's goal was created by a beautiful play **inspired by the imagination of the artist in his workshop**."
Pierre Ladouceur, *La Presse*, March 25, 2008, p. S3
"The return of Alexei Kovalev was one of the team's keys to success, and this is **one of the most beautiful accomplishments** of Carbo as a coach; he had the foresight to **give the artist** the latitude he wanted."
Marc Antoine Godin, *La Presse*, March 27, 2008, p. S2

"That's the **beauty** of the hockey playoffs, there's still another chance."

Cinthya Bérubé, *L'Acadie Nouvelle*,
March 28, 2008, p. 46

"Alexei Kovalev scored his 32nd and 33rd, **two gorgeous goals**, in addition to racking up an assist."

La Voix de l'Est, March 21, 2008, p. 30

On the other hand, there are other sports in which references to categories of artistry and artistic appreciation are not internal but rather external to the activities in question. Here, athletes don't seek them out for their own sake: they know they won't be judged by these criteria and that their success or failure doesn't depend on them. Best says these sports have an **aesthetic dimension**, and that this dimension is not intrinsic to the activity but rather secondary, extrinsic, or accessory, essentially existing in the eye of the beholder (the spectator). Accordingly, competitive sports, including hockey, have an **aesthetic dimension**. Whether or not the goal scored is elegant (lord knows Maurice Richard scored a few doozies in his day!) doesn't change the fact that the goal has been scored; the object of the game is simply to get 'er done.

But it is possible in sports with an aesthetic dimension that a goal, play, pass, or save may strike us as notable for artistic reasons: in the eyes of hockey spectators, the sport's aesthetic dimension can be manifested through any of these.

What is the significance of this? We can turn to philosophers who have written about the aesthetic experience for valuable insights.

Experience, attitude, and aesthetic judgment

Whether it comes to us when we're beholding a work of art or anything else, an aesthetic experience is something special that gives us pause. Everyone, presumably, has had such an experience and can remember it. Let's start from there and attempt what philosophers call (somewhat pompously) phenomenological description.

Imagine yourself in the presence of something that will create an aesthetic experience within you. It is directed towards your senses, but not just any senses: chiefly to sight and hearing (you probably wouldn't say that something you enjoy tasting, touching, or smelling is "beautiful").

But that's not the end of the story, because your reason and knowledge are involved.

This knowledge may well be minimal: even if I know nothing about music theory, I can still dig a solo by Charlie Parker and be moved by it, and Charlie Parker doesn't have to be an astronomer to be stirred by a beautiful sunset (and the astronomer would say that the sun neither sets nor rises; it's the horizon that falls!). But still, the knowledge we have of a given art form increases our ability to perceive and experience its beauty. An aesthete is someone who cultivates their taste for an art by going to the trouble of learning about it, the better to understand and appreciate it. Aesthetes are often highly passionate people; they want to know everything about the art's history, its creators, its techniques, and a thousand other things. The art lover—like the painter—is not necessarily someone who is moved by the sight of a picturesque landscape as much as the person who studies, understands, and masters the techniques of painting.

Here we have an experience that is sensory and, to varying degrees, intellectual. But countless other experiences would also satisfy these criteria, and what we have just described is certainly not sufficient to characterize an aesthetic experience. We're getting somewhere; let's carry on.

When we think about it, we note that the aesthetic experience creates within its experiencer something enjoyable and satisfying; it gives the experiencer what for now we will call a certain pleasure. It provokes reactions that we often express by saying that the work pleases us, charms us, delights us, or moves us. In the most powerful cases, we may even feel a deep sense of ecstasy in beholding a work of art. But whatever its power, this feeling is special. It is completely different from the pleasure we feel when we satisfy a need or desire: tasting (so to speak) the beauty of a John Coltrane solo makes us feel a "pleasure" that is rather different from those of eating, having sex, or buying some consumer product we really want.

We have to take this idea a bit further. When beholding a work of art, my attitude is one of disinterested appreciation or, you could even say, disinterested interest. The work definitely captures my interest, and while I am looking at it and enjoying it, all my attention is focused on it. But this interest is devoid of practical considerations, unattached to the pursuit of immediate or longer-term goals: in this sense it is disinterested. When I look at a painting and contemplate it, I don't wonder what I could do with it, what aim I could accomplish with it, or what need I could satisfy with it. (I might if I were considering it as an investment, say, but in that case, my attitude towards the painting would no longer be aesthetic.)

This aesthetic attitude also involves a momentary suspension of our usual relationship with the world, in which we pursue all kinds of goals based on practical interests. When I adopt an aesthetic attitude towards a sculpture, a performance, or a work of art, for a moment I am distanced from the "real world," and in that moment I am literally ravished by the work, which transports me to another dimension.

There's more. When I adopt this aesthetic attitude, I feel a special emotion that the piece of art produces within me, but I also formulate an aesthetic judgment about the work, typically declaring it a thing of beauty. This judgment is special for a number of reasons. And in formulating my judgment, I am definitely making a statement about myself (I'm saying what I like) but at the same time, it seems, making a statement about the world (I'm saying that this thing is beautiful).

We routinely formulate judgments in which we express our personal taste: for instance, we may say that we like a given dish or drink. But aesthetic judgment is different: it purports to describe a property of the world (the beauty of a given object). If one person who likes a certain culinary specialty is in the same room with someone else who hates it, there's no point in asking who's right or wrong: it's simply a matter of subjective taste.

As I say, aesthetic judgment is of a different order. It is presented as being applicable for me, but also for you and for everyone else: its intended universality is what makes it open to discussion. Popular wisdom dictates that we shouldn't discuss judgments of taste. Philosophical wisdom, on the other hand, teaches us that these aesthetic judgments are things we can, nay must, discuss even if beauty and the content of the judgment can't be reduced to any simple formula. Beauty is something we feel more than we prove.

I think that, essentially, all I have just described can be found in these breathtakingly magical moments in which hockey places us in the presence of beauty.

Consider the goal. As the play unfolds, I am transported to another level of contemplating the game. In an instant, my day-to-day worries have evaporated and my hopes of victory for my team become secondary. In beholding this play, I adopt an aesthetic, disinterested attitude. And I am utterly ravished. I feel the beauty of the game. This play is beautiful and I want to say so; I am compelled to formulate a judgment and to share it with you.

In my opinion, these moments aren't all that rare. I'd even say they're part of what makes hockey worth watching. And thank goodness for that. Because there is something noble about this type of attitude towards the sport that I dare say is on a higher level than simple fanaticism towards a particular team.

But it's also an attitude that must be learned and developed, just as aptitude for discussions in which aesthetic judgments are exchanged should be encouraged. I have a thought on this that I'd like to share with you.

As I mentioned above, I'd like to finish off this chapter with a proposal. And here it is: I submit that the National Hockey League should, as soon as possible, start awarding a trophy for the most beautiful player of the year, the person whose playing best glorifies and embodies the aesthetic dimensions of the sport and makes these felt by the spectators.

I don't find this idea the least bit out of place, and I hope that my readers will agree. Moreover, with the Lady Byng Memorial Trophy, awarded to the player who demonstrates the best

Kant's four formulas

Philosophers who have read this far will have already picked up on this: my presentation of the aesthetic attitude, experience, and judgment are inspired by the writings of the German philosopher Immanuel Kant (1724–1804), one of the most important theorists on aesthetics. Below are Kant's formulas, which sum up his thoughts on aesthetics. If I've done my job well, you'll find that they are a neat summary of some of the ideas I've been discussing:

1. Beauty is the object of a judgment of disinterested taste.
2. Beauty is what, without a concept, is liked universally.
3. Beauty is the form of purposiveness in an object, so far as this is perceived in it apart from the representation of an end.
4. Beauty is that which, apart from a concept, is recognized as object of a necessary delight.

sportsmanship, the NHL already rewards virtues that are distinct from those that are strictly athletic, competitive, and performance based.

Such an award would also put the spotlight on a certain dimension of hockey that, while neglected, is entirely tangible and deserving of attention. Adopting an aesthetic attitude towards the world in general and sport in particular (even for sports with only an aesthetic dimension) is one avenue to engage with the world around us, one that's different from the one imposed on us by the demands of the workaday, so often full of conflict and competition. To adopt this attitude is to reveal an indispensable part of what makes us human.

Finally, as we have seen, it is the spectators who perceive, recognize, and appreciate the beauty of the game. Awarding a prize for the most beautiful player would pay homage to the people who watch hockey and see within it things that the players typically can't account for but which, for the spectators, are an important part of their love for the game. The winner of this trophy could be determined by popular vote. Why not?

I will leave it to others who are infinitely more capable than I to settle the matters of organization and design that such an award would entail.

But if you want to know what I think the trophy should be called, I could answer you without hesitation: the Orr-Kharlamov Trophy. Both Bobby Orr (1948–) and Valeri Kharlamov (1948–1981) are, I think, unanimously recognized as being players of exceptional beauty. Also, associating the names of these two players, one Canadian and one Russian, representing the two countries that have valued and continue to value hockey more than any others would be a fitting way to acknowledge what has been endlessly affirmed by Plato and so many others: that beauty transcends people, societies, eras, and cultures.

Now I wonder who would win the Orr-Kharlamov trophy this year.

What do you think?

Further reading
On aesthetics
HUISMAN, Bruno, et al. (eds). *Les Philosophes et l'art: les grands textes philosophiques sur l'art*. Paris: B. Huisman, 1984.

KANT, Immanuel. *Critique of the Power of Judgment*. Translated by Paul Guyer. Cambridge: Cambridge University Press, 2000.

On aesthetics and sport
As far as I know, there is unfortunately no literature on the subject in French. So here are a few major texts in English.

BEST, David. *Philosophy and Human Movement*. London: Allen and Unwin, 1978.

> Best's ideas on the aesthetics of sport, some of which appear here, are mainly developed in pages 99–122 of that book.

HYLAND, Drew A. *Philosophy of Sport. Paragon Issues in Philosophy.* New York: Paragon House, 1990.

> Chapter 5 of this book provides a good synthesis of the works written on the aesthetics of sport to date.

MORGAN, William J., and Klaus V. MEIER. *Philosophic Inquiry in Sport*. Champaign, Ill.: Human Kinetics Publishers, 1988.

The book contains important essays and articles on the philosophy of sport.

The Great Drug Debate: Saturday Night at Chez Paulo

Normand Baillargeon

It's almost midnight on February 19, 2008. Just like every Saturday during the hockey season, I'm heading home from a night at Chez Paulo.

And also just like every Saturday, everybody in the "band of four" (as we call ourselves) was there: Chantal, a biology student; Jean, a dispatcher for a transportation company; Pierre, who studies literature and is writing his thesis on the poet Jacques Prévert, whom he quotes constantly; and me, an aspiring sports journalist. We're a motley crew as you can see, but we're really passionate about hockey, and our friendship runs deep.

The Canadiens won. Tonight's game was more than beautiful: it was a game we will all remember.

The Habs were playing the New York Rangers and trailing 5 to 0 five minutes into the second period. You might have expected they would more or less throw in the towel. We amused ourselves with the usual clichés to explain why the game was going so poorly: "*Eh! La puck roule pas pour nous autres, ce soir*" (the puck's not on our side tonight) and other dated expressions.

But against all odds, our *Glorieux* soldiered valiantly on. They made a miraculous comeback and, after three regulation periods, the score was now 5 to 5!

So it was into overtime. Off went the buzzer. No goals. The shootout had us on the edge of our seats. In the end, the Canadiens won the day with a goal by Saku Koivu! The owner of the bar

Hockey talk exported

In a culture like ours, in which hockey is such a big deal, it's not surprising that its vocabulary has slipped into everyday speech.

Here is a non-exhaustive list of expressions that have made their way into French:

Être (ou ne pas être) vite sur ses patins
Patiner
La puck roule (ou ne roule pas) pour nous autres
Donner son 110 pour cent
On ne peut pas toutes les gagner!
Travailler dans les coins
Un plombier
Pas pire, pas pire, pas pire
Jouser
Avoir (ou ne pas avoir) l'esprit d'équipe
Dans mon livre à moi . . .
Y'en aura pas de facile
Niaiser avec la puck
L'expérience d'un . . .
Mon toé là!
Accrocher ses patins
Définitivement
Être (ou ne pas être) un joueur d'équipe
La force (ou la dureté) du mental!
Il est fort ce . . . (N.B. and C.B.)

announced that drinks were on the house, which had never happened before. As the commentators reminded us many times over, this was the stuff of history: for the first time in its 99-year history, the *Tricolore* had recovered from a five-goal deficit and won.

So, like I said, it was definitely a night to remember. But I'll also remember it for an equally memorable debate the four of us had before the game. I'll record it here as best I can before I go to bed.

It all began when Pierre told us about a newspaper article he had just read (I can't remember which paper) saying that, according to a report published the previous January, a number of Major League Baseball players had used banned drugs to improve their performance. Éric Gagné, a Québécois, was one of the 87 players implicated in the report.

Chantal interjected, reminding us that the use of banned drugs was widespread in many sports besides baseball—with perhaps the most glaring example being cycling. Just by coincidence, she happened to have a *Scientific American* article on the subject with her.

If a picture is worth a thousand words, the graph she showed us was worth ten thousand. I can't remember it in exact detail, but basically it showed the average speed of Tour de France winners, which increased gradually from 1949 to 1990, presumably due to improvements in cycling equipment, training, and the athletes' diets.

Then, starting in 1991—and I here I do remember clearly as Chantal pointed at giant upswing on the graph—the average speed increased by leaps and bounds. This rapid progress couldn't just be from improvements in equipment, training, or diet. "How do you explain that?" I asked her.

The answer was obvious to all of us: drugs. "Yeah, but what kind of drugs?" Chantal wondered. We had no idea, but she did. She was in her element. Here's what I remember (I hope I'm being faithful to what she said).

For years, it had been common for cyclists to inject themselves with blood before a race—either their own blood (autologous blood doping) or someone else's of the same blood type (homologous blood doping). This practice increases the number of red blood cells that transport oxygen in the body, thus improving endurance and performance. For a long time, the authorities turned a blind eye to the practice, as the end result was pretty much the same as training in high altitudes. In addition, blood doping was complicated enough that at least some people didn't bother with it—all that blood to draw, all those bags to transport, all those needles to stick into their veins. In those days, the use of drugs and techniques like blood doping weren't considered forms of cheating. Yet.

All that changed in 1990 with the arrival of a laboratory-derived substance called rEPO. EPO is short for erythropoietin, a hormone produced naturally in the body. More specifically (and I can report this because I had Chantal look it up for me since these words were all Greek to me) it is a glycoprotein hormone that regulates **hematopoiesis**—a mouthful to be sure. Now, rEPO is a synthetic or recombinant version of the same hormone, hence the r. This substances increases, and I mean vastly increases, the relative volume of red blood cells in the bloodstream. In addition, athletes can simply carry little vials of the stuff and injected it under the skin. The effect is miraculous and very difficult to detect.

Jean then quoted an article in today's paper—er, yesterday's paper—stating that NHL managers vehemently denied that players were doping in their league.

We all burst out laughing. Jean went on to say that we weren't alone: the same article actually reported that fans are sceptical on this point, at least according to a recent survey that reports that "nearly half of Canadians believe that many or at least some NHL players use doping products" (I clipped the article).

Were all those people in the survey plus the four of us justified in our scepticism of the NHL managers' claims? I wasn't sure; my friends and I quickly agreed that we weren't qualified to take a position with any certainty.

But somehow our conversation took an unexpected turn, both in terms of the subject matter and in how we debated it.

We asked ourselves the following question: is it legitimate to prohibit athletes from using drugs? And as for how to prohibit them, we were forced to make conceptual distinctions and tackle normative issues that are, if my memory of mandatory cégep classes serves, the stuff of philosophy. Yessir, that night we were big-time philosophers. And while we didn't reach any definite conclusions, our evening did not disappoint—in fact, it felt useful and even enlightening. Who would have believed it?

We started off by deciding—at my suggestion, incidentally—that it would be helpful to define the boundaries of our subject. We quickly agreed to limit our discussion to adults practising high-level (e.g., Olympic) or professional sports (e.g., hockey, baseball, football). Because drugs can mean different things to different people, we also agreed discuss only performance-enhancing drugs (PE drugs)—setting aside anything to do with so-called recreational drugs (e.g., pot, hashish) and all the legitimate issues surrounding the status of alcohol and cigarettes.

List of substances and methods prohibited in- and out-of-competition in 2006 by the World Anti-Doping Agency and used by the International Olympic Committee
(Accessed at and adapted from: http://www.olympic.org/Documents/Reports/EN/en_report_1019.pdf)

III.PROHIBITED SUBSTANCES

S1. ANABOLIC AGENTS
1.1. Anabolic Androgenic Steroids (AAS)
   a. Exogenous AAS
   b. Endogenous AAS
1.2. Other Anabolic Agents

S2. HORMONES AND RELATED SUBSTANCES
1. Erythropoietin (EPO)
2. Growth Hormone (hGH), Insulin-like Growth Factors (e.g. IGF-1), Mechano Growth Factors (MGFs)
3. Gonadotrophins (LH, hCG), prohibited in males only
4. Insulin
5. Corticotrophins

S3. BETA-2 AGONISTS

S4. AGENTS WITH ANTI-ESTROGENIC ACTIVITY
1. Aromatase inhibitors
2. Selective Estrogen Receptor Modulators
3. Other anti-estrogenic substances

S5. DIURETICS AND OTHER MASKING AGENTS

S6. STIMULANTS
(Adrafinil, adrenaline*, fenproporex, furfenorex, and about 50 other substances)

S7. NARCOTICS
(Buprenorphine, dextromoramide, diamorphine (heroin), fentanyl and its derivatives, hydromorphone, methadone, morphine, oxycodone, oxymorphone, pentazocine, pethidine.)

S8. CANNABINOIDS
(E.g., hashish and marijuana)

S9. GLUCOCORTICOSTEROIDS

II. PROHIBITED METHODS

M1. ENHANCEMENT OF OXYGEN TRANSFER
(I.e., Blood doping, including the use of autologous, homologous or heterologous blood or red blood cell products of any origin; artificially enhancing the uptake, transport or delivery of oxygen.)

M2. CHEMICAL AND PHYSICAL MANIPULATION
(I.e., Tampering, or attempting to tamper, in order to alter the integrity and validity of Samples collected during Doping Controls).

M3. GENE DOPING
(The non-therapeutic use of cells, genes, genetic elements, or of the modulation of gene expression, in order to enhance athletic performance.)

> **III. OTHER**
> There is also a list of substances prohibited in particular sports. It includes:
>
> **P1. ALCOHOL**
>
> **P2. BETA-BLOCKERS**

Is it legitimate to prohibit high-level athletes from taking these drugs? That was the question on the table. We formulated, as clearly and forcefully as we could, all the arguments in favour of prohibition that leapt to our minds. Then, one by one, we tested them by trying to come up with reasons why they weren't convincing.

I'll try to summarize everything that was said.

We came up with five strong, persuasive arguments for prohibiting adult athletes from using PE drugs.[1]

Pierre came up with the first argument, which had to do with the health hazards that PE drugs pose for users. The drugs that the athletes take (e.g., anabolic steroids) purportedly have harmful effects on health, at least in the quantities in which they are taken. These presumed effects include physical effects (e.g., cancer, hair loss, masculinization in women) and psychological ones (e.g., increased aggression, mood swings). Therefore, it's permissible to prohibit the use of such drugs. True to form, Pierre concluded by referencing Prévert: "'It's all well and good to have an iron constitution—we always rust out in the end,' said Prévert. And there is a concern that PE drugs make athletes rust out sooner."

At first we thought the argument was pretty strong. But after we thought about it a little longer, we weren't so sure anymore. Chantal reminded us that the harmful effects of PE drugs on health aren't always clearly established—or, at least not as clearly as the

---

1. The arguments and counterarguments of this dialogue are inspired by Drew A. Hyland's presentation of the issue of drugs in sport in: *Philosophy of Sport, Paragon Issues in Philosophy* (New York: Paragon House, 1990), pp. 47–67.

health effects of cigarettes, for instance, which athletes are permitted to smoke. Guy Lafleur supposedly smoked during his professional hockey career. I countered by saying that we're talking about PE drugs, but Chantal responded that caffeine also enhances performance, as do many other substances that aren't banned.

Also, we sometimes ban practices that we consider equivalent to taking drugs, even when we know they are not drugs and are not harmful, like injecting yourself with your own blood.

Finally, even if we allow that certain drugs in certain quantities do have harmful effects on health, simply playing some of the sports in which they are banned can be inherently more dangerous. Boxing, football, mountaineering, and of course hockey are much likelier to cause injuries—often severe and fatal ones—than anabolic steroids.

In the end we agreed that this first argument wasn't as straightforward or persuasive as we initially thought. So we abandoned it, confident that we would find other, more conclusive rationales.

Jean put a second argument on the table. Athletes who decide to take PE drugs, despite the presumed risks to their health (whether or not these risks are real) and who are able to do so (because they can buy or otherwise access these products, etc.) have an unfair advantage over those who can't access them.

We were sure this baby was airtight. Then, when the four of us put our heads together, we concluded it wasn't—or at least that there were some holes in the argument.

For starters, was it true that users of PE drugs had an unfair advantage? Pierre framed the question like this: a sport is fair if its rules apply evenly across the board, for all participants. Once this condition is satisfied, what the sport does (and rightly so) is to show inequalities—that's kind of the point. These inequalities are not unfair provided the sport is fair in the sense we just mentioned. Wayne Gretzky and Guy Lafleur were better at hockey than most of their peers: this situation was unequal but not unfair, since all players were subject to the same rules. Athletes who train longer and harder and who outperform their fellow athletes as a result are unequal to their peers, but not unfairly so. A basketball player who is seven feet tall has a huge advantage over someone only six feet tall: is that unfair? There are plenty of sports where people who do weight training have an advantage over those who don't: should weight rooms be banned? It's certainly important to talk about fairness and unfairness, but claims that certain products provide an unfair advantage are far from being clear in all cases.

At this point, our faith in finding a rock-solid argument was crumbling. Thankfully, Chantal came to our rescue with the third argument.

She pointed out that in high-level sports, differences between individual performances tend to be extremely narrow: there's only a hair of a margin between the first-place runner and the second-place runner in the 100-metre dash, for example. The first-place runner gets all the money and glory, while the "runner-up" gets forgotten. This creates an incentive to use PE drugs, which may place athletes under pressure that borders on coercion. And that's unacceptable.

Mission accomplished! This felt like the clincher for sure.

But when the four of us picked it apart, this appealing argument didn't find unanimous support: at the end of the night, two of us (including me) agreed with it and two found it lacking. The naysayers said that, yes, there certainly is indeed pressure on other athletes to use drugs as well, but this situation is not unique: in any occupation out there, it's up to the individual to decide how much they're going to invest in the job. Some employees choose to work longer and harder than others. This doesn't mean there's undue pressure on those who are less invested. So why would this be the case for athletes deciding whether to use PE drugs?

Sigh. I'll humbly admit that it was I who found the next argument, our fourth. I was proud of it, but as we dug deeper, I began to change my mind. I'm not completely finished thinking about it, though. Here's the idea.

Sport puts people in competition with each other, and these people perform better or worse as a result of effort and work. Regardless, it's still people who are involved; this condition must be satisfied if we are to speak of sport in the first place. Accordingly, allowing drugs alters the nature of people and sport: it's the chemicals and technologies (which we rightly seek to disguise) that are now in competition with each other. If you take this line of reasoning to its logical end, it's possible to imagine a "bionic" man with super-powerful arms and legs. Such a man might skate at dizzying speeds and have an unbeatable slapshot—but many people would not consider this hockey player a person and might not let him (it?) play in the NHL. I think a league of super-robots might pique people's curiosity for a time, but in the end the fans would lose interest and seek out a game played by humans, with strengths and flaws, who are in the process of realizing human achievements.

I was surprised by the holes my friends were able to poke in my reasoning.

They made me see that you have to start with a clear idea of what is natural before you can oppose practices on the grounds that they're unnatural. But do we have such a clear and unambiguous concept of the natural? Bobby Orr played in the series against the USSR in 1976, and he was probably the best player in Canada at the time. This gentleman's knee was quite literally like jelly. He was forced to hobble on one leg during the day and stop going to practice altogether. It was just too difficult and too risky for him. But when the time came, he went on the ice and played just as magnificently as ever—aided by hefty injections of cortisone for his injured knee. The question is obvious: was this natural? And what about testosterone? That's a natural substance used as a natural component of anabolic steroids, but it's banned. As more and more examples were brought up, they created a cloud of ambiguity and vagueness that I was powerless to dispel.

It was Jean who came up with our fifth and final argument.

Jean had a little boy who was just starting to play hockey that year. Jean told us how much his son looked up to Saku Koivu, that he had a poster of him hanging on his bedroom wall, that he talked about him all the time, and so on. His concern had to do with the fact that hockey players are role models, especially for young people. Learning that Saku Koivu took PE drugs might encourage some of his fans to take PE drugs themselves, and it could also send the message that taking drugs is no big deal: after all, Saku does it. This case might have seemed abstract to some, but Jean was able to project it onto his own child. He concluded that this fact alone was a compelling reason to prohibit professional athletes from using PE drugs.

But once again, when we combed through it, the argument seemed less sturdy when we were through than when we began. We agreed on this much: we want the men and women our children admire to display positive moral and personal qualities; we want them to be intelligent, generous, sensitive, noble, articulate, and so on. But while we agreed that qualities like these are all desirable, they should not be a requirement. For if we decided to institute such requirements, where would they stop? Would we require athletes to be celibate or to abstain from alcohol? No? So why treat PE drugs any differently?

At the end of this lively debate, the room was split: two of us were on Jean's side and still thought his argument was good, while the other two disagreed.

As I mentioned, that's how our discussion went that night to the best of my memory. I promised myself I would write it down to keep a record of it, and I have done so. It is now very late and I must to bed.

It's been over a year since that night, and today I am picking up where I left off.

Throughout this time, I haven't stopped thinking about this issue of PE drugs, nor have my friends. We all agree that the issue we raised is a highly complex one, and certainly much more complex than we thought before we took a long, hard look at it and saw so many distinctions to be made, many of them quite subtle.

None of us claim to have settled the matter, but one thing's for certain: philosophers of sport, which I have been reading for the last year, have cast serious doubt on the banning of PE drugs. And people are starting to listen.

A recent editorial in the prestigious journal *Nature* claims that these bans are the relics of a bygone era and don't stand up to analysis.[2] More and more people feel that athletes should be able to take whatever drugs they like, provided that they are informed and

---

2. "A Sporting Chance." *Nature* 448 (August 2, 2007), p. 512.

receive appropriate medical supervision. In this case, as in so many others, we should seek to educate rather than to ban, and not simply rely on disseminating facts and leaving things up to choice. (I can hear Pierre quoting Prévert again: "When truth is not free, freedom is not true: today's truths are those of the police.")

My reading up on the topic taught me another interesting thing: your position on the issue of PE drugs may well serve as a litmus test for your position on a core issue in political philosophy. If you'll allow me, we'll close on a brief discussion of this.

Our society is a liberal one—not in the sense of the Liberal Party, but in the philosophical sense of the term. Specifically, this means that the state is not allowed to impose upon you any conception of what you should do with your life. Every adult is free to choose their own path based on their conception of the good life.

The corollary of this is that you cannot limit the freedom of an adult, even if it's for their own good, unless you absolutely have to in order to protect others. (Kids are a special case.)

This is how John Stuart Mill, one of the main founders of political liberalism, expresses and justifies the idea:

> The only purpose for which power can be rightfully exercised over any member of a civilized community, against his will, is to prevent harm to others. His own good, either physical or moral, is not a sufficient warrant. . . . [There] are good reasons for remonstrating him, or reasoning with him, or persuading him, or entreating him, but not for compelling him, or visiting him with any evil in case he do otherwise. To justify that, the conduct from which it is desired to deter him, must be calculated to produce evil to some one else. . . . In the part which merely concerns himself, his independence is, of right, absolute. Over himself, over his own body and mind, the individual is sovereign.[3]

If you fully share this liberal attitude, you probably think we shouldn't be allowed to prevent adult athletes from taking whatever

3.   John Stuart Mill, *On Liberty* (London: Oxford University Press, 1859), pp. 21–22.

Perronisms

Prévert isn't the only one who was creative with words. Comedian André Robitaille had some fun compiling some of the words of Jean Perron, who coached the Montréal Canadiens and the Québec Nordiques before becoming a sports commentator. The difference between Prévert and Perron is that Perron's creativity was involuntary, a stream of Freudian slips.

That doesn't make them any less funny, as you'll discover reading these unintended pearls of poetry we're calling Perronisms; Freudian scholars would be as incredulous as they are amused.

— *Faut pas chercher de midi à l'an 40!*
— *Vous m'enlevez l'eau de la bouche . . .*
— *On peut les compter sur le dos de la main.*
— *Ils peuvent se contenter chanceux!*
— *C'est de l'argent brûlé par les fenêtres.*
— *Il n'a pas inventé le bouchon à quatre trous!*
— *Ça m'a mis l'astuce à l'oreille . . .*
— *Je suis pas né dans un p'tit pain!*
— *Il s'est retrouvé les quatre jambes en l'air.*
— *Ils lui ont déroulé un plateau d'argent.*
— *C'est changer quatre 30 sous pour quatre piastres!*
— *Moi, je suis unanime là-dessus.*
— *Qui m'aime m'essuie!* (N.B.)

substances they please, including PE drugs. In this view, to do so would be to commit what some in political philosophy consider to be the sin of paternalism, that is, claiming to act for the sake of someone else's well-being, thinking that you know better than they do.

Others will counter that there are still many cases where the collectivity imposes things upon adults for the sake of their well-being. Apart from the usual and always reprehensible paternalism, some people feel that a moderate, justifiable version of paternalism should be allowed.

If you subscribe to this idea, you might try to justify the limitation of athletes' freedom to use drugs in the name of this moderate paternalism.

Who's right? I move we talk about it at the next hockey night at Chez Paulo, which has become our hockey-and-philosophy night many times in the last year.

To guide the "band of four" in our discussion, I made a list of the specific cases where our society has opted for moderate paternalism—and doubtlessly made decisions that purist liberals would denounce as paternalistic.

I plan to ask my friends to state their position on each of the following cases, and why:

Mandatory wearing of seatbelts in cars; mandatory motorcycle helmets; outlawing duels; prohibiting the purchase of certain drugs without a medical prescription; prohibiting swimming in certain areas; outlawing prostitution; legalizing pornography; giving children treatments against their parents' wishes; withholding pay for a pension plan.

The next hockey night is tomorrow, and it's shaping up to be a great one. Because we'll be having a discussion that my friends are sure to be interested in, of course—but also because the Canadiens are playing the Detroit Red Wings, which, according to our predictions, will hand the Stanley Cup over to us this year.

Not that any of the Canadiens use PE drugs, of course. Because nobody in the NHL does that.

Further reading
On drugs and sport in general
DE MONDENARD, Jean-Pierre. *Dictionnaire du dopage: substance, procédés, conduites, dangers.* 2ᵉ édition. Paris: Masson, 2004.
Philosophical debate on the prohibition of PE drugs
BROWN, W. M. "Ethics, Drugs and Sports." *Journal of the Philosophy of Sport* VII (1980). pp. 15–23.
> An article that has become a classic defending the legalization of PE drugs in professional sport. *The Journal of the Philosophy of Sport* will be holding a symposium which several authors including Brown will attend,

exposing various diverging opinions on the issue: Special symposium on Drugs and Sport, Volume XI, 1984.

LAURE, Patrick. *Éthique du dopage. La bioéthique en questions.* Paris: Ellipses Édition Marketing S.A, 2002.

On paternalism in political philosophy and in sport

BROWN, W. M. "Paternalism, Drugs and the Nature of Sports." *Journal of the Philosophy of Sport* XI (1984), pp. 14–22.

Overtime

A Game to Be Forgotten!

Jon Paquin

The following sketch depicts the life and work of some of history's philosophers; it is presented in a comedic and solely fictional context as a screenplay dialogue. It is the preliminary foundation for a film piece in which the characters' spirit would be revealed through the actors' performance. In this version, the emphasis is on the dialogue; physical descriptions of characters are intentionally left to the reader's imagination.

1. INT. – HOCKEY DRESSING ROOM – NIGHT

A spacious room with concrete walls painted sky blue comes to life. On the benches that line this last refuge of testosterone and clan mentality sit a group of men casually suiting up for a hockey game. Hanging on the wall is a TV screen. While intended for entertainment, it is bothering one of the players. The hapless player realizes that without his remote control the box will remain silent and lifeless. In the middle of the room sits a large table holding water bottles, pucks, rolls of hockey tape, and various tools; the table is being slammed repeatedly by one player attempting to break in his brand new hockey stick. In a small adjoining room, some of the men are showering before donning their uniforms. The various rituals are punctuated by frequent bursts of laughter; the rhythm of the preparations makes room for simultaneous conversations.

Dressed in goalie gear, ZENO OF ELEA is talking to himself in a rapid-fire manner. He leaps from side to side imitating the action of a goalie in front of the net (the glove save, the blocker save, and the knee save).

ZENO
Focus. . . Focus, Zeno! The puck does not move, therefore it cannot enter your net. . . It does not move; it cannot enter. . . It does not move; it cannot enter. . . Focus. . . Focus, Zeno! The opponents are not moving, therefore they do not threaten the wall blocking the net that is your body. . . They do not move; they are not a threat; they do not move; they are not a threat. . . Focus. . . Focus, Zeno! The hockey sticks that are thought to hit the puck are static. . . therefore the puck is motionless. . . The sticks are static; the puck is motionless. . . The sticks are static; the puck is motionless. . . Focus. . . Focus, Zeno. . .

HERACLITUS is sitting on the bench just in front of ZENO.

HERACLITUS
The puck may be motionless, but not you, eh?! You talk too much. You talk too fast. You talk too loud. . . Settle down, Zeezee!

ZENO
What's that, Hairy Boy? You want me to show you again how my tape balls fail to hit their target?

ZENO picks up old bunches of hockey tape from the garbage can under the table and takes a seat.

HERACLITUS
Dude. No. I don't want anything to do with it! And I told you already to stop calling me that. My name is Heraclitus.

ZENO starts shooting the tape balls at HERACLITUS's face and body.

ZENO
Eh, Hairy Boy? I know why they call you "The Obscure": because
everybody's so confused by your dekes and your puck handling
that don't amount to squat!
Eh, Hairy Boy? If you think everything is in constant motion, your
vision must be blurry. Hey! That must be why you're always trip-
ping on the ice. . . You can't see straight. . .
Eh, Hairy Boy? You gonna have a shower after practice? Oh right,
right, but it won't be the same shower it was last week or last
month, eh?!

HERACLITUS
For crying out loud, Zeezee! Cut it out. . . I've told you dozens of
times already. . .

ZENO
And I've told YOU dozens of times already. . . If you can logically
prove to me that my balls are hitting you, I'll stop shooting them. . .

HERACLITUS
I'm SO not in the mood for this right now. . . I'm warning you,
Zeezee, you're really starting to piss me off. . .

ZENO continues shooting tape balls.

ZENO
Eh, Hairy Boy? Oh, yeah, right. . . Some things change, some things
stay the same. Is that it? Like your wimpy little slapshot that's the
laughingstock of every goalie in the league!
Eh, Hairy Boy? It's like you were saying last time: "The path up to
their goal and the path down to our goal are one and the same.". . .
That would explain why you "scored" in our own net last game!
Eh, Hairy Boy? That's some conflict of opposites, isn't it? The guys
on the other team know how to play hockey, while you on the other
hand. . . Eh, Hairy Boy?

HERACLITUS (annoyed)
Zeezee! Zeno of Elea! I told you to settle down! You're starting to annoy me. If you don't cut it out right now, I'm going to become . . . I'm going to become . . . one mean dude! Then you'll regret it. . .

ZENO shoots another ball at HERACLITUS.

HERACLITUS picks up a puck and chucks it at ZENO, hitting him right in the chest protector.

ZENO (winces)
Hey. . . Not so hard. . . That hurt. . .

HERACLITUS
Is that so? Are you sure? Because, you see, I didn't see any puck move. . .
How about you, guys? Anybody else see it move?

The other players burst into laughter.

ZENO (more softly)
He's right, that's true. . . Focus. . . Focus, Zeno! The puck does not move, therefore it cannot hit you. . . It does not move; it cannot hit you; it does not move; it cannot hit you. . . Focus, Focus Zeno. . .

HOBBES is finishing putting on his shoulder pads while talking with DIOGENES.

HOBBES
Hey, I wonder if I have time to grab a poutine before practice. Diogenes! What time is it?

KANT enters the dressing room dressed in eighteenth-century garb with his hockey bag slung over his shoulder.

DIOGENES
Hobbes, my man, that's easy! Kant's just arriving, so it must be 6:30!

KANT gets out his pocket watch.

KANT
It is, in actual fact, 6:26.

KANT starts dressing.

DIOGENES
Hey, can I ask you something? Do you run your life like clockwork because you're sexually frustrated?

KANT
I see no connection between the two. Whatever do you mean?

DIOGENES (grinding his teeth)
Well, I mean, I'm just trying to imagine myself. . . going without women for that long, no company. . . no action. . . I mean, I'd be completely out of my mind, just raring to go!

KANT
I am satisfied with my perpetually peaceful life. . . reading, writing, dinner with friends. . .

DIOGENES
No one-night stands? No raging benders? No weekend getaways to Amsterdam in search of the Thing-In-Itself?

KANT
No.

DIOGENES (in astonishment)
I don't believe it. . . You're not, uh. . . You're not one of those. . . uh, ascetics, are you?

KANT
No.

DIOGENES
Ah! So women just aren't into you? Or maybe you're too scared to show them your little. . .

HOBBES (insulted)
Down, boy! Kant, don't listen to him! Diogenes, you dog! You're really scraping the bottom of the barrel! You dirty dog!

DIOGENES
What? I'm just trying to understand. . .

KANT
The only thing you need to understand is that I'm content to live simply.

DIOGENES
But that's just it. . . What could be simpler than getting laid?

KANT
Ah, yes. To the man who, er, "relieves" himself in public. . . I understand my choice of lifestyle may seem extreme. . .

DIOGENES
Whoa, whoa, whoa! Let's not start any rumours here. . . I mean, it may have happened a couple of times. . . But you know, it's not easy seducing a lady when you've got no wheels and you're dirt poor and living in a wine barrel. . .

HOBBES
All right boys, let's change the subject. I missed the last game. . . Can anybody fill me in on what happened?

HOBBES addresses BERKELEY.

HOBBES (mockingly)
Your Eminence?

BERKELEY
My son, my son. I can only explain things to you as I perceived them.

HOBBES
Yeah, I know! So, how did you perceive them?

BERKELEY (disgusted)
It was a game to be forgotten! The other team's coach, Niccolò, that sordid Italian mobster, put them up to all kinds of trickery to meet their ends. It was a confrontation from start to finish. And the referee acted accordingly. Justice and fairness?! Ha. Rawls was practically breathing through his whistle. . . Nietzsche was criticizing everything in sight and accosted the best player on the other team. . .

HOBBES
He attacked the idol of the Machiavellian Princes?! Who does he think he is, some kind of superman?

BERKELEY
. . . He was ejected from the game when he got out his hammer to strike the poor fellow. May God have mercy on his soul.

HOBBES
A hammer? . . . He got kicked out again?! What's up with him these days? It's been getting worse and worse. . . He's losing it, I tell you. . .

DIOGENES
. . . Yeah, he's had a tough go of it: he lives like a hermit, his health's in shambles, his best friend left with his girlfriend. . .

BERKELEY
. . . and that's not the end of it! Rawls also expelled our coach.

HOBBES
Rousseau got kicked out too?! Why?

BERKELEY
Bah! It's his same old story about liberty and the league feeling
unease. . . Rawls lost his patience. . . And, because it's not a first-
time offence, Rousseau's out for the rest of the season.

HOBBES
No way! The poor guy! He's going to feel persecuted for sure. . . But
who's filling in as head coach? Oh God! Tell me it's not Leibniz?!

BERKELEY
No, Leibniz is still assistant coach. . . actually, he should be arriving
any minute with the new coach.

*LEIBNIZ enters with DESCARTES. Both are wearing track suits
with the team colours.*

HOBBES
Ah! Speak of the devil. . .

LEIBNIZ
All right, boys! Listen up! This is the man who'll be replacing Jean-
Jacques. He's got a longstanding reputation for excellence in our
league. Gentlemen, I give you René Descartes.

DESCARTES
Thank you, Gottfried. You can all call me René. I know we're short
a few players today, but I still have some very important things to
say, so listen up. Together we're going to be starting from zero, you
hear me?

In one fell swoop, DESCARTES clears everything from the table with his forearm into a mess on the floor. The players stare at him, dumbfounded.

DESCARTES
We're going to build a solid foundation for this team. It's not working right now. You want to know what I see when I look at you? A bunch of snobs! You call yourselves men. Ha! You think you know everything! You allow yourselves be controlled by emotion and passion. Rousseau got kicked out because he didn't use his reason. . . "He didn't think. . ." Well, I think . . . therefore I am . . . your new coach. Starting right now, I'm the one who'll be calling the shots . . . with reason! What this team needs to get back on track is ORDER and METHOD! First of all, I'm going to implement a completely new strategy. . .

GORGIAS
Ha, ha, ha!

DESCARTES
What's so funny, Gorgias?

GORGIAS
Bah! It's just that there's no such thing as strategy! It doesn't exist! And even if there were, you wouldn't know the first thing about it! And even if you did know the first thing about it, you'd never be able to explain it to us! That's all!

DESCARTES
Oh! I see we have a comedian! Well, I'm not sure there's any such thing as a bench, but I can explain it well enough for you to understand that you'll be sitting on it all of next game!

DESCARTES turns to the rest of the players.

DESCARTES
Where was I? Snobs, every last one of you. . . Anybody else have a beef with my method? Anyone else care to interject?

Most of the players stare at the floor. DESCARTES slowly walks up to DIOGENES, who is tying his skates.

DESCARTES
You. Do you have anything to add?

DIOGENES
Yeah, actually, I do! Move aside. You're blocking my light. I can't see my laces over here. . .

DESCARTES seems fazed momentarily. Wordlessly, he takes one big step backwards.

DESCARTES
You, Blaise. Care to share your thoughts with us?

PASCAL
No coach, I'm fine!

DESCARTES
Thomas. Any comments? Questions?

HOBBES
Just one. Do I have time for a poutine before practice?

DESCARTES (enraged)
No! You don't!

HOBBES
All right, all right! Forget I said anything! We grant you all power and we won't say anything more about its enforcement. . .

DESCARTES
Good! This isn't Latin! I'm asking you to pay attention to what I say. . . in English. . . Now, one of our biggest weak spots on this team is lack of discipline. Gottfried, read us the stats from our last game.

LEIBNIZ
We lost 14 to 2. The other team scored 6 goals in power play and 1 when short-handed—that one was scored by Heraclitus. . .

HERACLITUS (annoyed)
Yeah, it was me! So I got mixed up! Everything was happening so quickly. And a goal's a goal, no matter who it counted for!

LEIBNIZ
. . . They had 78 shots on goal. We had 19. They won 68.4 percent of the face-offs; 76 percent of them were in the neutral zone, 66.6 percent at the start of the period, and 57.7 percent in our zone and their zone. They were in possession of the puck 76.3 percent of the time. They. . .

DESCARTES
Okay! Okay! Enough. How many minutes of penalty?

LEIBNIZ
There were a total of 143 minutes on the team, including several majors, a few misconducts, one game misconduct, and one match penalty.

DESCARTES
Let me see that!

DESCARTES grabs the clipboard with the game sheet.

DESCARTES
Even you, Immanuel! After 15 years in the league! You've never had any screw-ups. . . What happened out there?

KANT (ashamed)
I tripped the goalie!

BENTHAM
That's not true! You barely touched him!

DESCARTES
Ah! That's what I thought! He didn't deserve the penalty?

BENTHAM
Absolutely not! His action was of no consequence! The referees didn't see anything!

DESCARTES
All right! Immanuel, tell me clearly and distinctly what happened.

KANT
I was in front of the other team's goal, and the goalie antagonized me by hitting me in the calves. So I politely asked him to stop these disgraceful gestures that give our noble sport a bad name... And that's when he insulted me! He asked me whether I was still living in that hole in Königsberg! That's when I lost my temper... "This man shall fall," I told myself... So I placed my stick between his shin pads and gave it a quick jab.

BENTHAM
But you only tried to make him fall.

DESCARTES
Immanuel, did the goalie fall?

KANT (agitated)
No... but I wanted him to fall! It's the same thing! It's even worse!

BENTHAM
And after that, he rushed to tell the referee!

2. INT. – HOCKEY RINK – NIGHT

KANT approaches the referee RAWLS.

KANT
Mr. Referee, sir, I deserve to be punished.

RAWLS
Play on. There's no infraction. . .

KANT
Yes there is! I tripped the goalie!

RAWLS
I didn't see anything. . . Play on!

KANT
It was obvious! Clean your glasses, or . . . remove your veil . . . ignoramus!

RAWLS
Hey! Watch your mouth! I'm in charge here, and I say play on!

KANT slowly skates toward the penalty bench, lifting his arms towards the ceiling.

KANT
You don't control me! I contest your authority, with courage and resolve. From now on, the enlightenment will be my guide.

RAWLS temporarily looks up at the ceiling lights without under-standing. When he looks down again, he sees KANT approaching the penalty bench.

RAWLS
Oh no you don't! Get back here! I didn't give you any penalty!

KANT
But I deserve one! It's off the bench for me! Corrupt referee!

RAWLS
Okay, you want to disobey my orders?

RAWLS whistles.

RAWLS
Number 12, two minutes for unsportsmanlike conduct.

3. INT. – DRESSING ROOM – NIGHT

DESCARTES (sighing)
So, it was your fault! Immanuel, from now on, you're going to have to be a little less categorical with your imperatives . . . Let's forget about discipline for the time being. Instead, I'm going to teach you the guiding precepts of hockey.

BENTHAM
That's absurd! This isn't the peewees! We already know how to play hockey!

DESCARTES
Aha! There you go! You just violated the first precept: From now on you are to avoid precipitancy and only accept things as true that cannot be doubted.

HERACLITUS
Well, one thing's for sure about hockey: either you have it or you don't.

ZENO
And you don't have it! Eh, Hairy Boy?!

HERACLITUS
Pff! All I wanted to say was that hockey is a game of opposition.

DESCARTES
No! Hockey is a multitude of parts, a whole range of difficulties! That leads me to the second precept: divide every difficulty into as many parts as possible, the better to solve it.

BENTHAM
So, we just solve the problems we're given?

DESCARTES
There's more to it than that. . . Listen to the third precept: conduct your thoughts and actions in order, starting with the simplest objects and moving to the more complex ones.

PASCAL
That's easy! You start playing hockey by yourself, then you learn how to play with others and. . .

DESCARTES
It's harder than you think! You have to account for everything: skating, puck control, passing, shooting, defence, offence, strategy, discipline, sportsmanship. . . and more. You can't leave anything out. And that's the fourth precept: review the game so generally that nothing is omitted.

As the players are digesting all of this, an ICE TECHNICIAN enters the dressing room.

ICE TECHNICIAN
Hello Mr. Descartes, hello gentlemen. . . We're sorry, but there's a problem with the ice. It'll be an hour before you can practice. My boss asked me to let you watch the TV and also says you can use the Internet in his office if you wish. Here are the keys and the remote control. Again, our apologies.

The ICE TECHNICIAN exits.

DESCARTES
Well, are there any questions?

HOBBES raises his hand.

HOBBES
Now do I have time for a poutine?

DESCARTES (sighing)
Any questions about the precepts I told you about!

PASCAL
I see that it's an orderly approach, but what about feelings? What of instincts?

DESCARTES
Forget about them! Jean-Jacques may have let you waste your time with these, but not on my watch!

PASCAL
But reason has its limits! Why not bet on faith? And isn't it true that you need heart to play too?

DESCARTES
Forget about faith and heart! With well-directed reason, you can achieve anything. Now, if there are no further questions, I'll see you a little later on the ice! Until then, I'll leave you to meditate on everything I've said. . .

DESCARTES exits and closes the door behind him.

HOBBES
Our old coach said that the man who meditates is a depraved animal. . .

DIOGENES
Pff. . . Do you really think we're going to meditate? We're just going to watch TV to kill time.

DIOGENES walks towards the TV and turns it on as HOBBES watches him intently.

DIOGENES
Yeah, doofus! You have time to go get a poutine! And while you're at it, bring me back some fries . . . but not in a Styrofoam container, that's not environmentally friendly . . . Just use . . . uh . . . pita bread!

PASCAL
Listen! The news is about to start.

I would like to thank Jacques Vaillancourt and Mira Cliche for their suggestions on previous versions of this piece.

This text originally appeared in *Médiane* (Vol. 2, no. 2 and Vol. 3, no. 1).

Biographies of thinkers
Zeno of Elea (c. 490–430 BCE): A disciple of Parmenides, who advocated the use of reason rather than the senses in order to know reality. Zeno presented some paradoxes as an attempt to deny the existence of movement and change.

Heraclitus of Ephesus (c. 540–480 BCE): Nicknamed "The Obscure" because of his unclear writing style, he explained reality as being fire or "becoming," a perpetual change driven by the conflict of opposites. He wrote, "No man ever steps in the same river twice" to illustrate the idea that nothing is permanent.

Diogenes of Sinope (c. 412–324 BCE): Known as "the dog," he represented the cynic school, which rejected social conventions and authority, advocating for the independence of the individual. Diogenes is an inexhaustible source of anecdotes: it is said that he lived in a wine barrel with a bare minimum of possessions, that he spat in the faces of people passing by, and that he masturbated in the public square. Alexander the Great once asked Diogenes what he wanted, to which he responded, "Stand out of my sunlight."

Immanuel Kant (1724–1804): German Enlightenment philosopher who proposed "transcendental idealism," a theory of knowledge that differed from traditional rationalism and empiricism. He is recognized for having used reason to construct a very strict morality of duty. It is said that he was so regimented in going for his daily walk that people could set their watches to it. He is not known to have had any romantic relationships and rarely left his native city of Königsberg, where he grew up and taught. He was a friendly sort and was content to enjoy simple activities: meals with friends, reading, and writing.

Thomas Hobbes (1588–1679): English philosopher mainly recognized for his work in political philosophy. He revived the idea that "man is wolf to man." In such a context, characterized by ever-present mistrust and danger, he felt that citizens should concede their natural rights to a sovereign, and in turn receive the protection of their goods. He probably never enjoyed a poutine in his life.

George Berkeley (1685–1753): Bishop of Cloyne and idealist philosopher noted for his radical empiricism. The basic idea of his philosophy was that we can only experience impressions and ideas of things, and we cannot experience that which, in an abstract sense, is reducible to the existence of things.

René Descartes (1596–1650): French philosopher famous for writing the *Metaphysical Meditations* and *Discourse on the Method*, in which he set out four basic precepts to help people guide their reason. With the goal of starting at the very beginning and founding knowledge on solid bases, he used systematic doubt and kept only ideas that were "clear and distinct."

Gottfried Wilhelm Leibniz (1646–1716): German scientist, mathematician, and rationalist philosopher. His *New Essays on Human Understanding* popularized the concept of "monads," simple substances with no component parts. He discovered differential and integral calculus at the same time as Newton did.

Gorgias of Leontini (c. 487–380 BCE): Greek sophist who taught the art of rhetoric. He used logic to deny being. In his *On the Non-Existent*, he wrote that nothing exists; that even if something existed, we would not be able to know it; and that even if someone could know it, they would be unable to explain it to others.

Jeremy Bentham (1748–1832): English philosopher, a proponent of utilitarianism, which aims to achieve the common good by morally evaluating actions in terms of the pain and pleasure they cause.

John Rawls (1921–2002): American philosopher and professor of political philosophy at Harvard. In his book *A Theory of Justice*, he proposed a way to found a society that achieves a maximum of fairness by using notions such as the "veil of ignorance" and the "original position."

Blaise Pascal (1623–1662): French Philosopher, physicist, and mathematician. In his *Pensées*, he defended the Christian religion, criticized momentary pleasure, and framed human dignity as being reliant on the ability to think and wager on the existence of God.

Jean-Jacques Rousseau (1712–1778): Philosopher of Swiss origin who spent most of his life in France. In the context of the heightened rationalism of the Enlightenment, he criticized the vices of society and praised liberty, passion, and feeling and advocated for a life that was simpler and closer to nature.

Friedrich Nietzsche (1844–1900): German philosopher celebrated for his critique of religion, morality, culture, and philosophy. He taught readers "how philosophize with a hammer" to bring down idols, such as those ideals created by philosophers and people of faith. For him, the culmination of the will to power was in affirming the *Übermensch* (the superman). He went mad towards the end of his life.

Niccolò Machiavelli (1469–1527): Italian thinker and politician. In his book *The Prince*, he set out a pragmatic approach and taught political leaders the art of governing in order to gain and keep power, without regard for how.

Towards a Kantian Hockey

Chantal Santerre
(with Normand Baillargeon)

A Saturday night, in the winter of 2023

Granddaughter: "Grandpa, come watch the hockey game with me; the Montréal Canadiens are playing the New York Islanders."

Grandfather: "You know I haven't watched hockey since they banned checking."

Granddaughter (insistent): "But the captain of the Islanders is my favourite player. He can handle the puck like anything. I want you to see it. Do it for me. Come on, it would make me happy if you watched the game with me."

Grandfather (resigned): "Oh, fine. The things we do for our grandkids! I vowed never to watch hockey again. And lord knows I'm hard-headed."

A few minutes later, they are seated watching the game.

Grandfather: "Hey, where are all the referees? I can only see one of them. . . And what's number 8 doing? Did he just send himself to the penalty bench? And the Canadiens' coach: why did he say his own team's goal didn't count because it was offside? I don't understand anything anymore! But you were right about the captain of the Islanders: it is exciting to see him go at the net with that puck. Now that's what I call talent! Reminds me of Bobby Orr or Guy Lafleur. Ah! Guy Lafleur, now there was a. . ."

The girl's father, the grandfather's son, chimes in: "You know, Dad, hockey's changed a lot since you last watched it. It didn't just happen overnight, though. Things changed little by little, as people began to focus on the quality of the playing rather than the quantity of muscle. You see that player you like so much? Well, he's almost 40 years old. He's in great shape and still has a few good years left. And remember how Bobby Orr quit playing at 30 because of his problems with his right knee, which his opponents would go after to slow him down."[1]

~

Players sending themselves to the penalty bench? Coaches refusing to count a goal scored by their own team? A game with only one referee?

The grandfather in this story has discovered what we'll be calling Kantian hockey in this chapter, which is to say hockey played in an ethical spirit. That means following a moral theory developed by one of the most important and influential philosophers in history, Immanuel Kant (1724–1804)—hence Kantian hockey.

In this chapter we'll look at Kant's perspective on ethics and apply it to hockey in order to imagine what our national sport might look like under a Kantian approach.

We contend that applying Kant's ethics to hockey, even if it fails to produce all the results attributed to him in the imaginary scene above, would still represent a significant improvement to both the quality of play and the spectacle. Yes, the game might lose a bit of its rough edge, but what we lose in roughness we would make up for in subtlety—particularly because we would reduce all kinds of barriers that prevent true talent from shining through. In Kantian hockey, we'd get our excitement not from rough body checks and fights, but instead from the players' skills, the quality of their play, and the athletic and human virtues they display.

Considering how important hockey is to the myth and imagination of Québécois, and also how young children are when confronted with ethical issues on the ice, we feel that the dose of Kant we hope to inject into the sport could make a positive difference

---

1.   Translator's note: In this fictional scenario, the author refers to Orr's right knee. In reality, it was Orr's left knee that gave him the most trouble.

when it comes to morality in young people, specifically by providing them with athletes who model exemplary ethical behaviour.

Huddle! Here's the plan.

First off, we'll present the principles of Kant's ethics (section 1), which we'll refer to throughout the chapter. In parallel, we'll also present the utilitarian ethics, which is another major ethical system (perhaps the only one) that is frequently referred to in the search for solutions to ethical problems, especially when it comes to sports.

Next, we'll lay out the principles of Kantian hockey (section 2) and show how they might affect certain aspects of the game as well as the behaviour of some of the people involved (section 3).

We'll conclude by proposing a few ways in which we can help foster our preferred values and practices in the real world.

1. Kant's ethics and utilitarian ethics

Imagine the following situation. In the hospital where you volunteer, a sickly old man with no heirs pulls you aside and tells you that he's hidden $1 million cash. He tells you where to find the money and asks you to donate it to the Montréal Canadiens, his favourite hockey team, upon his death. You promise him you will. Moments later, the man is dead.

It so happens that you also know that the hospital is in dire need of an important piece of medical equipment that it cannot afford on its own and that costs, coincidentally, $1 million.

What do you do?

A utilitarian is basically someone who thinks that the right course to take should be determined by examining the positive and negative consequences that will ensue from an action, taking into account all the people who will experience these consequences and attributing equal value to each person. "The greatest good for the greatest number": this is the famous motto that utilitarians live by.

What would a utilitarian do in this imaginary scenario?

The utilitarian might reason as follows: the medical apparatus equipment would save lives, so purchasing it would have significant and highly desirable consequences for many people. The old man, for his part, is dead and won't suffer as a result of this decision; he'll never know. And finally, the Montréal Canadiens don't need the money that badly: the good it would do for the team is a drop in the bucket compared to the good the equipment would do for all those patients. Having reached the end of this calculation, the utilitarian would advise you to purchase the equipment even though this means breaking your promise to the old man.

Does this reasoning rub you the wrong way? Do you find it morally unacceptable? If so, you probably side with the ethical theories we call non-consequentialist. These theories posit that the morality of an act depends on something other than its consequences. If you search for such a theory, you will soon come across an ethical theory called deontology, which was proposed by Immanuel Kant (1724–1804) and is perhaps the most influential of the non-consequentialist ethical systems.

Kant would say that the consequences, in this particular case and in all others, have nothing to do with morality. He would tell you that a promise is a promise, and you should keep yours. In fact, Kant thought we should refuse to make promises we do not wish to keep, since a promise is by definition something we must keep.

The key word here is "must," and the morality that Kant proposes is aptly called "deontology"—from the Greek word "*deos*" meaning "duty."[2] This nomenclature points to an important part of what Kant affirms: that an action is moral when it is done out of duty.

In simple terms, here's what Kant suggests.

An action is moral if it is done with a good intention or will, and this good will is one that acts through duty in accordance with principles that our (practical) reason can apply.

To begin with, this means that if I give money to homeless people out of pity or compassion, I am not acting morally: I may be performing an action that matches what is required by morality,

---

2. This is why professional codes that set out members' duties and responsibilities are called codes of ethics or codes of deontology; they exist in order to protect the people who will use the services offered by members of these associations. Codes of ethics of the various sports associations are also based on an ethic of duty in the sense that they seek to establish prescriptions that we would want to see universalized.

but I am not acting morally. In order to do that, I must act out of duty according to the rational rule.

What rule is that? Kant thinks that we will determine this rule by asking whether an action conforms to what he calls the categorical imperative. It is crucial to fully understand what he means by this.

Certain things become duties if we desire certain other things. For example, if I want to become a doctor, then I must study. Kant calls this a hypothetical imperative (if X, then Y).

But for Kant, morality has to do with categorical duties, which are unconditional. These duties say, "You must. Period." In a given situation, we determine what the duty is by running all possible actions through the categorical imperative test. Here is one formulation: "Act only according to that maxim whereby you can, at the same time, will that it should become a universal law without contradiction."[3] This means that you must ask yourself whether you could universalize the principle you propose to follow. If you can, that's the way to go. Seen in this light, Kant's view actually resembles the old golden rule of morality ("Don't do to others what you wouldn't want them to do to you").

Back to the old man for a sec. Would we want people to make promises they have no intention of keeping? Kant says that admitting these acts is contradictory and that this action would kill the very institution of promising. Therefore, we have stumbled upon a moral duty: one must keep one's promises; one must do it because one must do it, end of discussion. And one shouldn't do it just to be well regarded in one's community, or because it would work to one's advantage in certain situations, and so on. Note also that this result was obtained through reason: Kant thought that we are rational beings for whom morality is not a matter of desire, happiness, or consequences, but of reason. The result (keep your promises) has no possible exceptions and is universal: we must keep our promises everywhere, at all times.

---

3. Immanuel Kant, *Grounding for the Metaphysics of Morals*, translated by James W. Ellington (Indianapolis: Hackett, 1993), p. 30.

Obviously, it's a tall order to live in accordance with these principles, and Kantian morality is rather strict and austere: some even call it rigid. Kant provides various formulations of his categorical imperative, and one of them humanizes the system somewhat: "Act in such a way that you treat humanity, whether in your own person or in the person of any other, never merely as a means to an end, but always at the same time as an end."[4] In other words: never use another human being; never treat someone else as a means to an end.

One final note: this line of thought figures into the ideals of the Enlightenment, the century whose spirit was summed up by Kant thus: "Have the courage to use your own intelligence." This statement is based on rationality, autonomy, and the recognition that that we are capable of giving ourselves our own laws.

The philosopher Alain summed up Kant's ethics as follows: morality is the knowledge that one is a spirit and that one is obligated to act ethically as a result. I couldn't have said it better myself. One contemporary philosopher, Alasdair MacIntyre, wrote that "For many people who have never heard of philosophy, let alone Kant, morality is roughly what Kant said it was."[5] In fact, after having learned about Kant's ideas on ethics, many people say this philosopher clearly articulates out loud all the things they already thought deep down in a more or less confused manner.

Time for a synopsis. The platform of beliefs proposed by Kant includes the idea that ethics is a matter of duties, which are to be performed unconditionally and that obligate us absolutely; it also includes the idea that one can use reason to determine the universal moral rules we must follow by asking ourselves whether the maxim we are considering following can be universalized.

Hopefully it's clear from this how the Kantian perspective differs from the utilitarian perspective. We think, for reasons we cannot fully discuss in detail here (but see the box below), that Kant is on the right side of this enormous debate and that ethics must be

---

4. Ibid.
5. Alasdair MacIntyre, *A Short History of Ethics* (London and New York: Routledge & Kegan Paul, 1966), p. 190.

Some criticisms of the utilitarian position

Utilitarianism essentially posits two things: first, that in order to judge the morality of an action, it's sufficient to consider its consequences and only these, and second, that consequences are to be evaluated in terms of what we will call (for brevity's sake) happiness and only in terms of this. We have stated above that both these positions are erroneous: in other words, to consider only consequences is an error, and to value happiness in a utilitarian fashion is also an error.

First let's consider what's wrong with examining consequences (to the exclusion of all else). Is this even possible? It's not always obvious. The first problem is determining what exactly the consequences of a given action will be. There are plenty of examples of actions that have unintended—and unpredictable—consequences. La petite Mafalda, in the comic strip of the same name, argued along these lines when she asked (more or less) what kind of a world this would be if Karl Marx had just agreed to eat his soup. This type of argument is interesting because, obviously, in not allowing us to predict the probable outcomes of the infinite options available to us with a certain assurance, the utilitarian perspective becomes hard to maintain. But that's not all.

Suppose that in a given context, an action X yields 100 hedons (units of happiness). Action Y also yields the same number of hedons, and the only difference between the two is that X requires us to lie. From a utilitarian standpoint, the two actions would be morally equivalent. This runs counter to our intuitions and suggests that perhaps there is more to the story than just outcomes.

Even worse, it's not hard to imagine cases in which the utilitarian calculus leads would recommend an action that would seem highly immoral. For instance, picture yourself in a city that is on the brink of imploding from racial violence. If you allow the crowd to hang a man you know to be innocent, the situation will be defused and you will have avoided a bloodbath. According to the utilitarian calculation, the man ought to be hanged.

Furthermore, utilitarians have been severely criticized for their reflex of considering only happiness (meaning their own hedonism). In simple terms, we don't seek happiness for its own sake: things that make us happy (or unhappy) do so because they align with our values (or not)—not the reverse. Contemporary utilitarians have come up with various methods to avoid these problems, but we will leave these for another day. (C.S.)

grounded in reason and duty rather than an examination of consequences to actions.

How does the Kantian view play out when applied to hockey? Read on.

2. Prolegomena to a future Kantian version of hockey

As a salute to Kant,[6] we propose three principles that could well serve as the platform on which to base a version of hockey modelled on Kant's ethics.

Let's examine each in turn.

First principle: Respect for rules

Every sport has its rules, and we commonly distinguish between two major kinds.

The first kind are called constitutive rules: these are basically the ones that defines the parameters of the game—they dictate the dimensions of the playing surface, delineate the spaces, specify how goals are scored, and so forth. In hockey, the constitutive rules cover various considerations like the maximum allowable curve on

---

6. This is inspired by ideas presented by David Cruise Malloy, Saul Ross, and Dwight H. Zakus, *Sport Ethics: Concepts and Cases in Sport and Recreation* (Toronto: Thompson Educational Publishing Inc., 2003).

a hockey stick, the exact size of the net, and thousands of other things.

But all sports also have the second kind, which are known as prohibitive rules: these are the rules that define and determine what's not allowed. In hockey, for example, there are prohibitive rules against hitting another player in the head, rules against high-sticking, rules against charging—all of which are precisely defined—and so on.

When a player voluntarily decides to participate in a sport, we have to assume (if indeed we are entitled to assume anything) first that he's aware of the rules of the sport, and second that he agrees to follow them. Indeed, Fraleigh speaks of this obligation imposed upon the players to honour the rules of their sport as they would a promise to fulfil their end of a tacit social contract.[7] Accordingly, we can be sure that playing in an honest fashion and following the rules means abiding by the promise the player made when he agreed to participate in the sport.

As we saw earlier, from a Kantian point of view, keeping our promises is a duty that can be founded in reason by examining the very nature of what promises are: our failure to keep them would abolish the very institution of promising. Similarly, adhering to the constitutive and prohibitive rules of a sport is necessarily inherent not only to the practice of the sport, but even to its very existence, because these rules are what define it in the first place.

Therefore, a commitment to abide by the rules, which is made by any person who voluntarily decides to play a sport, can serve as the first principle of a Kantian conception of sport in general and hockey in particular.

Kant leads 1 to 0!

Second principle: Respect for people
One of the formulations of the categorical imperative, as we will recall, calls us to "act in such a way that you treat humanity, whether in your own person or in the person of any other, never

---

7. Warren P. Fraleigh, *Right Actions in Sport: Ethics for Contestants* (Champaigne: Human Kinetics Publishers, 1984).

merely as a means to an end, but always at the same time as an end."[8]

This fundamental notion is filled with ethical implications. Its ramifications for sport are plainly decisive, as they impose a duty to treat one's opponent (and oneself) as an end and never a means.

To put it simply, this implies that Kantian hockey cannot exist unless there is a profound respect for human beings and unless everything else is subordinate to this.

By "everything else," we mean the many discussions and debates that will, in practice, be raised by the application of this principle. At what point, and by what practice exactly, is a player treated as a means to an end, either by someone else or by himself? How is this determined? Who decides? These questions are complex yet unavoidable, and we cannot answer them here. Suffice it to note three things about them.

The first is that hockey already has prohibitive rules that *mutatis mutandis* are completely in keeping with Kantian hockey, in spirit if not in letter. In practice, however, they too often go unrespected, both by players and by the authorities. This situation, and the message that it sends to players, coaches, referees, and spectators, is regrettable. Because of it, the exact rules of the game have become fuzzy and impossible to determine; they tend to vary according to the circumstances, the players involved, or even the location. When we have a rule on the books prohibiting fighting but sometimes let it slide, we send a mixed message. This doublespeak is present in many other practices that are theoretically illegal yet tolerated or even encouraged in reality. This is a huge barrier to the practice of Kantian hockey.

Our second note is that, while it may be difficult to apply certain principles (and we don't deny it), there are many specific, concrete cases in which their application poses no problem whatsoever—in which the implications are completely cut and dried—and yet the principle is still not followed. Hockey fans can think of many examples, but one clear-cut case would be a coach forcing an injured player to play while on medication in order to increase the team's chances of winning—even if playing in this

---

8.   Immanuel Kant, *Grounding for the Metaphysics of Morals*, p. 30.

> ### The report that collected dust
>
> Having decided it was important to address the issue of violence in hockey and its effects on player safety from a medical perspective, the Canadian Academy of Sport and Exercise Medicine produced a major report in 1988 on violence and injuries in ice hockey (Canadian Academy of Sport Medicine, *Position Statement: Violence and Injuries in Ice Hockey* [1988]).
>
> Recommendations of the report included:
>
> 1. That fights be banned from hockey altogether.
> 2. That a major program be established to help educate coaches, trainers, players, and parents in order to deinstitutionalize the currently accepted norms surrounding violence and injuries.
> 3. That the practice of boarding be banned from the minor levels of hockey that are not intended to prepare players for professional and international careers.
>
> The authors supported their recommendations as follows: "It is clear from most studies that body checking, high sticking and fighting for the puck are the most common source of injury of all types. It has been shown that body checking does not provide an outlet for aggression but, in fact, leads to increased levels of aggression and illegal acts." (C.S.)

state puts the player's health and career in grave danger. Such a coach would be treating the player as a means to an end.

Our third note has to do with being a good sport. Kant's second principle invites us to revive what in other times was called sportsmanship, understood here as respect for rules and consideration for one's opponent. At one time, this was considered extremely important in sports: what's standing in the way of us bringing it back in this day and age?

Most often the answer to this question (and correctly so, we feel) is the excessive emphasis that is now placed on winning. This attitude was nicely captured by Vince Lombardi, who said, "Winning isn't everything, it's the only thing."[9] In his book *Mortal Engines* (1992), professor John Hoberman, a keen observer of the contemporary sports scene, does a good job of explaining the evolution from sportsmanship to so much emphasis (too much, in fact) on victory:

> Traditionally, the rules of sportsmanship determined the relations between athletes, and their athletic abilities were less important than their honourable intentions; their muscles counted for less than their intentions. The nineteenth-century gentleman did not pursue his athletic training with the same determination as the contemporary athlete, even of the lower class, who sometimes must go as far as taking drugs. This ethos of honourable restraint has not disappeared, but it has ceded ground to the modern world's fixation on performance and productivity, which has replaced the ideal of sportsmanship. Indeed, the principle of performance has practically supplanted the ideal of restraint for athletes in the dominant ethos of elite sport.[10]

Hoberman suggests that this development, in which utilitarianism intermingles with widespread consumerism and materialism, takes us from a humanist view of the athlete to a conception of the athlete as merely a bodily machine. The attitude that we used to see only at the elite level appears today at all levels.

The Kantian perspective calls for a healthy reversal of these values and invites us to refuse to accept that the worst behaviours during a game can be considered, even if only implicitly or occasionally, acceptable means to reach this singular and absolute goal of winning.

After two periods of play, Kant leads 2 to 0!

---

9. Cited by David Cruise Malloy, Saul Ross, and Dwight H. Zakus, *Sport Ethics*, p. 118.
10. John Hoberman, *Mortal Engines: The Science of Performance and the Dehumanization of Sport* (New York: The Free Press, 1992).

> ## The Canadian Centre for Ethics in Sport (CCES) and sportsmanship
>
> "The notion of sportsmanship is a universal concept that underlies all sports. Without sportsmanship, sport is meaningless. Worse still, it can be a harmful experience for participants."
>
> "When our children interact with each other in sport, their capacity to make the choices required by sportsmanship develops along with their capacity to conceive of and distinguish what contributes to a gratifying and enriching life in society."
> (Source: http://www.cces.ca/forms/index.cfm?dsp=template&act=view3&template_id=122&lang=f)
>
> "Because of its crucial role in the moral development of members of our communities, sport must be ethical—and not only fair—for participants. The behaviour of individuals in sport, as well as the manner in which the sports system operates, must correspond to our notions of morality, justice, and respect for people and for human excellence."
> (Source: http://www.cces.ca/forms/index.cfm?dsp=template&act=view3&template_id=62&lang=f) (C.S.)

Third principle: Responsibility and duty

The notion of responsibility is obviously defined in relation to the role a person must fulfil and the tasks he must accomplish.

An athlete, like every other person, is responsible for his behaviour if he is autonomous and deliberately chooses to act in a certain way: his autonomy presupposes that he is free to choose and endowed with the ability to reason. For Kant, as we have seen, this autonomy and this rationality are two central elements of ethics that give us the courage to act as responsible beings and to use our own intelligence.

This sense of duty and responsibility is the third and final principle we would like to propose for a Kantian style of hockey.

The NHL and eye injuries

Hockey is a sport with an intrinsically high risk of injury: pucks, hockey sticks, and skate blades are all objects that can seriously hurt people, even if used according to the rules.

The Canada Safety Council (Conseil canadien de la sécurité, "Les blessures dans la LNH soulèvent des préoccupations," *Nouvelles* Vol. XLIV, No. 2, April 2000) is concerned about the NHL's inflexibility regarding protective gear. The wearing of masks and visors approved by the Canadian Standards Association (CSA) would reduce the number of serious eye and head injuries sustained by professional hockey players. In the NHL, players who don't wear masks account for 95 percent of all injuries to the eyes and face requiring medical attention (Canada Safety Council, "Smart Players Protect Their Eyes." https://canadasafetycouncil.org/child-safety/smart-players-protect-their-eyes. Accessed on July 19, 2008).

With this in mind, why does the NHL refuse to make safety equipment mandatory? Does it not have a responsibility to its players? Does it not have a responsibility to society in general? (C.S.)

As we have seen, when a hockey player or coach goes into hockey (whether amateur or professional), he freely accepts the tacit social contract to abide by the rules. Therefore, it is normal and consistent to assume he will be held responsible if he breaks the rules: no participant in the sport can blame anyone else or hide behind any excuse to avoid this duty and responsibility.

Players and coaches, like everyone else, must acknowledge that they are "absolutely obligated" to comply with the rules of the game they accepted by agreeing to participate in hockey and that they're responsible for their actions. In summary, Kantian hockey depends on the responsibility of every participant and their desire to do their duty.

The game ends with a decisive victory for Kant: 3 to 0!

What would such a game look like? This question would provide ample fodder for debate, discussion, and interpretation. We're going to give this game 110 percent by attempting to answer it in the following section. Break!

3. Kantian hockey: An overview

In Kantian hockey, all constitutive rules would of course stay the same without exception. The list of prohibitive rules would be expanded to include all unethical behaviours. Fighting, charging, high-sticking, all of which are technically prohibited but nevertheless tacitly tolerated because they're considered part of the game, would be strictly forbidden. Safety equipment such as helmets, visors, and neck guards would be mandatory, because not wearing them would place players at great risk of injury, which would not be respectful of their physical integrity. The nature of boarding and checking would substantially change and could even be removed altogether.

The league management would establish rules like these and others to protect the physical integrity of its players. Violent behaviour would be prohibited by very strict rules that, if broken, could see offending players banned from the league, thus sending a clear message about our refusal to accept these behaviours. Referees would be given more power to enforce the rules, thus ensuring that they feel supported in their work.

Coaches would insist that their players act respectfully towards their opponents and still demand the best of them with a view to winning honourably. Coaches would not abuse the power and authority they hold over their players by virtue of their role. Out of respect for all players, they would encourage their players to abide by the rules of the game and to respect the constraints and limitations that allow the sport to exist. They would also overtly condemn all unethical conduct.

Players would respect their opponents as much as they do their own teammates. They would not purposely seek to injure or otherwise hinder them by any means that contravene the rules. They would seek to outdo their opponents by the quality of their playing, their puck-handling ability, their speed, and their team's overall quality. They would take pride in demonstrating ethical behaviour. They would never be put in a situation where the rules say one thing and the opposite is tolerated in practice. They would always be able to identify what is expected of them, and these expectations would be universalizable.

The referees, of course, would enforce the rules, but all stakeholders in the league would understand and accept them; everyone would support the referees in their work.

The spectators would appreciate the beauty of the game, no longer constantly frustrated by players breaking the rules and referees not enforcing them consistently. They would enjoy a beautiful evening of genuine hockey that isn't constantly interrupted by boarding, slashing, elbowing, and interference calls. Finally, the spectacle they go to see would embody the values they themselves aspire to uphold.

We're definitely a ways away from this. How do we get there? We'll finish this text with a few modest proposals in response to this question.

Prospective: The game plan

In *Why Sport? An Introduction to the Philosophy of Sport*, Sheryle Bergmann Drewe reports on the results of a study she conducted with high-level university athletes. She asked them to cite examples of situations in which they faced ethical issues and explain how they resolved (or didn't resolve) the problems posed by these issues.[11]

As it turned out, the hockey players interviewed in the study were unable to identify a single ethical issue they faced in the practice of their sport.[12] They didn't deny that fights, vicious blows, breaches of the rules, and so on happen in hockey, but they felt that in spite of all that, these actions were justified because that's how the sport was played. Evidently, there's some important teaching

---

11.   Sheryle Bergmann Drewe, *Why Sport? An Introduction to the Philosophy of Sport* (Toronto: Thompson Educational Pub, 2003).
12.   Ibid., p. 95.

that needs to happen here. And so our first recommendation is just that: to educate people.

Our second recommendation is as follows: this education work could easily be supported by existing sports codes of ethics, in which Kant's influence is already apparent, particularly in terms of insisting on respect for people; protection against injury; the development of a code of ethics towards others; notions of justice, impartiality, and fairness; and appeals to an ethics of responsibility.

This brings us to our final recommendation. This teaching work requires a major paradigm shift on the part of all those involved in hockey, from parents to players, from coaches to spectators. Such a shift would make it possible to pass on the culture of sportsmanship we mentioned earlier.

If this is to be achieved, my inner Kantian can already see that a dose of virtue ethics, that other great ethical tradition begun by Aristotle, is called for. That tradition has the advantage of reminding us that if Kantian ethics defines what we must do and what approach we should take, it will be desirable to teach hockey players from an early age the meaning of sportsmanship the values that go along with it. These virtues, which we discover through reason and which we have a duty to follow, are learned, at least in part, by putting them into practice. In the same way that we become courageous by doing courageous acts, we become good sports by playing in a spirit of sportsmanship.

This last comment inevitably brings up the question of whether Kant's ethics can be easily reconciled with Aristotle's, both in theory and in practice. I'm not a philosopher by profession, so I should probably leave it to others to tackle this one. But I can't help thinking they would complement each other nicely!

Further reading
On Kantian ethics
Kant's conceptions of ethics are mainly exposed in the following two works: *Groundwork of the Metaphysics of Morals* and *Critique of Practical Reason*. There have been many editions of both.

LEQUAN, Mai. *La philosophie morale de Kant*. Paris: Seuil, 2001.
    Provides an accessible analysis of these texts.

On sport ethics

In addition to the works cited in the text, we recommend:

FRALEIGH, Warren P. *Right Actions in Sport: Ethics for Contestants.* Champaigne: Human Kinetics Publishers, 1984.

HYLAND, Drew A. *Philosophy of Sport. Paragon Issues in Philosophy.* New York: Paragon House, 1990.

MALLOY, David Cruise, Saul ROSS, and Dwight H. ZAKUS. *Sport Ethics: Concepts and Cases in Sport and Recreation.* Toronto: Thompson Educational Publishing Inc., 2003.

MORGAN, William J. and Klaus V. MEIER (eds.). *Philosophic Inquiry in Sport.* Champaign, Ill.: Human Kinetics Publishers, 1988.

> The second section of this book (pp. 139–373) is almost entirely dedicated to ethical issues in sport.

Kierkegaard and the Art of Goaltending

Charles Le Blanc

Introduction

The port of Copenhagen doesn't freeze over in wintertime. Already this says a lot about the practicality of playing a sport like hockey there. Of course, closer to the Limfjord, there are lots of ponds you could skate on, but the closest thing you'll find to sticks there are cattails. Besides, a frozen toad would never do for a puck—much too bouncy—and the Danes are so clean their country is completely devoid of "meadow muffins," which, as legend has it, were what Georges Vézina used to master the art of the pass. So, with conditions like these, it's no surprise that Denmark has no tradition of hockey.

The greatest philosopher of this hockeyless nation was Søren Kierkegaard, a feeble and slightly hunchbacked figure. Kierkegaard was a great proponent of walking (yet makes no mention of skating anywhere in his entire catalogue). He was an introspective sort, the type of guy whose gaze was cast downward physically and inward morally, and he didn't attach all that much importance to sport. His sullen disposition and incurable individualism would have made him a rather poor team player. All things considered, it may strike you as strange that we should turn to such a man as Kierkegaard, from such a country as Denmark, to better understand the delicate art of goaltending. But as we will see, his works contain many clues to this effect.

The concept of angst

We have Kierkegaard to thank for one of the most in-depth analyses ever written on the concept of anxiety, or angst as it is often translated.

Existence, with all the myriad situations that characterize it, offers humans an infinite number of possibilities. Looking back on my days as a young student in Germany, I remember drawing a breath of intoxicating freedom as I set foot in university for the first time. First of all there was the hodgepodge of students: the boys ill-shaven (environmentalists before their time) and the girls wearing thickly knit sweaters with roll-up collars that shielded anyone who laid eyes on them from all temptation. There was also an endless list of courses with so many enticing subjects to choose from that I just couldn't decide: a seminar on Antigone, that course on Plato's *Timaeus*, this course on the relationship between nature and art in classic German texts, and on and on. What option could I select without immediately knowing I had sacrificed something of what I could fully become as a human? With Antigone, I would have honed my sense of duty; with *Timaeus*, I would have glimpsed the world's soul and understood that madness and ignorance are what cause the maladies of the soul; and with the German classics, my every sigh would have become pregnant with meaning. Any one of these choices could have been decisive for me, for my personhood. Certain kinds of knowledge are so special that they shape us as individuals. There is no Platonic concept of human after which all concrete human beings are modelled, no ideal mould in which we are all cast. Rather, there are a variety of *concrete* concepts—beauty, truth, art, love, duty, and so on—that form the multitude of *concrete* humans and that we all come from: you, me, everyone.

To put it briefly, my student years were ones of *possibility*—I could still dream of doing this or that, being this thing or that thing, going here or there. But I found myself bombarded by this mishmash of possibilities all at once, and I was paralyzed. The seizing up of the human soul when faced with what it *could* do but with no certainty about the *result*, that clamminess in the palms, that lump in the throat, that's *angst*.

Kierkegaard defined angst as *the lived experience of possibility* of that which might be *but which is not yet*. Angst is fuelled by the fact that its object is not determined and cannot be identified *objectively*.[1] Kierkegaard developed these ideas in a book he published in 1844 under a pseudonym, as was his custom—in this case Vigilius Haufniensis (literally, the Watchman of Copenhagen). He says that humans, who are constantly confronted with the possible, are permanently in a state of angst, and this angst outweighs their freedom to act—a bit like me, as a poor student in Germany, who on the spur of the moment could have dropped out of school and gone hiking through the Harz mountains, or answered the call of the sirens (which in Lower Saxony, as I recall, wore thick sweaters with roll-up necks). In other words, I could have done whatever I wanted. *Possibility, freedom, and angst are all intrinsically linked.* Together, they form a sort of triumvirate of the human condition.

Kierkegaard adds another essential feature to his interpretation of angst. If humans didn't have minds, they wouldn't be able to appreciate the possibilities that already accompany their place in the world. The human mind, which is capable of great things (although more readily applied to petty affairs), makes us fully conscious of the possibilities that surround us. If we had no mind or intellect, we would not experience angst. Kierkegaard concludes by saying that *angst is linked to the very spirituality of humans* and suggests that "If a human being were a beast or an angel, he could not be in angst."[2] If he were an angel, he would know the cause of it; if he were a beast, he would not know the power of it.

All of this plays into the exercise of evaluating the goaltender's performance in hockey. I have always felt that using statistics to measure a goaltender's worth was profoundly superficial, as if the best save percentage or the number of goals against per game were somehow the true measure of a player. Personally, I feel that the level of angst is the best benchmark to use in evaluating the talent

---

1. This is what distinguishes *angst* from *fear*.
2. Søren Kierkegaard, *The Concept of Anxiety: A Simple Psychologically Orienting Deliberation on the Dogmatic Issue of Hereditary Sin*, Kierkegaard's Writings, VIII, translated by Reidar Thomte, in collaboration with Albert B. Anderson (Princeton, N.J: Princeton University Press, 1980), p. 155.

of the goalie, who I also think is the most important player on the team. Or at least, he's the only one who isn't allowed to screw up. It is precisely on this denied right to err that the goalie's fundamental state of angst rests. Out there on the ice, skaters are permitted the occasional slip-up. In a pinch, there's always a teammate there to pick up the slack and save the play. The goaltender, by contrast, has no such margin, as this would lead to a goal for the other team. Now, consider this carefully: even though the goalie's right to err is denied him, *error remains within the realm of possibility*. The possibility of screwing up is, in a manner of speaking, made stronger by its own negation, which is why I say that *angst is the fundamental state that defines all goalies*. And if angst is the fundamental state, then angst is what should be used to evaluate performance.

A detailed study of the way in which angst acts on goalies would provide a truer metric of their workmanship and help us to finally understand the mysteries of certain miraculous saves. The phenomenology of angst has a promising future as a discipline in hockey. I'd like to visit a few brief examples to show you what such a phenomenology might look like.

Without a doubt, Tony Esposito was one of the great goalies of professional hockey. The famous number 35 of the Chicago Blackhawks was nicknamed "Tony O" because of his record 15 shutouts in one season (his rookie season, no less: 1969–1970). Yet despite all his talent, this man cannot be considered the greatest goalie in hockey history. He certainly exhibited a high degree of angst, of course. As evidence, I'll mention that he was one of the people who developed the "butterfly"[3] style, a style that is certainly well suited to the angst-ridden. This collapsing onto the self, with the legs at angles and the arms free to cover the upper part of the net is an inherently angsty gesture. The goaltender does not face the object he fears (the puck), but instead passively waits for it to hit him as he sinks into himself—one of the classic symptoms of angst.

Since we know there is a relationship between the art of goaltending and angst, it would seem that the substantial improvement

---

3. The great Glenn "Mr. Goalie" Hall must also be acknowledged as another pioneer of the technique.

in goalies we have seen over the last 15 years or so is directly pro-portional to the angst they experience; this is consistent with the rise in popularity of the butterfly style in professional hockey. However, Esposito's angst lacked a key feature that would have made him a truly out-standing goalie, if you'll pardon the pun. That element is the mind. Without dominance of mind, Kierkegaard teaches us, angst cannot be complete.

Patrick Roy was another great goaltender. But those who place him as the greatest goalie of all time don't understand angst. Either that or they haven't read the Danish philosopher (or this chapter). I don't deny that Roy was a highly angst-ridden goalie early in his career and when he won the Stanley Cup for the first time. His many tics show what an angsty sort he was. But, in time, he over-came them. The only way to conquer one's tics is to understand what triggers them. The instant Roy became aware of the cause of his angst, it converted into *fear*.[4] To my knowledge, this makes Roy a never-before-seen case in hockey's fabled history. He will still be associated with a certain type of angst because of his butterfly style. But the mind has never been the driving force or dominant char-acteristic of this player, who is noted for his aggression and fits of anger. So, regardless of what his stats say, he cannot be considered the greatest goalie in history, as angst played only a secondary role for him.

According to the idea I am developing here, namely that angst should be the yardstick we use to evaluate and judge goalies and in some sense explain the inspiration for their art, the greatest goalie of all was Ken Dryden. Some will object, pointing out that Dryden did not use with the butterfly technique, preferring a stand-up and side-to-side style. For this reason, the angstiness of his condition is disputed by some. But those people have not read his book *The Game*. Every page of this volume is practically dripping in angst. The book tells the reader all about his difficulties adapting to being on the team, his feeling of being an exception, his deep insecurity about being able to deliver a performance worthy of his teammates,

---

4. Introversion is the typical reaction of angst. The typical reaction of fear is vio-lence. Insofar as a player is fearful, he is violent. Insofar as he is dominated by angst, he is calm.

and more. Feeling like you're in over your head, believing your situation (and therefore your fragility) to be exceptional, having doubts about the *possibility* of succeeding: these are the three conditions inherent to the angsty. Everything about this goalie screams angst, right down to his trademark pose, standing upright and casually leaning on his stick. So suffocated was he by his angst that he needed to rest or else he would have snapped. And add to all this Dryden's domination of mind. He was—and still is—the only scholarly goalie in hockey history. With degrees in history and law, Dryden has a mind of the highest level imaginable, which makes him, *de facto*, the angstiest of all. For all these reasons, the honour of the greatest goalie of all time goes to him. Thus we have seen how a reading of angst can be fundamental in evaluating the work of a goaltender.

I have one final observation about angst in the context of hockey's gatekeepers. To borrow from Heidegger, whom all self-respecting philosophers are virtually required to mention these days, angst is the goalie's *being-in-the-situation*. It shows how every goalie is deeply embedded in a temporal situation that determines his *historicity* as a goalie.[5] Angst is what engages the goalie, makes him connect with the inner workings of the game, and allows him to respond *per anticipatio* to the opponent's dekes, for everything in angst is *per anticipatio*. The very definition of angst is being fearful in the face of an uncertain future, an undetermined risk. This makes angst a fear *per anticipatio*. In a sport where the puck travels over 175 kilometres an hour, you need a little anticipation. Therefore, the goalie *is in* the angst as much as he fuels it. One could even say that the calmer the goalie is, the less afflicted he is by angst, the less able he is to participate in the game and stick out his leg pad at an unexpected but nevertheless providential moment. The more angst-afflicted a goalie is, the more pregnant his *being-in-the-situation* is, the more talented he is, precisely because angst is what characterizes the hockey goalie. And this analysis—which will no doubt play a definitive role in the future of our national

---

5. Here it can be seen that the history of hockey goalies is inextricably linked to the history of angst.

sport—would never have been possible without the great Søren Kierkegaard.

The mask, or the selective pseudonym

Kierkegaard always had a poetic rapport with his writings.[6] His philosophical works were published exclusively under pseudonyms. He saw himself merely as the "stage prompter" for the opinions put forth by his characters who, although they were created by him, represented only themselves. Victor Eremita, Johannes the Seducer, Frater Taciturnus, Johannes de Silentio—all of these figures were and at the same time were not Søren Kierkegaard. This second-hand discourse constitutes what is called *indirect communication* in Kierkegaardian philosophy. The use of pseudonyms distances Kierkegaard from his text and gives him full licence with his characters, who in turn are free to follow their logic. That's why the Danish thinker could say that there wasn't a single word in any of the books written under fake names that really came from him.[7] This use of these literary masks plays into a broader theme that hinges upon whether it is possible to communicate the truth of subjectivity, the truth that counts not only for reason but for all of existence. Pseudonyms provide a distance that, paradoxically, cuts to the heart of basic issues in life's journey by showing that these problems aren't theoretical but actually represent *concrete possibilities of existence* embodied by the pseudonyms.

There is a clear link between this masking effect of Kierkegaard's use of pseudonyms and the hockey goaltender, for whom the mask plays a similar role.[8]

Conventional wisdom dictates that the goalie wears a mask to protect himself. This is true. But protection isn't the main reason why

6. See Søren Kiergaard, *Miettes philosophiques; Le concept de l'angoisse; Traité du désespoir*, translated by Knud Ferlov and Jean-Jacques Gateau (Paris: Gallimard, 1990), p. 217, note.

7. Søren Kierkegaard, *Post-scriptum aux miettes philosophiques*, translated by Paul Petit (Paris: Gallimard, 1989), p. 424.

8. It would be worth investigating whether Jacques Plante, the inventor of the goalie's mask, was an avid reader of Kierkegaard. Because of his interest in the mask, I believe I can affirm not only that he was a reader of the Danish philosopher but also that he was probably one of the great Kierkegaardians of the twentieth century.

the mask was introduced into the world of hockey. Jacques Plante, the famous Montréal Canadiens goalie, wore a mask during training but wasn't allowed to wear it during games. He noticed that when he wore the mask, the players seemed intimidated; they were less self-assured, and had more difficulty "threading the needle," to use a dated expression.[9] Meanwhile, Plante himself gained confidence. When he had the mask on, he became another person and was no longer afraid of exposing his inevitable signs of fatigue, pain, and weariness. The mask—which certainly also protected him—concealed his signs of weakness from his opponents. The advantage is obvious. It's no surprise that it was quickly adopted by many goalies.

In addition to cloaking the fragility that all goalies naturally have—which, as we have seen, is derived from the angst that is inherent to their position—the mask finally gave the goalie the opportunity to express his personality as a player, to indirectly communicate (that is, to express through the mask) the *fundamental traits of his concrete existential individuality*. Of course, such a feat of individuality could only be fully realized in a society where the individual was more important than the masses, the collective. This explains why the goalie's mask didn't catch on in Eastern countries. Of course we remember the mesh helmet worn by Vladislav Tretiak and, more recently, Dominik Hašek's rather neutral helmet, which was likely reminiscent of the Soviet era. The norm in North America was to individualize the mask as much as possible, which effectively became the Kierkegaardian pseudonym of any self-respecting goalie.

The first mask that comes to mind is obviously that of Gerry Cheevers. Cheevers drew a stitch-mark on his mask every time he was hit in the face with a stick or a puck, to show everyone that he feared neither action nor roughness. This mask was actually pretty intimidating, and much of Cheevers's success can be attributed to it. It literally fashioned his personality as a goalie. Dan Bouchard also had a rather distinctive mask when he played for the Atlanta

---

9. It's essentially for this reason that the directors of the horror film series *Friday the 13th* made its maniacal killer, Jason (note here the fine mythological link with Jason and the Argonauts), wear a hockey goalie mask. The directors may have used Gary Bromley, former goalie of the Vancouver Canucks, as inspiration. See the mask he wore during the 1980 season.

Flames in 1976–1977, which he designed it himself. It added some interest to his style that hasn't been seen since, especially after his religious conversion. He doffed his mask in favour of a mesh helmet—a metaphor for the confessional booth—which is why his teammates on the Québec Nordiques called him "*Le Curé*" (the priest). The mask worn by Terry Sawchuk from 1962 to 1972 for the Detroit Red Wings was downright terrifying. In designing his mask, Sawchuk drew inspiration from the poem by Paul Laurence Dunbar (1872–1906), "We Wear the Mask."[10] Many people have interpreted Sawchuk's mask—correctly, I think—as a sort of goalie's support for the African-American Civil Rights Movement. Because of his mask, Sawchuk, a white man, can in some sense be considered the greatest African-American goalie in hockey history, thus demonstrating the full extent of the hockey mask's pseudonymous power.

As these few examples prove, the mask is a form of *indirect communication* of the goalie's personality, his aspirations, or even his existential state. It is the outward expression of his innermost personality. But it is also the *creation of a new personality* in the sense that it imbues the player with a personality that he may not have had to begin with but that he wishes to have and that unquestionably has a direct influence on his playing style and goaliehood.[11] Furthermore, the mask affords the goalie a certain distance from his angst. Note the nuance: *taking a certain distance from*

---

10. We wear the mask that grins and lies,
     It hides our cheeks and shades our eyes, —
     This debt we pay to human guile;
     With torn and bleeding hearts we smile,
     And mouth with myriad subtleties.

     Why should the world be overwise,
     In counting all our tears and sighs?
     Nay, let them only see us, while
     We wear the mask.

     We smile, but, O great Christ, our cries
     To thee from tortured souls arise.
     We sing, but oh the clay is vile
     Beneath our feet, and long the mile;
     But let the world dream otherwise,
     We wear the mask!

11. Heidegger and his school would doubtlessly speak in terms of the goalie's
     being-in-the-world.

it does not mean casting it aside. Nothing can fully rid the goalie of his angst, because, as I have argued, angst is his most basic and fundamental state. Taking this step back helps him to channel his angst as a constructive and positive force, and to concentrate on his technique, on the concrete aspect of his work, and also on the most eminently *existential* aspect: style. Here again, discerning philosophical eyes may spot a deep-seated Kierkegaardian influence.

The stages of existence and the styles of goaltending

For Kierkegaard, existence presents the individual with possibilities that place him in a relationship with himself, with the world, and with the absolute (God). These are the three fundamental possibilities of existence. Kierkegaard accounts for these three types of relationship in his philosophy of stages on life's way: "There are three spheres of existence: aesthetic, ethical, and religious."[12]

Similarly, hockey has three fundamental styles of goaltending, which correspond to the goalie's bodily position in response to the possibilities offered in the course of a game: *butterfly*, *stand-up*, and *toes-up*.

In the aesthetic stage, the individual has a contradictory relationship with the world. His relationship with reality is essentially an idealistic one: he does not accept the world as it is. The aesthete—what we call someone who is in the aesthetic stage—lives only for the moment. Each pleasure leads to another, but the individual never experiences satisfaction of his desire. And this ceaseless search for pleasure, this impossible quest, generates angst. Therefore, because of the angst embedded within it, the aesthetic stage is the natural stage of all goalies. In goalie terms, this stage is associated with the butterfly style—not just because of the natural elegance of this style, or its flashy and spectacular quality, but also because the collapsing onto oneself that it involves, as we noted earlier, is an expression of angst.

Next comes the ethical stage, which is characterized by engagement in existence. Where the aesthete procrastinates, the ethicist

---

12   Søren Kiergaard, *Concluding Unscientific Postscript to Philosophical Fragments*, p. 339.

jumps into existence with both feet. This concrete engagement, this way of being upright, and not being kept upright, as Marcus Aurelius put it, corresponds to the stand-up style. Since this style requires the player to master his angst, if not rid himself of it entirely, it's unsurprising that it has vanished from professional hockey.

In the religious stage, the final stage of Kierkegaard's existential philosophy, the individual understands that his weaknesses and sins are sources of individuality. In coming to understand his limits before the Absolute, the individual also becomes aware of the unique character of his individuality. In hockey, the religious stage corresponds to the toes-up style. This style was most popular from the late 1960s to the early 1980s, as it was a transitional step towards the butterfly style that now predominates. The toes-up style has been abandoned, and the explanation is simple. While very effective at blocking rebounds, this style bespeaks great assurance, steadiness, and confidence, which are completely foreign to angst. Going down on one's side demands little thought or introspection, and therefore no precipitous return to the throes of angst. This corresponds to the religious stage, as the goalie prostrates himself only when he senses his limits being pushed by his opponent, when there is no alternative but to do so. And what is religion but the end of alternatives?

We could delve deeper into this very clear link between the Kierkegaardian philosophy of stages on life's way and goaltending styles, but that would be beyond the scope of this chapter.

My conclusion to this chapter would be incomplete without a formulation of its overarching thesis: *angst is the essential condition of the goalie; the mask distances him from his angst, and this distance allows him to develop his style*. In a nutshell, this is the fundamental Kierkegaardian dialectic of goaltending in hockey.

I'll add that I also believe that Hockey Canada should incorporate intensive readings of the works of Søren Kierkegaard in its exercises for young goaltenders. This would make budding goalies more aware of the role angst plays in their game and encourage them to view their aesthetic in a new light. Wouldn't it be interesting to hear a goalie launch into a passage from Kierkegaard's

Diapsalmata in his next interview, after removing his mask painted in the image of the great Danish philosopher?

Further reading

Unfortunately, there are not yet any works that deal with Kierkegaard's importance to hockey or the phenomenology of angst in the sport. However, I would recommend Kierkegaard's work *Fear and Trembling*; the title alone hints at goaltending. I am not aware of any readings of this text from a sports perspective. Of course, *In Vino Veritas* by the same author is a must for any self-respecting garage league player. And anyone who travels frequently during the regular season will already be familiar with *The Seducer's Diary* and *The Spontaneous Erotic Stages*.

Shootout

Haitians, Hockey, and Some Philosophy of Culture

Rodney Saint-Éloi
(with Marie-Célie Agnant, Dany Laferrière, Rita Metsokosho, and Jean Morisset)

At first blush, Haitians and hockey don't seem to have much in common. But when Normand Baillargeon approached me about contributing to this collection, I immediately accepted—because it's almost impossible for me to tell him no, given the trademark drive and pluck of this man who endeavours to turn the words "hope" and "rebellion" into something concrete. So accept it I did. I told myself that hockey and philosophy weren't a bad choice in terms of subject matter—for an immigrant, they even hold an exotic appeal!

For the first time, I'm in the odd position of doing what others do when they pontificate about things that are far outside their experience or culture. Like those journalists who spend a week as tourists in the Caribbean and take themselves for specialists on the region.

This distance, this relative foreignness, is of philosophical interest. It ties in with the colossal concept of "culture," which we use to refer to socially constructed and defined ways of doing, feeling, thinking, and behaving. While culture has long been bandied about by ethnologists, sociologists, and anthropologists, the concept actually originated in philosophy. Through it, we understand the relativity of customs and learn to relativize our own cultural practices, to stop thinking of them as universal or valid for all of humanity. Relativization is always an interesting exercise, and it can be quite revealing philosophically. It often teaches important lessons about openness and modesty.

Yes, here I go philosophizing. Nothing like a little on-the-job training!

I will venture into this territory and dig beneath the surface of this disconnect. I'll start by discussing Haitians' relationship with sport. Then I'll recount how I was first introduced to hockey before sharing my perception of Québécois' relationship with their sport. As you'll discover, I learn best by listening to others—so I wanted include the voices other writers in the mix: two Haitians (Marie-Célie Agnant, Dany Laferrière), one Québécois (Jean Morisset), and one Aboriginal of the Mingan nation (Rita Mestokosho). Each will partake in the discussion below to by telling about their relationship with sport in general and hockey in particular.

Hockey is obviously not my national sport. It had no place in my childhood or the fantasies thereof. For all Haitians, the word "sport" is synonymous with soccer, and soccer carries with it a certain cultural relationship.

Indeed, soccer occupies a major place in the Haitian imagination, but not because of our national team: Team Haiti—when it exists—never does very well in international competitions. Soccer is Haiti's number one sport by proxy, via a sort of projection onto countries where soccer is king. Haitians cheer for other countries' teams: Brazil, Argentina, France, and Germany (in order of importance). So when they talk sports, the issue of otherness and references to other people and cultures immediately come into play.

Because of this effect, most Haitians identify as Brazilian, Argentinian, French, or German. They import nationality and identity to say that they support the team of Brazil, Argentina, and so on. Discussions are passionate and make for a lively back-and-forth of players' names, team names, bits of gossip, failures, and successes. It's common to see buses driving through the streets decorated in honour of Ronaldo, Ronaldinho, or Bebeto. Pelé and Maradona are de facto heroes of the national pantheon. For the 90 minutes of game time, an entire people gets swept up in dreams of winning by enveloping itself in cultural symbols from away: flags,

My father's take on sport
Marie-Célie Agnant

My father's take on sport was that it was the only area of life that crossed all borders, even religious and political ones. He even went so far as to say that age-old conflicts were drained of their strength on the soccer field. He would preach this to anyone who would listen. Often this was my mother, who became literally ill when I left to go on a school ski trip, because she knew that I would never miss even the tiniest opportunity to hit the slopes.

Mother had lived for many long years in this country of snow and ice, but for her, doing sports meant bathing in a shallow river. Father said it was a matter of cultural references. Father pleaded, Mother sighed. Father saw sport as a panacea. He said it was a seedbed in which friendships that transcended time could grow, a place where the bonds of brotherhood couldn't help but form.

Mother had a hard time understanding Father's infatuation with hockey night. She said she didn't like the fighting, which she thought was completely divorced from any expression of friendship or brotherhood.

Father would rebut that this violence, which was reserved for the hockey rink and therefore contained, was in some sense an outlet for a deeper kind of violence, a latent aggression that many of us only barely detected. Perplexed, Mother would look at him and shrug. There was begging in her eyes. She could sense that the time was coming when all her arguments combined wouldn't amount to a grain of sand compared to Father's passion. One day, the scales tipped. Father picked me up very soon after school. He looked happy, and I knew why. He had just enrolled me in hockey. I was worried. I was caught between the joy I knew I would have lacing up my new skates and improving my game, and the insurmountable terror I knew Mother would have.

At the store, Father was feverish. I had to have—we had to have—the finest pair of skates, the toughest helmet, the most softly padded mitts. The truth was that he saw himself as the one who was rushing out onto the shiny ice. I shared in his joy, although I couldn't decide whether I wanted to play for my own reasons or to give Father the chance to live out what, despite my being just seven years old, I knew was a fantasy.

By the end of my first week of practice, I was all bumps and bruises. I made sure to keep my scratches hidden to spare Mother the pain of seeing them. The camps were formed. In Father's eyes I was a hero; in Mother's, a victim of passion, or rather of transplanted passion. She said Father had always dreamed of being a star soccer player. But that hadn't been in the cards for him. He had had to leave his country, his dream bundled in a bindle. I was his only son; it was up to me to help him forget this hurt, and most of all to prove that his theories were correct: "Sport and intermixing are the antidotes to the identity problems that plague our society. There needs to be more room," Father the math teacher preached, "to play sports, all sports. That's the only way a new society, a more fraternal and closely knit society, can be born. The world is changing," he lamented, "and we stubbornly insist on remaining strangers to one another." Time after time, he used this sermon to persuade Mother to watch the hockey game with us on TV. Father wouldn't have missed a game for the world. "Your mother's cultural references are stuck in place, my son," he lamented. Father saw hockey games as the expression of genuine communion between people of all ages and walks of life. Mother said she could take it or leave it. I drifted between their disagreements until one day when, out of laziness, I hung up my skates for good in the basement closet.

food, portraits, etc. Consensus is easy only in sport. Take electricity, for instance: in Haiti, it is a fiction. Being absent from most households, electricity is what metaphysicians might call an unassignable noun. No one can explain this state of affairs. No one receives statements or apologies from the official electricity provider. Everyone simply accepts it. However, there is one thing people do demand of the authorities, and on this point everyone agrees: that during the World Cup, or anytime there's a big soccer match on, everyone should have access to electricity—or at least be notified of the utility's schedule and service capacities.

Take a red-letter day in the world of soccer (like when Brazil plays Argentina or any other international championship): in Haiti, these days are holidays. Don't break your arm; you won't find a doctor at the hospital to treat you. Don't bother trying to pay your taxes; the office is closed. School is also out for the day; no self-respecting teacher would bother going in. And for goodness' sake don't die on a soccer high holiday: the undertaker is out. Death can wait till the next business day. After the match, the city bursts into song and dance. The carnival and busy crowd—several days' worth of celebrations—take over the streets.

So soccer is a stoker of the passions—and Haitians' passion for sport is historically much stronger than their obsession with politics has been over their country's two centuries of existence. Politics turns with the seasons and its characters come and go, but sport is timeless. Everywhere you go in the country, people talk soccer; radio rebroadcasts stand in for cockfights and boxing matches. To listen to people in the street and sports reporters talk so intensely about soccer, you might think you're in the land of soccer supremacy and that soccer courses through the veins of all Haitians. But to see our team play so badly, you'd discover that fantasy trumps reality in this case. In any case, in a climate like ours, there's no room for another sport. Which is why I said earlier that Haitians and hockey don't seem to have much in common.

This is my cultural baggage. These are my avenues to sport. So how have I taken to hockey? What struck me, surprised me, or shocked me about how Québécois relate to their national sport?

My hockey education

It was my twelve-year-old son Aimé who first really introduced me to hockey one afternoon in June 2008. I was spending the day with writer Rachid Djaïdani, who describes himself as a "kid from the French suburbs of Algerian and Sudanese origin." I was watching my son as he watched the game. I had no idea that hockey mattered so much to him. I had assumed that as an immigrant (or at least the son of an immigrant) he, like me, would have a different take on the sport than his peers, a sort of bird's-eye view. But apparently not: it's amazing how our own children can surprise us! It's also amazing just how quickly they absorb the host culture. Our children have their own ideas about things, and often they find their way in life in spite of us. I had thought Black people would be interested in sports that Black people played, like basketball, football for sure, the 100-metre dash, and so on. And I had also thought that hockey was a White sport that was played by people who were built for the cold. But I was wrong: my son is a bona fide hockey devotee. He's got it down pat: the vocabulary, the season, everything. Aimé started making fun of Rachid and me (neither of us knew the first thing about the game, and we couldn't have named an NHL player to save our lives).

"Come on, that's not the ball, it's the puck. . ."

"But it's a little ball," Rachid shot back mockingly.

"No, it's called the puck."

"Two brothers on the same team? That's can't be true," I said.

"Yep, they're brothers, and they're amazing! Sergei and Andrei Kostitsyn."

"No Black players in this sport. They must be racist," Rachid said.

"The American teams have lots of Black players. . ." Aimé replied and effortlessly spouted off a list of names.

Richard and I were beat. We were content to watch the game. The Canadiens lost. The Philadelphia Flyers won. Oh well!

The Canadiens! Now there was a word that had piqued my interest. After the game was over, I left my son at home and went out walking in the streets of Montréal, where Canadiens flags were everywhere in sight in spite of the loss. I thought back to my arrival

Nature and culture: Blacks and sport
The concept of culture becomes even more philosophically interesting when you factor in its relationship with human nature. But explaining cultural traits in terms of nature can be a slippery slope, and the history of sport provides ample reminders of this. For a long time, the discrimination that Black athletes faced in the United States was justified by claims that its purpose was to spare Blacks the humiliation of competing with White athletes, who were taken to be superior. The outright racism is palpable. Yet later, when Black athletes were allowed to play in White leagues and it turned out (as was often the case) that they dominated the sport in question, no one said they were naturally better at it.

It's not easy to take a firm position on all these issues. Currently, it's clear that athletes of African origin or with Black ancestors do in fact dominate in certain sports, especially running events. And it seems clear that few Black people excel in hockey or play in the NHL due to cultural reasons.

That said, it's also interesting to note that nobody gives a hoot as to whether Asians dominate in ping pong! (N.B.)

at Dorval airport in May 2001. The immigration officer had forced me to choose between Québec and Canada. I had thought that in leaving Haiti I would be free: free to move throughout the world. Free in how I could live in my chosen country. Naïvely, I had thought that the two entities were the same thing, the same country, the same (rather charming) White people, with their linguistic and cultural diversity, and so on. But the officer gave me a quick primer. There's Canada. There's Québec. And they're not the same thing. For the first time, through hockey, I thought I understood that the term "*Canadien*" wasn't derogatory, that it didn't necessarily mean those maudits conservative Anglophones, who were, incidentally, decent folk. They went to church. They took good care of their spouses and pets. They worked hard and paid their taxes and voted for politicians on the right. They played golf and helped their fellow man. They respected the sacred laws of the market, curried favour with friends in high places (Sarkozy-style), and spoke in favour of reasonable accommodations to Blacks and Arabs. Had I been lied to? It wasn't my fault! My initiation began when I thought the two worlds were interchangeable. I was humbled, letting myself be looked down upon by the world, and by this immigration officer who was teaching me how to live in Québec like a Québécois . . . and to forget about *les Canadiens*, who were perhaps detestable. But as I listened to this man, I quickly understood that the Québécois and the Canadians didn't like each other and didn't really live in the same country. "Well, this must be the school of life," I said to myself. Or, as the writer Sergio Kokis put it so well, "It's a hard job, exile!"

As I walked the streets, I saw the Québécois flying the Canadiens flag, and even though their team had lost the game, they acted as though they belonged to a history that was larger than themselves. Not bad for a people resigned to being second-class citizens. As long as the game lasted, they were utterly and completely wrapped up in their history.

I continued to wander through Montréal-Nord. It was almost 9:00 p.m. I wanted to see how invested the people of that community were in this game. Like true Blacks and immigrants, they naturally wouldn't care, I assumed. Wrong again! The whole borough of Montréal-Nord felt surreal. The streets were empty. There were no cars blasting hip hop music! The sidewalks and laneways were still. The gangs stayed home. Demands for jobs, justice, and dignity; attacks against racism and exclusion; roving gangs of desperate youth; battles of profanities; street fighting for survival—all had ground to a halt. Must be a truce, I thought. They had given up, they had defected from the battle. They were on a hockey break to gain perspective on themselves. They had obviously been drinking during the game: the air smelled of cheap beer. Even behind the curtains I could sense the players' exhaustion; I could hear people making bets as I walked. Some had seen the game as their big chance and risked everything they had on it.

The sacred game of hockey
Dany Laferrière

I know nothing about hockey. I arrived here in 1976 during heyday of Guy Lafleur, who was known as *Le Démon Blond* in those days. He never wore a helmet. You can define eras in terms of politics and sports. Politically, we talk about the Great Darkness, the Quiet Revolution, and the Referendums. In sports, we talk about the Maurice Richard days, the Guy Lafleur days, and the Patrick Roy days. I went to a hockey game once. It was wintertime. That really gives you the feeling of being in the North: the players are skating on ice inside while it's winter outside. It has no relationship with the South. For me, hockey is really the other extreme. I can relate to soccer, which is played outside, on the grass, with the body. Soccer is a graceful game of the body; hockey is a brutal game of the mind. Hockey is also a sacred game. It's played in a temple. Soccer is a pagan game. It's played in a stadium. Hockey has religious references like the Sainte-Flanelle. Also, you can't start playing it as an adult; you have to learn it as a child. My childhood is in another place, in a little Southern city sandwiched between the sun and the sea.

I hear Aimé's voice in my head. Naturally, he is talking about hockey:

"In Port-au-Prince, I didn't know anything about hockey. For me, the only sports were soccer and baseball. I started watching hockey here with my Québécois friends. They taught me about the game, and I like it. I don't really know why. I even bought myself a hockey stick (a CCM Vector) and started playing with my friends in the neighbourhood. I've scored lots of goals. My best memory is this one time at school when I got past three guys, even though I didn't score . . . My friends dreams of playing hockey in the big leagues. I don't. But I do like watching it. I think the two best players are Henrik Zetterberg of the Detroit Red Wings and Alexander

Ovechkin of the Washington Capitals. And the best player on the Canadiens is Andrei Kostitsyn."

Funny. The person who first taught me about hockey was my own son. I have to keep learning by asking questions, by using my imagination, and by weaving a narrative of integration through hockey as a fantastical game. How does one break free . . . when one is young and Black and hungry for the world, what choice does one have: will it be the factory or the faculty? That doesn't apply anymore. There are too many doctors and doctoral candidates from our communities who can't find work. . . How does one shed light on these tiny invisible peoples? The prisons will take them in . . . but I would think they need other places to go than that. How does one live one's whole life here and never get asked "Where do you come from?" How does one remove the sting from the word "immigrant"? How does one be Québécois in diversity: *pure laine*. . . pure Afro. . . pure Latino. . . pure Arab. . . or mixed fabrics. How does one walk in the parks of Montréal-Nord without getting stopped because of racial profiling? As I write this, I hear this story on the news:

"Fredy Villanueva, 18 years old, died on August 9 in a park in Montréal-Nord during a police intervention after being shot three times. His death has triggered a protest that escalated into a riot the following day."

Side note: can you imagine an armed police officer targeting a middle-class kid in a park in Westmount or Outremont? That would never happen, you might say, and you'd be right. We all believe, or make believe, that young people from nice neighbourhoods aren't involved in drugs or crime. They're at home snug in their beds! They were born into the right families and have the support of the institutions founded by their fathers. No need for policemen to keep the peace. Their private security guards are on patrol, and their housekeeping staff know the children's names by heart. This two-tier society is losing touch with the virtues of citizenship. It was the young people from the nice neighbourhoods who helped me understand what an immigrant was and how better to define one. An immigrant is a traveller without a suitcase, motherless and fatherless and penniless. If the immigrant falls, he

Black players in the NHL
1958–2013
 1. Willie O'Ree, 1958
 2. Mike Marson, 1974
 3. Bill Riley, 1976
 4. Tony McKegney, 1978
 5. Bernie Saunders, 1979
 6. Ray Neufeld, 1980
 7. Grant Fuhr, 1981
 8. Val James, 1981
 9. Brian Johnson, 1983
10. Dirk Graham, 1984
11. Darren Lowe, 1984
12. Eldon "Pokey" Reddick, 1986
13. Steven Fletcher, 1987
14. Claude Vilgrain, 1987
15. Paul Jerrard, 1988
16. Mike McHugh, 1988
17. Graeme Townshend, 1989
18. Reggie Savage, 1991
19. Dale Craigwell, 1991
20. Darren Banks, 1992
21. Donald Brashear, 1993
22. Nathan LaFayette, 1993
23. Sandy McCarthy, 1993
24. Fred Brathwaite, 1994
25. Craig Martin, 1994
26. Joaquin Gage, 1994
27. Jason Doig, 1995
28. Jarome Iginla, 1996
29. Anson Carter, 1996
30. Jamal Mayers, 1996
31. John Craighead, 1996
32. Mike Grier, 1996
33. Rumun Ndur, 1996

34. Sean Brown, 1996
35. Kevin Weekes, 1997
36. Peter Worrell, 1997
37. Georges Laraque, 1997
38. Jean-Luc Grand-Pierre, 1998
39. Tyrone Garner, 1998
40. Francis Bouillon, 1999
41. Bryce Salvador, 2000
42. Nathan Robinson, 2003
43. Trevor Daley, 2003
44. Ray Emery, 2003
45. Sean McMorrow, 2003
46. Greg Mauldin, 2003
47. Anthony Stewart, 2005
48. Dustin Byfuglien, 2005
49. Gerald Coleman, 2006
50. Joel Ward, 2006
51. Johnny Oduya, 2006
52. Shawn Belle, 2006
53. Nigel Dawes, 2006
54. Mark Fraser, 2006
55. Kyle Okposo, 2007
56. Robbie Earl, 2007
57. Chris Beckford-Tseu, 2007
58. Theo Peckham, 2007
59. Kenndal McArdle, 2008
60. Chris Stewart, 2008
61. Derek Joslin, 2008
62. Wayne Simmonds, 2008
63. Paul Bissonnette, 2008
64. Evander Kane, 2009
65. Maxime Fortunus, 2009
66. P.K. Subban, 2009
67. Ryan Reaves, 2010
68. Akim Aliu, 2011

69. Emerson Etem, 2012
70. Devante Smith-Pelly, 2012
71. Darren Archibald, 2013
72. J.T. Brown, 2013
73. Seth Jones, 2013
(N.B. and C.B.)

doesn't know whether there will be somebody to help him back up. The immigrant lives in fear of never being able to fall. . .

Young people, according to the narrative they have constructed for themselves, find that the only way out of their poverty is to play hockey. What? Yes, with hockey you can break free. Everybody's watching. Remember, Québec came into being with The Rocket and The Comet (the illustrious Maurice Richard). And one day these tiny invisible immigrant peoples will avenge history and its justice. Yes, one day we will hear: Laferrière to Agnant, Agnant to Saint-Éloi, Saint-Éloi to Bekri, Bekri to Péan, Péan to Benjamin, Benjamin to Kimato, Kimato to Kotto, Kotto to Dominique, Dominique to Ollivier, Ollivier to Chebbi, Chebbi to Mouamed, Mouamed to Milla, Milla to Jean-Louis, Jean-Louis to Shakib, Shakib to Saint-Éloi, Saint-Éloi shoots! What a shot! He scores! The Canadiens are making a comeback. And when that day comes, the NHL will resemble Côte-des-Neiges.

For the last two or three decades, various philosophers, notably Charles Taylor, have urged us to remember the importance of this requirement of recognizing culture and everything else that contributes to forming a person's identity. Taylor writes: "The thesis is that our identity is partly shaped by recognition or its absence, often by the misrecognition of others, and so a person or group of people can suffer real damage, real distortion, if the people or society around them mirror back to them a confining or demeaning or contemptible picture of themselves. Nonrecognition or misrecognition can inflict harm, can be a form of oppression, imprisoning someone in a false, distorted, and reduced mode of being."[1]

Here is not the place for me to discuss the merits or potential constraints of this idea, which opened the door to multiculturalism and communitarianism. But it is certain that multiculturalism has helped take cultural heritage that has tended to be overshadowed and bring it out into the open. This has benefitted not just these cultural communities, but also the whole world and truth itself.

We have seen this in hockey. In the book *Black Ice*, George and Darril Fosty recount the extraordinary yet unknown story of the relationship that Blacks have with hockey in Canada.[2] They tell us that at the end of the nineteenth century—before the NHL even existed—Nova Scotia had an informal league of Black hockey players! The teams were made up of Africans and people who had fled the slave trade or their descendants. They played for a crowd of mostly White people, who were both numerous (up to 1,500 per game) and enthusiastic.

There is so much more research to be done on the presence of Blacks in hockey. Why not start with a book on the Black Rocket?

Now for some voodoo! Haitians take up hockey and soccer becomes all the rage in Québec. Wait for history to offer us a Québec society that is diverse, open, generous, and strong, a society that can welcome the Other with the earnestness of a sorcerer. Bravo! The twenty-first century will either be the century of the conquest of immigrants and the transmigration of cultures, or it won't be. Here's hoping it will. When it does, we'll sit down together and watch the hockey game, toss around strange-sounding names, and

---

1 Charles Taylor, "The Politics of Recognition," *Multiculturalism*, edited and introduced by Amy Gutmann (Princeton: Princeton University Press, 1994), p. 25.

2. George Fosty and Darril Fosty, *Black Ice: The Lost History of the Colored Hockey League of the Maritimes, 1895–1925* (Halifax, NS: Nimbus Publishing, 2008).

The Black Rocket

Towards the end of the 1940s, in Québec, Herb Carnegie was a living legend in certain circles: they called him The Black Rocket. He was a huge star in the provincial and senior leagues. Along with his brother Ossie Carnegie and Manny McIntyre, he was part of the exceptional Black Aces line. But it was Herb who garnered most of the fans' attention. People marvelled at his extraordinary speed and offensive talent, which allowed him to single-handedly change the outcome of a game.

Herb Carnegie should have played in the NHL. He would have been the league's first Black player.

But unfortunately, prejudice and racism prevented him from doing so, even though the NHL had no official policy of racial discrimination like so many professional American sports teams did at the time. Conn Smythe, then owner of the Toronto Maple Leafs, reportedly said these remarkable words: "I'll give anyone $10,000 today if they can turn Carnegie white." (N.B.)

fly dozens of flags on our cars that say no to intolerance, racism, and exclusion. The life lesson here is that hockey, in forged fiction, will not only have been a display of strength, violence, and muscles: it will have been a display of a transformative mythology in which we can "look to tomorrow."

About the authors

Normand Baillargeon has written a great many articles and books on a wide variety of topics: education, philosophy, anarchism, poetry, politics, and economics. When he finds the time, he enjoys watching YouTube videos of Bobby Orr, his favourite player. To this day, he holds a grudge against everyone who deliberately attacked Orr's knee, ordered this to be done, or looked the other way when it was done.

Anouk Bélanger is a professor in the sociology department at the Université du Québec à Montréal (UQAM). She is interested in popular cultures, including that of hockey in Québec, which is one of her areas of research and teaching. She firmly believes that hockey and the Montréal Canadiens are popular expressions that not only are relevant in understanding certain dynamics at play in Québec society, but also participate in these dynamics.

Christian Boissinot teaches philosophy at the Collège François-Xavier-Garneau. He is a diehard fan of the Nordiques and of scientific hockey, even though the person he shares his life with thinks that the Maple Leafs are based in Edmonton and that every hockey player ought to be given his own puck to prevent fighting. His only claim to fame in the hockey world is being the first person to ever sell pepperoni sticks at the Colisée de Québec. He secretly dreams of driving a Zamboni.

Jean Dion thought he would one day skate like his idol Bobby Hull the first time he took to the ice. After a career of one game at the

Atom B level, he concluded that athletic ability was highly over-rated and decided to become a journalist instead. He believes we should teach our youngsters that everything was much better when there were only six teams and people played without helmets or masks. One highlight of his career as a hockey fan stands out: eating a so-called hot dog (in a baguette) at a Paris Français Volants game, and choking on it upon hearing the words "*deux minutes de prison pour surnombre*" ("two minutes in prison for surplus"). His life's ambition is to prove beyond a reasonable doubt to an unreasonably incredulous world that Alain Côté's goal was good.

Jean Grondin is a professor in the philosophy department at the Université de Montréal—mainly because his career as a hockey player didn't pan out. The (conservative) world of hockey has been somewhat resistant to his ideas on metaphysics (*L'universalité de l'herméneutique*, Presses universitaires de France, 1993; *Du sens de la vie*, Bellarmin, 2003; *Introduction à la métaphysique*, Presses de l'Université de Montréal, 2004; *L'herméneutique*, Presses universitaires de France, 2006). This hasn't stopped him from playing hockey with his students by participating in the annual interfaculty hockey tournament, in which he has helped secure his team's perfect record: not a single win, eight years running (but two tie games!).

Mario Jodoin is a labour market economist who specializes in analyzing trends in the professions. He has run a friendly hockey pool franchise for over twenty years and doesn't care a lick about the salary or the style of the players he picks—just as long as they rack up lots of points!

Charles Le Blanc was destined for a brilliant career as a goalie, but too early on conquered his angst so well that it turned into fear—a rather counterproductive thing to be feeling in front of the net. He spent several years in Germany and especially Italy to cure himself as a philosophy student. At age 40, fully cured of his fear and firmly back in the grips of angst, he returned to Canada and was shocked to discover that he was now too old to play Midget AAA hockey. In desperation, he became a university professor. He still teaches without a mask, but it is rumoured that he never goes out without his jock.

Jon Paquin is a teacher at the Collège François-Xavier-Garneau in Québec City. He has written several educational works for college-level philosophy courses. For a long time, he debated whether to pursue his current career or be a goon for a hockey team.

Tony Patoine finished a master's thesis on sport and nationalism at the Université de Montréal in 2008 (okay, the thesis was just an excuse to talk about hockey). When not teaching philosophy at the Cégep du Vieux Montréal, he blogs about the "big issues" surrounding the Montreal Canadiens and hockey in general at danslescoulisses.com. He also attempts to play like the Swiss player Mark Streit on the ice (with limited success). Finally, to spice up his life, he married a nice girl from Saskatchewan whom he met at the Bell Centre in 2007 at a Canadiens game (the Florida Panthers won 1 to 0). That's all that was needed to convince him that his son was sure to be a cross between Maurice Richard and Gordie Howe.

Julie Perrone is a historian and a Ph.D. graduate of Concordia University. She has also written about the 1972 Summit Series, the great Howie Morenz, and the Québec hero Maurice Richard. More than anything else, she is proud of her ability to impress her friends with useless statistics and dusty old anecdotes about hockey.

Rodney Saint-Éloi was born in Cavaillon in southern Haiti and has lived in Montréal since 2001. He divides his time among writing, publishing, literary tours, and conferences. He founded Les Éditions Mémoire in Port-au-Prince in 1991 and Les Éditions Mémoire d'encrier in Montréal in 2003. He is clueless about hockey in particular and sports in general. The proof? All his writer friends he asked to contribute to his chapter weren't any more knowledgeable than he was. The publisher of this book will surely honour him with certification as a Grade A dunce.

Chantal Santerre teaches business administration at the Cégep de Saint-Hyacinthe and is a great admirer of Immanuel Kant's works, especially his ethics. She has indelible memories of the great years of the Lafleur-Shutt-Lemaire line, whose plays were almost as great as Kant's ethics. In collaboration with Normand Baillargeon, she has published *Mémoires d'un esclave* by Frederick Douglass, *C'était demain* by Edward Bellamy, and *D'espoir et de raison: écrits d'une* *insoumise* by Voltairine de Cleyre. All are published by Lux in Montréal.

Jean-Claude Simard is a teacher at the Cégep de Rimouski. He writes, "So why is a philosophy prof so interested in hockey anyway? My father introduced me to the national sport when I was a child. For him, a Saturday night without watching *La Soirée du hockey* was unthinkable. His passion for the game was a sight to behold. How could I forget his rage when the Canadiens got crowded into their zone? 'Get out of there, get out, you dirty. . .' (Decency prevents me from sharing the rest.) Hearing such venom spew out of such a mild-mannered Catholic amazed me. 'If only I could grow up to play such a holy sport,' I thought. Unfortunately, I was the seventh and youngest boy in a family of fourteen children. So, after my older siblings had outgrown the few pairs of skates we had in the house, I would have been better off with butter knives. Surely to compensate for this, I developed a passion for analysing the sport, a passion that has never faded. Go Habs go!"

Fannie Valois-Nadeau is a doctoral candidate in communications at the Université de Montréal. After finishing her thesis in sociology at UQAM, in which she studied the discussion forums on the Montréal Canadiens, she now works on practices of memory that have appeared as part of the team's hundredth anniversary. Memory, sport, and popular culture are her primary areas of study. She takes a cultural studies approach in her work.

Daniel Weinstock directs the Centre de recherche en éthique at the Université de Montréal. He has written nearly 100 academic articles on ethics and political philosophy that are much less important than his contribution to this book. He recently published a short book entitled *Profession: éthicien* at the Presses de l'Université de Montréal. The most important chapter of that book, on the ethics of offsides, was tragically cut. He is a diehard Montréal Canadiens fan and has still not gotten over the Larry Pleau's defection to the World Hockey Association in 1972.

Philosophica

The *Philosophica* series presents essays by contemporary authors who offer philosophical reflections on current societal, cultural, artistic, religious and political themes. A place of debates, meetings, discussions and rigorous expression of thought, *Philosophica* is an agora where ideas meet.

Previous titles

Charles Le Blanc, ed., *Laïcité et humanisme*, 2015.

Thomas de Koninck, *Questions ultimes*, 2012.

Réal Fillion, *Foucault and the Indefinite Work of Freedom*, 2012.

Jean-François Mattéi, *Le procès de l'Europe. Grandeur et misère de la culture européenne*, 2011.

www.press.uottawa.ca

Printed in October 2015
at Imprimerie Gauvin,
Gatineau (Québec), Canada.